Here's what professionals and the media ar

"This is a book I think you need to read! It brings together importan
wide variety of sources, and walks parents through questions, issues ɛ
may face...[it's] hands-on approach will help parents...improve dynamics in their family."
Dr. Laura Schlessinger
As featured on her nationally syndicated radio show

"*Please Stop the Rollercoaster!* is like a well-organized college-level class on dealing with teenage offspring, wrapped up in an easy-to-use workbook. Parents searching for a lifeline will feel they've grabbed onto something substantial with this book."
ForeWord Magazine

"This is an outstanding book on the subject of raising teenagers. Your book is an inspiration to other families, to build connections through all circumstances. This is a wonderful guide of hope through all times."
Positive Parenting Magazine

"I was greatly impressed by *Please Stop the Rollercoaster!* I thought it a wonderfully helpful guide that goes right to the core of the real challenges that face the parents of teenagers. The book is amazingly clear, rich, and comprehensive, and I found it a true pleasure to read."
Anthony E. Wolf, Ph.D.
Get Out of My Life, but First Could You Drive Me and Cheryl to the Mall?

"*Rollercoaster* really gets it! I learned a lot from the book and believe parents everywhere could benefit tremendously from reading it. The book is easy to read, and the author has a sense of humor, which is so crucial! This is an excellent book written by a wise and witty woman."
Edward Hallowell, M.D.
The Childhood Roots of Adult Happiness
Instructor in Psychiatry, Harvard Medical School
Founder, The Hallowell Center for Cognitive and Emotional Health

"*Rollercoaster!* is just what our community was looking for. It provides the framework for parents to create a community that will support them throughout the teen years."
Paula Nelson, Co-Chair
Parent Engagement Network,
Boulder, CO

"*Please Stop the Rollercoaster!* provides the structure for parents to engage in a highly valuable text-based discussion program where they learn together and discuss their concerns. It is easy for us to manage and parents have been enthusiastic about the program!
Libby Moore, Principal
Marblehead Middle School, Marblehead, MA

"This is a wonderful resource! All parents who want to understand their teenager more, and re-establish effective communication, will find this book to be a very helpful and useful guide."
David Gleason, Psy.D.
Psychologist in Private Practice, Concord, MA

"*Please Stop the Rollercoaster!* was invaluable in providing both content and structure to our parenting discussion groups. Using the book for guidance, we were able to discuss our concerns, stories, and help each other as parents of teens. We learned so much and came away from each meeting with different ways to think about situations and how to manage them."
Sally Lewis, Chairman, Community Action for Youth, Acton, MA

Comments from parents of teenagers:

"*Please Stop the Rollercoaster* is a 'reader's digest' of parenting information. It's everything you need to know in one condensed book so that you don't have to weed through the 'gazillions' of parenting resources out there.
Terry Bromfield, Newton, MA

'This book is a springboard for great ideas."
Nancy Gardiner, Trumbull, CT

"...sensible, straight forward and fastidiously researched--Everything one needs to know to parent teens more effectively. Committed parents will be comforted to know that they are not alone in their struggles and concerns."
Kate Frank, Albuquerque, NM

"This book, more than any other parenting book I've read, gets people talking. It's the beginning of a dialogue that will help you through the rough spots of parenting your adolescent."
Carole Heaton, Medfield, MA

"If you are going to read just one parenting book, read this one!"
Amy Drinker, Marblehead, MA

"Both the book and the program have provided my wife and me with invaluable guidance on how to knock down that persistent, teenaged wall between our kids and us, and keep it down."
Winslow Pettingell, Concord, MA

Please Stop the Rollercoaster!

How Parents of Teenagers Can Smooth Out the Ride

Sue Blaney

ChangeWorks
PUBLISHING

ACTON, MASSACHUSETTS

Excerpts from GET OUT OF MY LIFE! BUT FIRST COULD YOU DRIVE ME AND CHERYL TO THE MALL? by Anthony Wolf. Copyright © 1991 by Anthony E. Wolf Ph.D. Reprinted by permission of division of Farrar, Straus and Giroux, LLC.

Excerpts from UNCOMMON SENSE FOR PARENTS WITH TEENAGERS, by Michael Riera, copyright © 1995 by Michael Riera. Reprinted by permission of Celestial Arts, P.O. Box 7123, Berkeley, CA 94707.

Excerpts from RAISING TEENS: A SYNTHESIS OF RESEARCH AND A FOUNDATION FOR ACTION, by A. Rae Simpson, Ph.D. copyright © 2001 by A. Rae Simpson and the President and Fellows of Harvard College. Reprinted by permission of A. Rae Simpson.

ZITS cartoons copyright © Zits Partnership. Reprinted with Special Permission of King Features Syndicate.

Excerpts from THE PARENT'S TAO TE CHING by William Martin, copyright © 1999 by William Martin. Appears by permission of the publisher, Marlowe and Company.

Excerpts from ALWAYS ACCEPT ME FOR WHO I AM by J.S. Salt, copyright © 1999 by J.S. Salt. Used by permission of Three Rivers Press, a division of Random House, Inc.

Excerpt from EVERYDAY MIRACLES; HOLY MOMENTS IN A MOTHER'S DAY, copyright © 1989 by Dale Hanson Bourke. Used by permission.

My sincere thanks to these publishers for permission to quote from their works. SB

Published by
ChangeWorks Publishing & Consulting
P.O. Box 3085
Acton, MA 01720-7085
978-264-0692
www.PleaseStoptheRollercoaster.com

Printed in the United States of America

Table of Contents

Children Naturally Love Life

Your children naturally love life.
Their love of life is spontaneous and unconscious.
It delights in every nuance of light
and color.
It wonders at every shape and form.
It dances in their bodies
without self-consciousness.
They are not taught this love.
It cannot be taught,
only lived.

If you live this love for your children
you will guide them,
but never demand a certain response.
You will welcome them,
But never smother them.
You will give birth to them,
but never possess them.
You will nurture their dreams
and guard their self-respect.
They will honor you naturally,
not because of who you are,
but because of who they are.

Don't worry about how your children treat you.
Concentrate on how you treat yourself.
If your children see in you
a sincere celebration of who you are,
they will return eventually
to their natural joy,
in themselves and you.

From *The Parent's Tao Te Ching, a New Interpretation*
by William Martin

A note from the Author...
Reflections on this Parenting Journey

When this book was first published in 2003, I was still in the midst of parenting my teenagers. It's a journey unlike any other—full of anticipation, excitement, pride and joy mixed in occasionally with unbearable heartache, embarrassment and even fear. Now that my children are both in their twenties, I've gained a perspective about this journey that I couldn't see before. For one thing, the teen years were over before I knew it. The rough days have faded in my memory, and I realize they were simply bumps in the road. My teens and I survived our mistakes and we can look back now on many of them and laugh. Now I'm welcoming home my twenty-something young adults and wondering why I ever worried about either of them.

My intent with this book is not tell you how to parent, but to walk along beside you to provide some guidance, relevant research and key questions. As I've spoken to parents and educators around the country I've not found parents who are disconnected from their teens; rather, parents who care deeply and are trying their best. I have deep respect for the wisdom, sensitivity and capability I've seen parents bring to this effort. I understand that parents may struggle over various issues during this dynamic time in life, but I've also observed that their feelings are remarkably similar. We have an opportunity to learn from one another, and when we share our parenting journey with our peers, it does get easier. It is my mission to help connect you.

And I hope to stay connected with parents like you through my book and companion website. This book has initiated parent discussion groups across America, and I'm proud to say it has positively impacted thousands of parents who are raising teenagers. It has provided the framework for parents' discussions as they learn together, improve their relationships with their teens, and support one another in their own communities. My hope is it will do the same for you.

Sue [Ireland] Blaney, Certified Professional Behavior Analyst, communications expert and parent of two recent-teenagers, has over 25 years experience in training and marketing. She is the founder of ChangeWorks Publishing whose mission is to empower, educate and connect parents of teenagers.

Contributor JoAnn Campbell: JoAnn Campbell is a high school assistant principal in Massachusetts. She is also an instructor in the Simmons College Master of Arts in Teaching (MAT) program. She is pursuing her doctorate at Boston University with a concentration in Administration, Training, and Policy.

Acknowledgements

This labor of love has benefited from the encouragement, enthusiasm, and contributions of numerous people. First, my thanks and recognition goes to our original parenting discussion group: Patrice Rochette, Pat Loria, Judy Paavola, Cindy Soule, Sharon Smith-McManus, and Valerie McGovern. You've been wonderful partners in this exciting adventure. Were it not for a critical phone call at a critical time from JoAnn Campbell, this project may not have reached the point of publication. JoAnn not only provided friendship and enthusiasm, but offered vision as well as concrete contributions. I am very grateful. Casey Mitchell was my "right hand man" in many ways, and provided vital input as well as her brilliant creative touch.

I'm grateful to the many people who took the time to provide valued comments, suggestions, and contributions: Pat Nelson, Dr. David Gleason, Paul O'Leary, Suzanne Zellner, Gwyn Thakur, Marcia Felth, Liz Lampros, Anne Seni, Sharon Brown, Abby Sexias, Bonnie Petrovich, Linda Braun, Mac Reid, Kathy Bowen, Emily Hutcheson, Marga Hutcheson, Amy Loria, and Amy Drinker.

My thanks to my professional crew: Jennifer Bixby for copyediting, and Lois Wisman and Annie Cronin for their cover design.

And, my family deserves my recognition and thanks. I love you, John, Wes, and Kara.

Author's note: The references to teenagers in this book use "he" and "she" interchangably. Please adjust to fit your family.

Why you need a parenting program

Use this book as a guide, or program, to facilitate your own learning, to clarify your beliefs, gain confidence, and be a better parent.

It didn't happen all of a sudden. But, all of a sudden, I felt as though I was dealing with someone I didn't even know. My son didn't change overnight, but rather as the seasons change, like a series of storm clouds that blow through over several weeks. One day I realized we were in a new and different season.

Parenting kids going through adolescence is a wondrous, frightening, challenging, stimulating, and exciting time. And few parents prepare for the challenge.

When we change jobs, we usually receive some training for the position, and it is recognized that we need time to learn our new role. In parenting, however, we're working in a constantly changing situation and, too often, take no time out to consider *what* has changed and *how* our responses should reflect that. Few parents take advantage of training programs that are targeted to them during their child's adolescence, perhaps because they are so deeply involved in knowing their child that "training" does not feel like the appropriate answer. I can understand why that approach does not strike a chord with many parents.

We've included research and expert opinions for you; we provide guidelines for your discussions and some exercises to make you think.

What do parents of teenagers need? Our relationships with our teenagers and our roles as parents are changing dramatically during our child's adolescence. As parents, we need several things to help us through this period:

- **Confidence:** parents who are confident in their role and understand their teen will be able to provide appropriate guidance,
- **Knowledge:** parents who are knowledgeable about adolescents and their world are equipped for the ride,
- **Connections:** parents who are connected can support one another, benefiting their teens and their communities.

Become conscious of the way you parent. Be intentional about your words and actions.

This book provides a guide to help you meet these needs. You can read this book and do the exercises on your own, or you can use this as a guide for a parenting discussion group program. Either way, I encourage you to discuss the issues with colleagues, peers, and your child's other parent if that is possible. Discussing these important topics is the best way to gain input and become informed. This can be as simple or as in-depth a process as you choose to make it.

Why you need a parenting program (cont.)

This program is flexible enough for you to fit what you learn into your values, and your family.

This program will help you focus on priorities. Parents are over-stressed today in a wide variety of ways. Those who have the desire to read many of the excellent books that are available on raising adolescents, just can't seem to find the time. And getting just one expert's point of view may not be enough information for you. *Please Stop the Roller-coaster!* allows you to explore the voices of many experts. And with this format you can spend your time differently: rather than investing your precious time just reading, you spend less time reading and more time examining and discussing issues with your peers.

Designed to facilitate the kind of parenting in which you want to engage, this program is not a "training course" that teaches you the "right way" of doing things. On the hard days, I find myself sometimes wishing there were one "right way," one answer that would solve my current dilemma. But in fact, there are as many shades of gray, as many ways of solving the challenges of raising teenagers, as there are kids. So my goal is to help you to illuminate the right way for you and your family. You're the expert on your child. We begin there and build on that.

Effective parenting requires your involvement—there is no way around it.

But, although there is not one "right way" in terms of values and beliefs, there are "rules for engagement" in parenting that have proven to be most effective. And "engagement" is what it comes down to. You can't do a good job as a parent and not be directly involved with your teens. There is no easy way out, and the challenges of the job have probably brought you to these pages. We'll talk a lot about effective parenting throughout this program.

Prepare in advance for the inevitable "crisis" when quick decisions are required.

Too many times parents must respond during what seems like a crisis. We are put on the spot regularly and need to make quick decisions and fast judgments as our teens grow. We'll explore key issues and help you identify the choices you have, enabling you to make the best decisions in times when quick answers are required.

Our focus is on the issues most families face. Serious issues should receive professional attention.

Many teens dance with dangerous behavior. Most are confronted with serious and dangerous choices that adults find frightening. There may be times you should seek professional advice rather than getting help from your peers. Serious issues such as eating disorders, depression, dangerous sexual activity and substance abuse are some of the highly specialized areas that require special information and professional assistance. This program focuses on the areas common to all teenagers—especially the wide majority whose behavior falls within the "typical" range.

Why you need a parenting program (cont.)

Your teenager needn't be threatened by your involvement in this program. In fact, many teens see it positively that you are investing your time and energy in improving your parenting skills.

One point I'd like to emphasize is that you can do this work while respecting the confidentiality of your teenager. Even though we encourage discussion, your kids needn't be uncomfortable thinking that you are talking about them behind their backs. You don't need to share private information. Please view this as an opportunity to explore parenting and learn about adolescent development without sharing information that makes others uncomfortable. These are not therapy groups. That said, the more you invest in this process the better your experience will be.

The topics addressed in the eight chapters that follow cover the main areas of knowledge with which parents of teens should be familiar. You'll find experts quoted throughout the chapters, and you may find yourself stimulated to read more of the authors' work. I hope you will! New trends and issues constantly emerge in our fast paced culture, and our website (www.PleaseStoptheRollercoaster.com) should be consulted for current, relevant topic information. In addition to a wide range of articles, there are sections of the website that are specifically designed to provide information and tools to supplement this book.

How to use this book   If you elect to do this program on your own it's simple—just read the book and do the exercises. When you come across questions and issues you want to discuss, find someone to discuss them with: your spouse, a friend, even a walking buddy. I urge you to take your time and work through the material slowly. That way you'll get the most out of it. There is a lot of "rich dessert" here, so take your time.

A discussion group can meet for eight sessions, or an indefinite length of time. You can customize it to your own interests and needs.

Another option is to create, or join, a parenting discussion group. This book can provide the curriculum for either a self-directed group that runs like a book group, or a group that is facilitated by a discussion leader using our secular, Christian or Jewish Leader's Guides. This is a wonderful way to get parents thinking, talking, and connected with one another. Use whichever model feels best to you. Participating in such a program can be positive for everyone. All it requires is an openness to learning, a willingness to share your experiences and insights, and the desire to be a better parent. That's all.

Benefits await you and your teenager   So whether you elect to join a group or read this on your own, the better informed you are, the more thoughtful and intentional you are in your words and actions, the smoother you can make your ride.

Why you need a parenting program (cont.)

Our group remains deeply connected and continues to get together.

My friends and I created a parenting discussion group that had a great impact on our experiences and stress level. And we didn't just meet for eight sessions, but for over two years! We increased our understanding about parenting and adolescent behavior in a way that truly impacted ourselves and our families. We explored ways to improve communication when we felt left out and shut down. Often I learned the most from the people who were the least like me; I always benefited from a different point of view. Although we emphasized that no one was expected to share confidential information, we also reinforced our commitment to group confidentiality in each meeting. This created a safe haven for conversation, self-discovery, and for processing the significant changes we were experiencing. We shared much laughter and a few tears. We value and appreciate all that we learned and experienced together.

Your teenagers are one step closer to "out the door" with every day that passes.

Just do it! Don't spend too much time "thinking" about how you can use this program. If you want to improve your parenting and positively impact your relationship, you can start *today*.

Use this book:
- **To read on your own** It's easy to read and do the exercises on your own. You can explore these issues further with your peers.
- **To create an informal, self-facilitated parenting discussion group, along the lines of a book group** By discussing issues together you'll help each other "smooth out the ride."
- **As the course material and workbook for a facilitator-led program** View our website or contact us about obtaining our secular, Christian and Jewish Leader's Guides; we offer training sessions in person and by telephone.
- **In school programs to engage parents and get them talking and learning** Many middle and high schools yearn for ways to connect the parents of their students with the school community and with one another. Everyone benefits—schools, parents, and students.
- **To enhance relationships and connections** Faith-based groups find this program is a vehicle to connect parents as they support one another.

Enjoy!

My hope is that what you learn here about yourself and your teenager enhances your relationship. And I hope that you develop a precious and valuable connection with your parenting peers...one that helps you to bring the best of *you* to these exciting years.

How to use this guide

Please Stop the Rollercoaster! isn't like other parenting books. It's a curriculum, workbook, course reading material and guide all in one. Here's how you can use it:

On it's own, this book provides the reading material and serves as the workbook for a parent discussion group. All the material you need is here in this book, and we supply and update supplementary and more current information on our companion website. This text is used by all participants in both facilitated and self-directed groups. In Christian or Jewish groups, the facilitator will customize the program for the faith setting using material in the selected Leader's Guide.

Readers may also want to read the book and initiate discussions on their own. For those who don't have the time or desire to join a formal discussion group, this program is designed flexibly enough that you can use it with a walking buddy, or any way that suits your needs.

This guide provides you with the content you'll need to meet *four* objectives:

- **Learn from the experts.** We provide many excerpts from top experts in a variety of fields who will inform you, teach you, and help you think in new ways. (Many readers use this information to guide them to books they will read in their entirety, and you can find additional sources at our website.)

- **Challenge and clarify your beliefs.** Unexamined and unchallenged beliefs may undermine your best intentions. The way you were raised may not be the way you want to raise your kids, yet it is normal to unconsciously fall into patterns of behavior from our past. This program is designed to raise to a *conscious level* your choices and approaches. Challenge your beliefs—you may learn a new way to approach a problem, you may emerge with new ideas, you may learn *why* you believe what you do. You will need to know this because, at some point, your child is likely to challenge your beliefs.

- **Learn from others through discussion.** Plan on making discussion a part of your experience. The sharing of stories, experiences, and points of view helps you to be open and to learn. There should be no expectation of sharing confidential information about your family; rather, there is much to be explored together as you learn about adolescent development, experiences, changes in parenting roles, and strategies.

- **Learn from yourself.** We will also guide you to do some written reflection as a way to work through various ideas and thoughts. We provide room here in this book to do some of this writing and encourage you to make use of it. Writing your thoughts is an effective way of processing issues and ideas, and it can be a tangible way to see your growth.

How to use this guide

Reader instructions   There are eight chapters, each with a different focus, each containing exercises to guide you to reflect on key issues. Although the exercises won't take much time, they are important, and will help you to gain the most insight. Pay particular attention to the "take-aways." By writing down what you've learned and how it applies to your situation, you identify your own priorities and action steps.

For those of you in discussion groups Group members will each need their own book so they can read the entire chapter and complete the exercises in preparation for the meetings. The next few pages address some of the issues involved in creating and running discussion groups, as well as instructions for group leaders. Information about our Leader's Guides and training for discussion leaders is available along with additional information and support materials on our website.

Quotes   Read what the experts have to say.

Exercise   Exercises are an important part of this program because they require your involvement. You'll have many opportunities to think and write about issues, opinions, experiences, and feelings. Much of what you are asked to write is for your use only, but occasionally it may be shared and discussed at group meetings. Exercises are to be completed by each group member before group meetings unless other instructions are given. (Occasionally, for instance, exercises include group activities.)

Issues to examine and discuss   We provide questions as guidelines to help you think further about important issues. If you are in a group, you can use these questions as the basis for your discussions. If you are not in a group, you should pursue conversations about the issues that are important to you.

Take-aways   At the end of each session, identify and write down what you've learned and what was relevant to you. Articulate how that will translate into action.

A "window" into the adolescent world   These are quotes or excerpts that come from teenagers and their world; they are meant to enlighten you and expand your understanding of their point of view.

This book is designed to be used with our companion website: www.PleaseStoptheRollercoaster.com. We keep this book principles-based and put the more current information, as well as helpful tools, on the website. Be sure to check out the "Tools for Groups" area.

Offering this program in your community

If you are considering bringing this program to your community, you probably have many questions about anticipated results, funding, promotion and recruitment and models.

Why offer this discussion group program? Helping parents means you are helping teens. Connecting the two is obvious. Parents who are engaged, confident, and informed are more effective at keeping kids in school, off drugs, and behaving well. Notable research in the area of parent involvement in education points out that in order for parents to be involved in their kids' education they must have a degree of "efficacy." This is what this program addresses: it helps parents gain a sense of empowerment and confidence as they learn about teen development and improve their skills in parenting.

Communities benefit when parents are connected with and communicating with one another. *Rollercoaster!* discussion groups are a natural way for parents to expand their networks, develop new friendships, learn to know their children's classmates and friends… and to establish communication patterns that benefit their teenagers on many levels.

Funding options: The costs associated with this program are reasonable and should not be a detriment in any case. We encourage parent contributions to cover the costs associated with it; this is a simple way to demonstrate their commitment to the program. Some schools have covered part or all of the cost of the books, and there may be funding opportunities available if you are willing to do some work. The Department of Education's Office of Safe and Drug Free Schools is one such government department that offers grants to support efforts in keeping kids safe and healthy. There is often a parent component to these programs, and in some communities this funding has helped to support the (optional) leader training and the administration of the *Please Stop the Rollercoaster!* program. Also, in some faith communities grants have been used to support the program. We welcome qualified individuals to charge for their services as they facilitate this program.

Selecting the best delivery model: This program can run in a self-directed fashion just by following the suggestions in this book; alternatively, it can be led by a formal facilitator using our secular, Christian or Jewish Leader's Guides. We've found that participants will self-select, choosing the model with which they feel most comfortable. In various communities the program has been offered using both models, allowing interested parents to sign up for whichever type of group they prefer. Many times, author Sue Blaney will help to build interest by speaking to parents in a workshop to launch the program.

How to promote the program: We offer as much help as we can to make the promotion and recruitment process as easy and turn-key as possible. Promotional materials are available for free download from our website, and some are included with the Leader's Guides. We add to this area frequently and invite your suggestions. Visit the "Tools for Groups" area of www.PleaseStopTheRollercoaster.com.

We welcome your comments and feedback so we can improve our program and services for you.

Forming a parenting discussion group

Creating a discussion group If you decide to create your own self-directed group, it needn't be complicated or difficult. Ask two friends. Ask them to ask two friends. Be open to people you don't know. Before you know it, you'll be ready. But be thoughtful about planning the make-up of your group because that will be important. Here are some recommendations:

- **Create a group of 6 to 10 people.** Smaller than that may not give you the diversity of opinion and viewpoint that will facilitate enlightening discussions; larger than that may limit everyone's ability to participate in the group discussions. That said, we've had groups as small as 3 and larger than 10. This program is flexible—make it yours!

- **Go for diversity.** This is a chance to open yourself up to new ideas. You know how your friends think. Being friends, you are likely to think in similar ways. We urge you to reach out to a more diverse group. This is a great way to expand your circle.

- **Consider gender.** Groups may be composed of all women, men, or a combination of both. Ours was a women's group, and we loved it. There's a comfort and camaraderie that is likely to develop that can be wonderful and supportive. On the other hand, having both fathers and mothers can add a wonderful dimension.

- **Gather parents of girls and parents of boys.** Our one recommendation with regard to gender is to try and have parents of both boys and girls. Even if you personally have only daughters, learning about their peers of the opposite sex will greatly enhance your understanding of your child's world.

- **Consider age.** You may want to be conscious of the ages of the adolescents; juniors in high school are dealing with different issues than eighth graders. This doesn't mean you can't have a group with children at different teenage stages, but you may find additional ways to support each other if you are experiencing similar situations. This program can help parents of teenagers at all stages of development.

- **Set expectations and norms.** Talk about group expectations and rules, and discuss expectations for attendance, frequency of meetings, administrative duties, and structure for the meetings. You will also want to cover in advance how to handle those who may dominate discussions. Don't let feelings fester; establish norms for discussing group process from the very beginning. Visit our website for useful tools in this area.

- **Rotate leadership.** We recommend having one or two discussion leaders for each session. Rotate throughout the group membership evenly. This way, everyone shares the responsibility, the work, and the opportunity to influence group process and discussion. (This won't be necessary for those participating in the facilitator-led model. See our website for more information about the Leader's Guide and training options).

- **Identify one group coordinator.** One central coordinator can help smooth communication and simplify organizational items.

Forming a parenting discussion group (cont.)

Here are some suggestions based on what we learned:

Meeting place   There will be as many options for meeting places and time as there are groups. In our experience, we tried meeting in our homes in the evenings, but found we preferred not to meet there because we didn't want to make our teenagers feel uncomfortable. We found several alternatives: a church room, a school room, and we eventually settled in a conference room at a friend's business.

Frequency of meetings   As for frequency, we found every two weeks to be about right for us, although a weekly commitment would also be effective. The key is to keep up momentum and focus, because that is essential to the success of your experience. Although some people gravitate toward a monthly frequency, this is not what we recommend. A group that meets only monthly runs the risk of losing momentum, and unless they are careful they won't even get through the whole book in one school year.

Duration   Plan for each meeting to last about two to three hours. However, this book provides more content and discussion questions in each session than you can cover in that amount of time, which gives you flexibility to customize your approach for your group's needs.

Keep the conversation focused   As much as we loved getting together to "chat," we quickly learned that if we were too "loose" about the topics and agenda, group members would find themselves drawn into other, more pressing commitments. Keep focused on the *learning* and your group will complete its mission.

Take-aways and tips   I've noticed that sometimes parents want *answers,* and they get itchy when discussions about difficult issues have no clear resolution. In this program you will develop your own answers, the ones that feel right for you and your family. We have created "tips" sheets for some chapters that are downloadable from our website in the "Tools for Groups" section. Also, use these sheets to discuss and develop your own tips.

Keep your timeline flexible   There are eight chapters, or sessions, designated in the book, but you may find them too "meaty" to get through in eight sessions. You may want to spend two sessions per chapter, or decide on the amount of time you want to spend on each topic depending on your particular interests and needs. Make it work for you—there are no hard and fast rules here.

Forming a parenting discussion group (cont.)

Group Leadership in self-directed groups: Unless you have a formal facilitator, we recommend that all group members take turns as discussion leaders and play a role in running the meetings.

Here is an overview of what session discussion leaders need to do:

- Establish the priorities for the meeting. Ask each member to identify the most important discussion issues they wish to cover in the meeting from the "Issues to examine and discuss" page at the end of each chapter. Begin with each person's top question and go all around the room. Then discuss the questions of secondary interest, and so on. (Alternatively, the leader could select the issues to discuss, if that is preferable.)

- It may help to create a time line for the meeting so that you can cover each topic and discussion point appropriately while keeping the meeting on time.

- Make sure each person has the opportunity to contribute to the discussion.

- Occasionally, you may want make use of a white board, or a flip chart. The leader should identify and plan for these needs in advance.

- The leader should be responsible for ending the meeting 10 minutes early to give everyone a chance to write down their "take-aways." If you have time, share them.

- If your group chooses to sign a confidentiality agreement at the beginning of each meeting, the leader should make sure that happens. However, no one should feel obligated to reveal personal information.

- Be sure the leader is identified for the next meeting.

@   **There are additional tools and resources on our Web site: www.PleaseStoptheRollercoaster.com in the "Tools for Groups" area.**

Getting the most out of this program on your own

Here are some suggestions on how you can get the most out of this program if you choose to read the book on your own:

- **Take your time.** Resist the temptation to read the book cover to cover; be sure to invest the time to answer the questions and identify take-aways. By doing the exercises you'll retain more information, and create behavior changes that will yield results. Take time to explore the program contents so you can observe your surroundings with new eyes.

- **Initiate discussions about the issues that resonate with you.** You can do this in such a casual way people won't even know what you're up to, unless you want them to know. It's important to talk about the issues, and the questions that you have, because it helps you to clarify your beliefs and it opens you up to new points of view. Have these conversations in as formal or informal a setting as you choose, but be deliberate about having the discussions. Try and discuss issues with your child's other parent, with your friends and family, with your child's friends' parents, with teachers, coaches, administrators. Everybody has something to say about adolescence.

The "you" factor If you're on a rollercoaster ride raising your teenager, you're going to have to isolate the challenges *you* own, because that's where you can have the most direct influence. We are focusing on *parents* in this program, while we learn about adolescence and how to best support our teens. Isolating out the "you" factor is not difficult to do, if you are honest with yourself. We'll provide guidance as we visit this theme throughout the book.

If you need to process situations or issues on your own, here are some initial suggestions. (If you're in a group you can help each other by doing this together).

- Try to isolate your emotions and look at the situation objectively. Recognize your emotional involvement; how much of your reaction is about you and your emotions, expectations, and needs? How is that coloring this situation?
- Take into account all that you know about adolescent development. Is this situation reflective of your child's developmental stage? Is he acting in a developmentally appropriate manner? Does that change your response?
- If you do nothing what's likely to happen?
- What's the worst that can happen?
- What would be the best possible resolution?
- Is action required on your part? Why? What kind of action?
- Identify your options.
- If your friend were in this situation with his teenager, what would you suggest to him?
- What is your role in this situation? Pull back and take a look at the big picture. What's really going to be best for your teenager and how might that be achieved?

In thoughtful preparation

Complete on your own before you start this program. Either write a letter to your adolescent about why you are reading this book (it is up to you whether or not you share this letter with your child) *or* write down what your vision is for yourself upon the completion of the program. What do you hope to get out of this process? Are you open to learning new things? Are you willing to change your behavior if necessary? If you are participating in a discussion group, you may want to share this with each other.

I am told that parenting a teenager is a whole new experience in parenting - Throw out the old rules.

As my children are going through this ride and so I am, I want to be so effective and so helpful as possible. In addition I think that teens these days are dealing with more "dangers"

Before you begin

One of Stephen Covey's contributions to the world in *The 7 Habits of Highly Effective Families* is his advice to "begin with the end in mind." Before we explore the important topic of adolescent development, we need to examine what our objectives are, not just in this program, but in what we hope to achieve as we raise our children.

Resiliency is the word that many professionals use to describe the characteristics that we hope to help our children develop. Robert Brooks and Sam Goldstein, authors of *Raising Resilient Children,* articulate some of the traits of resiliency: the ability to deal more effectively with "stress and pressure, to cope with everyday challenges, to bounce back from disappointments, adversity, and trauma, to develop clear and realistic goals, to solve problems, to relate comfortably with others, and to treat oneself and others with respect."[1]

Applicable as a goal in all the stages and phases of our children's growth, "resiliency" embodies our objectives as we discuss the development of adolescents. Brooks and Goldstein suggest particular "guideposts" that need to be embedded in the mindset of parents who foster resilience in their children. They are:

- Being empathetic

- Communicating effectively and listening actively

- Changing "negative scripts"

- Loving our children in ways that help them to feel special and appreciated

- Accepting our children for who they are and helping them to set realistic expectations and goals

- Helping our children experience success by identifying and reinforcing their "islands of competence"

A resilient teenager can handle the bumps in the road without being overly traumatized. This quality of resilience may well be one of the most important qualities for a human to strive for, as it plays a key part in one's ability to cope with life's ups and downs.

Before you begin (cont.)

- Helping children recognize that mistakes are experiences from which to learn

- Developing responsibility, compassion, and a social conscience by providing children with opportunities to contribute

- Teaching our children to solve problems and make decisions

- Disciplining in a way that promotes self-discipline and self-worth[2]

Revisit this list from time to time. Be thoughtful about how you are applying what you learn to the overall objective of raising adolescents who are resilient, know they are loved and supported by their families, and are prepared to enter the world as young adults.

Adolescent Development

A scenario

Inside and out, your teenage daughter is changing dramatically. Seemingly overnight, she has grown four inches, gained sixteen pounds, and is exhibiting womanly curves. She seems uncomfortable in her own skin; even her walk seems different. In addition to the external changes, she seems paranoid about everything: her appearance, her friends, your words and actions. She is critical of you and quick to be "mortified" by your every move. It's as if she thinks she's on camera all of the time. Life is either "unbelievably fantastic" or "the absolute worst." There is no in between. It seems that when she is around other people, she is more comfortable and mature. At home, she seems to fall back into childish behavior and outright laziness. This blur of change is confusing, frustrating, and fascinating you at the same time.

Have you noticed the signs of physical and psychological development in your teenager?

Chapter One: Overview and objectives

One of the biggest reasons parents find raising teenagers challenging at times, is because we don't understand what is behind their behavior. We're going to focus our attention on adolescent development in this chapter, so you will gain a perspective and understanding about the developmental realities of adolescence. What is this experience like for our teenagers? What is normal? Why? How are teenagers different from children? From adults? What can parents expect from teenagers during this period? The more you understand the teenager's reality, the better equipped you are to use this insight to support your child and to help your relationship. We will look at development with a focus on several different areas: physical and cognitive development, self-discovery and developing identity, teenagers' views of parents, spiritual exploration, friends, and fears.

Objectives

In this chapter you will:

- Explore, learn about, and discuss the developmental process along with issues and dynamics experienced by adolescents.

- Learn about the teenager's search for self-discovery and identity.

- Examine how their developmental process includes changes in their views of adults in general, and parents in particular.

- Become attuned to the messages in their youth culture (such as in their music) that reflect topics of importance and relevance to them, such as their search for self-discovery.

> *"Flunking a test and getting dumped by a boyfriend or girlfriend within a couple of days is analogous to an adult's losing a job and a spouse in the same time period."*
> Riera[3]

Chapter One: Instructions

Reader Instructions

How to get the most out of this chapter:

- Complete the letter/vision exercise on page 12 in the Introduction.

- Read all of Chapter 1; you may want to highlight the areas that are the most relevant to you.

- Prepare the exercises on pages 25, 33, and 34.

- Give special attention to music, both from your generation and your teenager's, that provides examples of the adolescent search for identity.

- Examine the issues and questions on page 39. Discuss the most relevant questions with a friend, spouse, or in your parenting discussion group, if you have one.

- Be sure to write down your "take-aways." These insights will help you translate your intentions into actions.

If you have a parenting discussion group:

Group Recommendations/

- If your group hasn't met before this, you'll want to spend some time getting to know one another and discussing goals and ground rules. There are documents to help you on our website including a "First Meeting Blueprint" and "Maintaining Smooth Group Dynamics."

- If anyone has brought in music they wish to share with the group, listen and discuss.

- Ask each group member to identify which of the issues on page 39 they wish to discuss.

- The facilitator for the meeting can guide the group discussion to ensure that the issues of greatest interest to group members are examined and explored, and that all group members participate.

 Be sure to access supplementary and current information on this topic at www.PleaseStoptheRollercoaster.com.

A view of adolescence

The changes are dramatic and virtually constant during adolescence.

How do you want to view adolescence? It is not a disease. It is a normal stage of life and an important part of development. It can also be said, however, that adolescence is an existential crisis—of major proportions—and it is to be experienced without the benefit of adult perspective. Think about it: absolutely everything is changing in the world of a teenager. Their bodies are undergoing dramatic changes over which they have no control. They begin to think in new ways as they gain cognitive capabilities that entirely change their view of, and interactions with, the world around them. Teenagers feel an irresistible pull away from their families and begin to relate with a new sense of urgency to their peers. They try on different personas in their search to discover who they really are. And some do this amidst fear and pain, pain they cannot admit even to themselves, about separating from their family and entering into the larger world. Teens gain a new perspective about their family of origin as they begin to see, with clarity, that their parents are flawed, as are most adults. The world is tempting, exciting, enticing, frightening, and overwhelming all at the same time. And, as they go through these fundamental changes and growth spurts, they must still manage to study and stay focused on grades and their other activities. Sounds challenging, doesn't it? And teenagers do tend to take others along on their rollercoaster ride, as we parents can attest.

Our teenagers can confuse and puzzle us. Children who were peaceful and happy as youngsters can turn into screaming door slammers seemingly overnight. Parents wonder about what is happening inside the heads of children who spend hours behind closed doors, moody and uncommunicative, or others who spend hours on the telephone—what could possibly warrant so much discussion?

Parents marvel at the outward changes and how quickly they occur.

And how about the physical changes that occur? The contrasts between the shapely bodies of many girls in junior high and the boys who still resemble little kids can be confounding. If it can be distracting for adults imagine how it must feel to the kids! And what is it about summer vacation—is it my imagination or do most students grow at least 3 inches in the course of 10 weeks?! How does that happen?

As our children enter middle school parents often find themselves struggling to understand what is happening. We find it difficult to figure out what constitutes "normal" behavior because the teenagers' behavior varies so widely. The best of parents find it challenging to know what to do—how to support a child who one moment pushes you away, and the

A view of adolescence (cont.)

next moment wants to cuddle up. The contrasts between their public and private persona can be particularly vexing.

Understanding what's behind the behavioral changes enables parents to provide needed understanding and support.

As I've already told you, sharing our confusion and concern brought the women who formed my parenting discussion group together. Once we better understood what was happening with our kids, we were able to smooth out our ride *and* give the support we so wanted to give. I clearly remember our relief when we read in Anthony Wolf's book *Get Out of My Life, but First Could You Drive Me and Cheryl to the Mall?* that teenagers' behavior in public was a better representation of their real level of maturity than what we saw at home. His discussion about their "baby self" gave us an understanding about behavior that had been puzzling. And it deepened our curiosity to learn more about this developmental process.

"Why do friends seem more important than family, all of a sudden?" "How can I support my son when we can't seem to have a civil conversation?" "Why is she so self-conscious? She never cared about her looks so much before." "They seem so loud and obnoxious when they are together as a group!" "Why is it my friend's daughter seems so mature when mine seems so young, and moody and fragile?"

Adolescent experts help us gain insight into the developmental process.

These are some of the questions we set out to answer. We found many wonderful explanations in the books and resources we accessed, and I'll quote from a number of these adolescent experts in this session. You may want to read more of these books, and I encourage you to do so. Consider this a start, a "Cliff's Notes" version of adolescent development.

Be observant. Listen more than you speak. Try to get into your teenager's shoes. Once you understand what is going on, what is driving these changes, you'll be better equipped to provide a calm eddy for your teen, a safe place where she can gather strength and grow as she prepares to move on.

A glimpse into their world

Let's begin with the big picture. Regardless of whether your child is just beginning the journey through adolescence, or you're in the midst of the college search, it benefits parents to have an understanding of the journey as a whole. What is it about the process that makes it a challenge for many of us? What can we learn from the experts to help us put this into perspective?

Ava Siegler, Ph.D., author of *The Essential Guide to the New Adolescence* gives us a look at the big picture that begins to provide a perspective on the process.

The Five Developmental Tasks of Adolescence (these are usually sequential):

Separating from old ties   The adolescent needs to separate from parents, and see them as real people with strengths and weaknesses. He needs to develop his own sense of self, of independence, of power. This results in mixed feelings for parents: "sadness at the loss of childhood, nostalgia for the days when we were needed, anxiety about whether they can manage without us, anger at being replaced by peers, relief that their child is growing up normally, happiness that they got this far, safely."[4] Does this very mixed bag of responses sound accurate to you?

Creating new attachments   The adolescent needs to fill the emotional gap left by parents and prepare himself for lasting love and companionship attachments. It is as difficult for the teenager to shift the attachment and admiration for parents to people outside the family circle as it is for parents to accept. Early social experiences can be painful, but he "learns what he wants from a relationship, what sorts of people he gets along with, and what kinds of people he can't bear, and he'll learn how to maintain his own sense of self, while still being able to stay connected to another."[5]

Establishing a mature sexual identity and a mature sexual life   The adolescent establishes his sexual identity and begins to pursue love outside the family circle. Siegler observes: "Teenagers are rarely capable of a deep and abiding love and loyalty to each other in early adolescence, but they are learning to form relationships. Teens tend to be serially monogamous."[6]

Formulating new ideas and new ideals   As the teenager becomes more independent and autonomous, she reexamines parental influence and standards, integrating them with new concepts from her peer group. As religion, values, and other core beliefs are scrutinized, this "process of self-definition" can easily cause conflicts with the family. As they reach late/post adolescence, they may or may not return to their parent's values.[7]

Consolidating character   The adolescent integrates aspects of tasks 1-4 and is able to function as a "capable and productive adult."[8]

You can probably see all five of these steps as you reflect back on your own development.

A glimpse into their world (cont.)

Mary Pipher's *Reviving Ophelia* may have reached the elevated position of a "classic" in adolescent-focused literature. She provides a wonderful framework for our discussion of adolescence, as descriptive for boys as it is for girls:

E

> Adolescents are travelers, far from home with no native land, neither children, nor adults. They are jet setters who fly from one country to another with amazing speed. Sometimes they are four years old, hours later they are twenty-five. They don't really fit in anywhere. There's a yearning for place, a search for solid ground.
>
> Mary Pipher, *Reviving Ophelia: Saving the Selves of Adolescent Girls*, 52

The developmental areas in which teenagers grow are rarely synchronized. You've seen it: kids who may be physically ahead of the curve can be behind emotionally. Strong abstract thinkers may have underdeveloped social skills. What's difficult for adults is to understand, is how to relate to this ever-changing adolescent. Should you relate to the mature, rational 16 year old or the part of her that is as undeveloped emotionally as a six year old? It can be confusing!

Author's note: Books that are referenced often will be introduced in the following way. Additionally there are many excellent books that are referenced once or twice; they can be found in the Selected Bibliography section.

> Mary Pipher, PH.D., provides an informative, provocative, and sometimes alarming view of adolescent girls' experiences in *Reviving Ophelia: Saving the Selves of Adolescent Girls*. While offering meaningful insight about adolescent girls' development, she also discusses the "girl poisoning" society in which we live. A well known text that withstands the test of time, this is not only a "must read" for parents of girls, but by parents of boys and teenagers themselves. Much of what she says about our society, and about adolescents, applies to boys, as well as to girls.

Teenagers take on a veneer, an attitude, that intentionally separates them from adults. This veneer is sometimes used as a weapon—it increases their separation from the adult world as it protects them, masking their self consciousness and vulnerability.

Passion fills the lives of teenagers. The world is exciting. They don't want to miss anything. Their world, sometimes, even takes on a desperate quality. Accompanying this is a sense of exposure and vulnerability, which can increase their sense of desperation.

Physical and cognitive development

Girls generally mature earlier than boys; in fact, in early adolescence girls are roughly two years ahead of boys in physical maturity. In high school this evens out and the boys catch up in their physical maturity.

Physically, girls will usually be well into puberty by age 13, and by age 15 for boys. The physical changes, of course, happen over a number of years around this average midpoint. Boys will typically double their physical strength from age twelve to age seventeen.[9]

We are all aware that hormones play a large part in driving this growth process; hormones are mind chemicals that act on the brain and tell the brain to change the body. In boys, the main hormone is testosterone, an anabolic steroid which helps to beef up the body. In puberty, testosterone levels soar to 20 times their level in girls.[10] Of course hormones play a big role in girls' development, as well.

But hormones seem to be getting less attention lately as new research is shedding light on the brain development that occurs in growing teens. (We'll talk more about this in chapter 5, and this is a subject we explore regularly on our website.)

Cognitively, one of the most dynamic ways in which adolescents mature is in the growth from concrete thinking to abstract thinking. This affects their academic life as well as their social world. Michael Riera's description below is the best I've seen to explain this phenomenon.

E

Along with these physical changes is a profound shift in cognitive processes. Swiss psychologist Jean Piaget called this the move from *concrete operational thinking* to *formal operational thinking.* This shift can be compared to the difference between watching a movie on a four-inch black-and-white television and seeing the same movie in a state-of-the-art theater with surround-sound and interactive capabilities. Concrete operational thinking is limited to the present and to physical reality; formal operational thinking handles abstract concepts, ideas, and possibilities….

…Your teenager's inconsistent behaviors and attitudes are often the result of rapid switches between concrete and abstract thinking.

Michael Riera, *Uncommon Sense for Parents with Teenagers, 12*

Michael Riera, Ph.D, offers *Uncommon Sense for Parents with Teenagers* which provides no nonsense advice and some of the most useful insights I've seen. Previously a high school counselor in California, his direct experiences in working with thousands of teenagers helps to provide an air of credibility and even calmness to his commentary—his book is one of the best on the topic of teenagers, and particularly focuses on high school students.

Physical and cognitive development (cont.)

One way in which young teenagers demonstrate their "concrete" thinking is in their need to "categorize" people. To illustrate this point Pipher says: "People are assigned to groups such as geeks, preps and jocks…. Teenage girls are extremists who see the world in black and white terms, missing shades of gray."[11] It's not hard to miss examples of black-and-white thinking every day, when living with teenagers. Flip-flopping back and forth between friends, activities, preferences…we learn to accept it as normal at this stage.

Because they frequently finding it easier to express what they don't want, rather than what they do, dealing with teens can, at times, be frustrating and difficult. Sometimes they read meaning into comments and glances that was not intended, which can be the cause of strife and misunderstanding.

Teens live at the center of their universe, and have difficulty seeing others' points of view. As egocentric as this seems, it is a developmental stage, it does not indicate the inappropriate selfishness of which they are sometimes accused by parents.

Feelings become all important as teens engage in what Pipher calls "emotional reasoning," where feelings get so intertwined with reality and truth, it becomes difficult to distinguish it. Pipher says teens believe if they feel something, it must be true. "If a teenager feels like a nerd, she is a nerd. If she feels her parents are unfair, they are unfair."[12]

Teenagers become intensely self-conscious. One friend of mine likened it to living under spot lights. "How would you like to give a dinner party in a store display window?" she asked us. That's what the scrutiny feels like to them. One psychologist called it "imaginary audience syndrome."[13]

This extreme self-consciousness is connected to the development of abstract thinking. It allows teens to learn from their experiences, and to apply lessons learned to other, similar situations. This is beneficial as they navigate the social scene in high school. On the other hand, Riera points out "the curse of self-consciousness is that it also becomes a tool for self disparagement or guilt, some of which is necessary, but much of which is excessive. This means that teenagers not only experience pain in the moment, but they can re-experience pain for a long time afterwards.[14]

Mom, I want to have little parties together and put makeup on each other, paint our nails over a bag of popcorn and talk about guys. Don't just say, "I'm too old for that stuff, honey."[15]

Michelle, 14

Physical and cognitive development (cont.)

E

> To sum up, this shift into abstract thinking, accompanied by a rush of hormonal changes, can (and often does) change a person overnight. Imagine waking up in a body that has new physical dimensions and new sexual desires, with a mind that conceptualizes the world in drastically new ways and that carries an overwhelming sense of confusion about all these feelings—all without prior warning! This is the world of the adolescent.
>
> Michael Riera, *Uncommon Sense for Parents with Teenagers*, 15

As parents, we need to be aware of teens' self-consciousness and fear of humiliation. There are times when we can support them by helping them get out of situations gracefully, avoiding humiliation.

A simple developmental time line:

- Seventh graders look to conform with peers.

- Eighth graders want to stand out to a point, but their "pose" must be just right.

- Freshmen girls are way ahead of boys; both boys and girls are trying to find their niche and to identify their group of friends. They are beginning to renegotiate their relationships with adults.[16]

- Sophomore boys and girls are reevaluating relationships, activities and values. They have embarked on an "extreme search for identity."[17]

- Juniors tend to experiment more seriously; they are looking for lasting friendships. They are idealistic and romantic.[18]

- Seniors are on top of the world, and comfortable there. They may be somewhat bored with the present, and anxious about the future.[19]

E

> Just like earlier teen subcultures peopled by beatniks, rock 'n rollers, and others, members of the hip-hop generation adopt a shocking veneer not just to unnerve adults, but to cover the acute self-consciousness and painful vulnerability of being an adolescent. To most kids, this is a "style."
>
> Patricia Hersch, *A Tribe Apart*, 88-89

Physical and cognitive development (cont.)

Have you seen signs of the shift to abstract thinking in your child? What have her teachers noticed?

School easier

Noticing his sense of humor as it matures is also a good way to identify his developmental progress. What have you noticed in this regard?

Sarcastic, quickwitted

Is your child still in the "black and white" phase of life, or are shades of gray emerging?

more black+white

The physical changes are easier to detect. Keep track of their growth statistics from their annual physicals; my son grew 5 inches and gained 23 pounds in one year! Has your son or daughter had a big growth spurt, or is it still in front of him or her?

slow + steady

Self-discovery/identity

Adolescence is a time of major transitions and psychological change. It is the time of life when children begin to turn away from their childhood, from their dependence on parents, and develop their independence. This means the security from their former life gradually becomes a thing of the past as the teen begins to take responsibility for her own survival. It is an exciting time—but it can also be very scary. Life, survival, independence—this is for real. Parents can find appropriate ways to respond if we see what is at stake from the adolescent's perspective. This is big. The process can make teenagers feel very exposed, very vulnerable.

In order to manage this change successfully, teens begin to disallow their childish feelings, as they work to enhance their sense of independence. At times this is not an elegant process, as you've most likely seen. Parents feel the shift from being the trusted savior to being the last person on the face of the earth with a good suggestion. It is that if the child accepts the parent's suggestion, the child has somehow given away her opportunity to stand on her own—to make her own choice successfully. Can you see how parents, through no fault of our own, can come to represent feelings that the child must now reject? This is a healthy transition, it is what their growth is all about. We really can't take this rejection personally.

E

The course of preadolescent childhood is played out in the continuing struggle between the mandate to grow up and the wish not to. On the one hand is the "baby self" which desires only the nurturing it has enjoyed for years. All pleasure. No fuss. "After a hard day at school let me unwind and fill up with good stuff. Let me watch television and eat Doritos. I definitely do *not* want to hang up my coat."

Parents see their children act immature, irresponsible, lazy and demanding, because the home is the natural realm for expressing the dependent, babyish mode of functioning.

But there is the other self beginning to develop slowly—the independent, mature self. This self reaches out and seeks gratification from meaningful interaction with the world. It sets forth to accomplish something, to develop competence. It is willing to deal with stress, to take on responsibility. It is even willing to hang up coats—but only at school, or at Grandmother's house. It is usually on view only *away* from the home, unseen by parents.

Normal development pushes toward an ever-decreasing role for the baby self. Adolescence is no more than the first, most traumatic stage in this ongoing struggle, exacerbated by the new awareness of sexuality and the mandate to separate from parents, to avoid unacceptable feelings of dependence. Once people reach adolescence and, ultimately, adulthood, most have resolved this conflict by choosing a life of growth and separation. This "decision" is what we label maturity. This is what's supposed to happen. Ultimately, they can even act nice toward their parents. But not during adolescence! Then, they very much remain children when they are home. And often, rather nasty children. This is a crucial point: operation in the baby-self mode is a way *not* to separate from the parents.

Anthony Wolf, *Get Out of My Life, But First Could You Drive Me and Cheryl to the Mall?*, 15,16

Self-discovery/identity (cont.)

Teenagers feel an unconscious contradiction: they really do want to be left alone, but parental controls act as a kind of security blanket for them that sometimes feels very, very good.

Some children have a smoother transition than others. It seems that those who are most comfortable acting independently have the smoothest transition. Wolf says, "Some children need to cling, often provoking endless and senseless battles. Children who are not so good at functioning on their own will probably have a tougher adolescence than their peers."[20] What about the parents who don't support their kid's attempts at independence? The adults in a child's life can make this process easier, or much more difficult.

Kids need to be comfortable at home; they need the opportunity to recharge their batteries, to save up their energy for their forays out into the world. They need to retreat into their world at home regularly. Home should provide them with a sense of safety and a healthy calm.

For these adolescents, they are embarking on nothing less than their search for identity and self-discovery. Although an individual process, this takes place under the scrutiny of their peers. Teens will often experiment with roles, with behavior and with priorities. They may compare their external self with their internal self and ask "Is this me?"

Membership in a group allows teens a place for self-discovery as they are asserting independence from parents. After she is clearly "in" the group, she may, in time, step away as she proceeds with her own process of self-discovery.

Anthony Wolf, Ph.D., psychologist and family therapist, offers some of the best insights for parents of teenagers in *Get Out of My Life but First Could You Drive Me and Cheryl to the Mall?* He does it in a way that is accessible and understandable for almost anyone. His inimitable humor adds a dimension frequently missed in this genre. If you purchase just one additional book, this is the one you need.

Don't worry so much if you don't have the answer to a question I may have. Just keep helping me find the answers.[21]

Charlene, 17

Self-discovery/identity (cont.)

Look to teenagers' music for insight into their struggles for self-discovery. Christina Aguilera, in one of her songs, asks when the girl she sees in the mirror will reflect who she is inside.[22]

Music is called the language of the soul. It communicates feelings, experiences, and moves us on many different levels. It provides a sense of community, as people gather to listen and experience music together. Music provides a connection between people, common ground, shared language. Or it can be used to exclude others and drive them away.

Patricia Hersch describes music's ability to provide a desired mask for young teenagers:

E

That music, the hallmark of their age group, has a style that is all they are not: confident, outspoken, brash, packaged in a deep rhythm and attitude that says things he wouldn't dare say, speaks of doing things he wouldn't dare do. It takes away thinking, awkwardness, transforms the room by its overwhelming beat and volume.

Patricia Hersch, *A Tribe Apart*, 129

"83" written and sung by John Mayer[23]

Here I stand 6 feet small
And smiling cause I'm scared as hell
Kind of like my life is like a sequel to a movie
Where the actor's names have changed
Oh well

"Dancing Nancies" The Dave Matthews Band[24]

I am who I am who I am well who am I
Requesting some enlightenment
Could I have been anyone other than me?

"Choices" by Asher[25]

How long will it take you to decide
What you're gonna do?
Right now is the moment where you will
Choose your destiny

Self-discovery/identity (cont.)

This struggle for identity is sometimes discussed in psychological terms that are difficult for the average parent to understand. But, whether you understand the psychological roots of behavior or not, you certainly have seen many people struggle with the basic issue of developing enough confidence to stand up to pressure from others. I'm sure you've seen this dynamic played out many times over your years as a teenager; sometimes we still see adults struggle with it. Although the pressure is great to conform, I've seen kids sometimes admire one who has the courage to stand alone. One fourteen-year-old girl whom I know is admired by kids and parents alike because she marches to the beat of her own drum. This kind of self-assuredness is uncommon among younger teens.

Mary Pipher does a good job of helping to explain how it happens that some kids lose their sense of self, and consequently their self-confidence, as they demand approval from the outside world. Again, this can apply to boys as well as girls; she says: Girls have a choice: they "can be true to themselves and risk abandonment by their peers, or they can reject their true selves and be socially acceptable."[26] We all see too many girls who choose the safe route, and follow the crowd's expectations for them. To follow one's authentic self may require more courage and maturity than many girls can muster, especially as younger teens.

This choice is significant because self-esteem (and authenticity) is based on the acceptance of all thoughts and feelings as one's own. Girls, and boys too, lose confidence if they "disown" themselves. Pipher observes that if all their validation comes from the outside they can be "vulnerable and directionless children—happy when praised and devastated when ignored or criticized. They can become like sailboats without centerboards; their self-worth changing with the wind."[27] This can so distort their perspective and self-image that they are no longer able to hear their own voice or to discern their own right and wrong in the world around them.

The establishment of a personal identity and *the confidence to project it,* are part of the adolescent journey. But, even for the teens who stay connected to their authentic selves, this is a bumpy ride. They will make mistakes, they will misinterpret reality, they will change their sense of who they are and what they are passionate about—that is all part of this process. However, the teenagers who are somewhat self-reflective, who find their originality supported and applauded, who know they are loved unconditionally, will find it easier to stay "centered" while they navigate this ever changing landscape.

Development and gender

I have found it difficult, many times, to understand my boy. I have felt left out, confused, concerned … and challenged to find a way to communicate. When I speak with other mothers of boys, they, too express similar feelings. Mothers of girls may have a different experience entirely, and now that my daughter is a teenager I can see fundamental differences in the way my two kids experience adolescence, manage school and particularly, relate to their parents.

A boy will tend to retreat behind closed doors. And if he's forced to emerge into a more "public" part of the household (kids have to eat!) he'll do his best to maintain this masked self behind an attitude of disconnection, sulkiness and one syllable grunts. This is common behavior. Challenging as it is for parents to understand, Anthony wolf offers some explanation:

E

Above all, teenage boys become very private. They do not like to talk to their parents. In fact, they do not want their parents to know anything about what is going on in their life. The main reason is their sexuality. These feelings are an enormous part of a teenage boy's world. And this sexuality is something that he very much wants to keep separate from his parents. But it is also so much a part of him that the only way to keep it separate from them is to keep *himself* separate. The internal taboo against mixing sex and parents is so strong and the role of sexuality in a teenage boy's life is so pervasive that he is forced, for the most part, to shut his parents out of his life.

Anthony Wolf, *Get Out of My Life, but First Could You Drive Me and Cheryl to the Mall?*, 28-29

So that is what the retreat behind closed doors is all about?!

Additionally, Wolf points out, boys are frequently not comfortable with intense verbal debates. Girls may stay and fight—loudly—but boys often don't.

E

Boys rarely develop the skills or the emotional capacity to stay with strong verbal scenes. The typical adolescent boy history includes few direct child-parent screaming matches.

If boys do become emotional with their parents, they tend to get very emotional. These occasional instances are often accompanied by a punched hole in the wall or a broken screen door flung open too violently as the boy storms out of the house. Boys avoid confrontation for the excellent reason that they can't handle it. They get too upset. It's either fight or flight, and at home they usually do the latter—which is good.

Anthony Wolf, *Get Out of My Life, but First Could You Drive Me and Cheryl to the Mall?*, 31

Development and gender (cont.)

Many girls, on the other hand, behave very differently. I hope Wolf's description doesn't describe anyone you know, but if it does, his explanation might help. Experienced parents have seen the verbal gymnastics with girls; parents who are going through the adolescence of their first child will learn a lot from his explanation. We can begin to see how boys' interactions with their families is fundamentally different than that of most girls.

E

Girls deal with the psychological dilemma of adolescence differently from boys. Like boys, adolescent girls find it totally unacceptable to feel attached to, or dependent on, their parents. But girls do not withdraw. Unlike boys, they do not have to. Instead they fight. It is with girls, not boys, that parents experience the supreme disruption of adolescence. Sweet, cooperative daughters turn, often rather suddenly, into hysterical, shrieking monsters.

Girls solve the problem of living at home, and yet successfully combating their totally unacceptable feelings of love and dependence, by fighting everything. . . .

Anthony Wolf, *Get Out of My Life, but First Could You Drive Me and Cheryl to the Mall?*, 33

"Shrieking monsters?" Ouch!

But the fact that a girl stays engaged, that she is in contact with her parents, can help parents have a better sense of what is going on. And once parents understand what is behind this unsettling dynamic, they can relax a bit and learn to go with the flow.

E

A battling teenage girl can certainly be more of a strain on parents than a disappearing teenage boy. Yet this battling is not as bad as it seems. Though they are disagreeing and criticizing, they are nonetheless staying in contact. By fighting, they maintain an ongoing relationship with their parents. They are using their parents for support. Boys more or less do not. They are unable to. (Perhaps this isolation contributes to the fact that boys' suicide rate is more than triple that of girls.) As a result, even though girls' adolescence is more tumultuous, at least at home, they also get more support. Girls can have it both ways. They can keep their dependency going via their continuing contact with their parents, however stormy, but they also get to feel that they are independent. Boys, because they isolate themselves and have nobody to lean on, are forced to deal with problems more on their own. They are perhaps more vulnerable to serious problems. If there is a consolation for adolescent boys, it is that some years later, in early adulthood, they seem to have an easier time leaving home *for good* than do many girls....

Anthony Wolf, *Get Out of My Life, but First Could You Drive Me and Cheryl to the Mall?*, 35-36

Behind the mood swings

Have you marveled at the mood swings? Do you sometimes wonder how the same child can be so loud at one moment and so quiet and reserved another? This seems to be one of the hallmarks of adolescence, one that has long puzzled me. Again, Mary Pipher offers a rich explanation of this interesting developmental dynamic. She differentiates between what she calls the "surface structure of behaviors and the deep structure of meaning. Surface structure is what is visible to the naked eye—awkwardness, energy, anger, moodiness and restlessness. Deep structure is the internal work—the struggle to find a self, the attempt to integrate the past and present and to find a place in the larger culture. Surface behaviors convey little of the struggle within and in fact are often designed to obscure that struggle..."[29]

Much of the conversation in which teenage girls engage is a process of examining details of events for underlying meaning; "What did that look mean?" "Do you think he understood what I meant?" "Did she look angry when I said that?" "Did he notice me?"

Pipher points out that this helps to explain the coded messages we receive, but don't always understand. Questions which appear, on the surface to be straight-forward, may actually be masking questions of much greater importance. "Can I go to an unchaperoned party" may actually mean "Am I ready for sexual experiences?" "Can I stop going to church?" may mean "Do I have freedom enough to make my own spiritual choices?"

So, as teenagers are, on one level, processing this "serious deep-structure work," they need to release the tension and do so by behaving in sometimes opposite ways: silliness, loud boisterousness, high energy intensity that is actually a release, a welcome break. Adults do this too; after the intensity of a hard day at work a good workout, or brain-dead relaxation in front of the television can be a welcome break.

But, with teenagers it can become difficult to understand what it going on. You can see how easily miscommunication and misunderstanding can occur if teens are processing events with a different focus than what is apparent on the surface. And, at any one time it may not be evident exactly what their focus is—are they evaluating events and comments at the "surface" level or at the level of deep meaning? As this can be confusing for their peers, it can certainly explain much of the poor communication with parents.

If we pierce our body or make graffiti art, it's not to offend others but to express ourselves. If a kid grows his hair long and then shaves his head, he's just experimenting with his own personal style. It's fun to paint your face, wear weird clothes or do something crazy with your hair. It's just a form of personal expression, a confirmation that you exist. [30]

Cullen, 16

Behind the mood swings (cont.)

No doubt you've disapproved at times of the manner in which teenagers do express themselves. Is it body piercing, tattoos, blue hair, gothic dress…? What are your hot buttons? Many parents are too quick to judge the outside of the package, and this is an easy mistake to make. Personally, I've found experiencing this stage as a parent has forced me to open up in ways that I could not previously conceive. I remember about 6 years ago marveling at a mom who sat in our church on Sunday with her son who wore hair meticulously pulled into a dozen 3″ spikes, each spike tip carefully bleached blonde. I wondered what she felt like and how she could take him seriously. Lately, however, I've grown to appreciate her ability to see through that façade into a boy who was, perhaps anxiously, trying to find his unique voice.

What examples can you identify where your child may be working on developing his or her identity? Can you see role experimentation? What examples can you identify that may actually be "coded messages" masking examination of deeper issues?

choosing new friends, choosing to be a student, being cool but then silly.

I love it when you watch a movie with me. It's such a good feeling knowing that you want me to be with you. Sometimes I don't think you want to be around me, but when you sit with me and give me a hug your love runs right through me.[31]

Will, 16

I need your support when I make decisions, even if you don't agree with me.[32]

Nancy, 13

The threat of flawed adults

We've all felt our kids' disapproval. Our pants are too short, our hair isn't right, we talk too loudly and embarrass them. We never claimed to be perfect, though, so how dare they make us feel so incompetent! Sometimes our feelings do get hurt!

The dynamic is tough on all of us as we, as parents, fall off the pedestal. But, again, it's part of a normal developmental process. If teens think that adults are without flaws, that sets them up to believe perfection is necessary for adulthood. Although adults know this is not true, it can be an intimidating prospect for kids. It is a healthy developmental step for adolescents to recognize that adults are flawed but are still worthy of respect. And it is helpful for adults to be realistic about their flaws and help kids to understand perfection isn't a prerequisite for healthy and successful adulthood.

Michael Reira offers some insightful comments into this dynamic:

E

They begin to see their parents as real people—complete with human foibles, inconsistencies, and bad habits. This realization is at first terrifying. Suddenly, the people who several years earlier seemed omnipotent are exposed as really no different from the rest of the adult world—or from the teenager, except that they are older and more experienced....

Now, for the first time, many adolescents feel truly alone, and may for a brief while turn on their parents in angry rejection for being human. They are scared and vulnerable. And if vulnerability isn't safe, anger is the easiest alternative. In anger, one is active and seemingly in charge, instead of being in the more passive and potentially humiliating state of vulnerability. And teenagers, more than any other age group, will go to extremes to avoid humility and vulnerability.

Michael Riera, *Uncommon Sense for Parents with Teenagers*, 29

Have you experienced a sense of falling off the pedestal? What has it been like for you? How might you ease the "fall?"

Hard - told I'm a spaceshot, don't know
Things.

Spirituality, ethnicity, and conscience

The process of self-discovery often includes spiritual exploration and experimentation. Beliefs that have not been challenged before come under intense scrutiny. It's not at all uncommon for teenagers to try out new beliefs, new communities. Sometimes these communities are spiritually based, but not always. Musical groups can attract kids who become deeply devoted groupies; think of the "dead heads" from a previous day. Additionally, new interest may emerge in learning about and connecting to their ethnic heritage. All of these are ways of self exploration, of trying to match the external person with the internal, and to fit the person into the world at large.

Teenagers also begin to develop their own conscience, voice, and values. This is a process that can be painful for teens and their families, as the parental voice he has been raised with is challenged and scrutinized. Wolf points out that "Often the teenager's own conscience can be stricter and more demanding than the parents'. Some teenagers drive themselves far beyond our expectations."[32]

E

Part of adolescence is the development of one's own set of values. It is a sorting-out process, deciding what to accept from the parents' values and what to reject. The finished product at the end of adolescence is a set of values that are distinctly the teenager's own. But early on that process can be very confusing. Inevitably it can include stupid battles in which children fight about things parents never said and in which parents seem totally unable to correct this confusion.

Anthony Wolf, *Get Out of My Life, but First Could You Drive Me and Cheryl to the Mall?*, 83

When you combine this search for spiritual identity (and the development of their own values and conscience) with their need to separate from parents as they gain independence, you can see why some teenagers challenge parents to their core. The drive for independence can express itself in ways that parents find difficult to understand—a teenager may make his own decision and then *change it* if it happens to be what his parents wanted. Sometimes, even, she will do the ex*act opposite* of what she wants to assert independence! Wolf sums it up nicely when he says, "To have made a right decision because of parental advice is often for a teenager less desirable than to have failed on one's own."[33]

Friends

We've discussed the teenagers' change in focus from family to the world outside, and for teens, the most important component of the world outside is *friends*. Teenagers care intensely about friends because this is where they gain a large part of their sense of self. Many teens measure themselves by the friends they have—their self-esteem is tied to their popularity. Even though many kids hate school, they want to be there because it is where they find their own kind. They have a thirst for the activity, the connection, and the "mirror" it provides. As they move toward independence they need to see themselves in the world of their peers.

A teenager's first romantic interest can sometimes cause a parent to stretch because first loves may be in sharp contrast to the family. Ava Siegler points out the more *foreign* the choice (religion, ethnic background, reputation), the easier it is for the adolescent to move away from his previous dependence on his parents. ("It's hard to kiss a girl who looks like your Mom.") Much later in adolescence, he will be able to make a choice that is more integrated with aspects of his parents and background.[34]

Typically, in early adolescence, kids belong to groups of the same sex, which, as they get a little older, merge into heterosexual crowds. Later, crowds divide into heterosexual groups. And finally, groups break down as teens begin to date. Research shows that girls are more likely than boys to have a best friend, and a larger portion of girls' friends belong to the same social crowd.

E

Newly adolescent girls, forced by their adolescence to separate from their parents, are not confident. In time, they may be. But the young teenage girl feels the ever-present threat that she could lose it all. This underlying insecurity gives rise to much cruelty. At the same time, teenage girls make strong, almost loving attachments to girls that they admire, which often creates intense jealousy. The result of this combination of insecurity and strong attachments is an unparalleled nastiness. It is most clearly observed in the phenomenon of junior-high cliques.

Anthony Wolf, *Get Out of My Life, but First Could You Drive Me and Cheryl to the Mall?*, 42-43

And boys? What is this experience like for them?

E

Cool replaces tough. Coolness—the capacity to be in style—is a kind of sexualized, downbeat version of tough. The need to be cool, to be in style, is probably the closest that boys come to teenage girls' obsession with looks. But this concern is different in that it is not nearly so demanding. One does not really have to be cool. Many boys do care about how they look and act, but mainly that caring has to do with trying to get girls, not with peer acceptance. For the most part, how a boy looks and dresses is not so much an issue of status as it is one of identification. How you look and dress indicates which general group you belong to: preppies, maggots, whatever.

Anthony Wolf, *Get Out of My Life, but First Could You Drive Me and Cheryl to the Mall?*, 45

Fears

The fear that drives adolescents, more than any other, is the fear of being alone. As they loosen ties with their families, an emotional void opens, which intensifies their fear of aloneness. It must be filled with peers, yet in order to achieve their desired level of peer connection, they must measure up. So they add on another fear—fear of rejection. Much of their emotional life is focused on taking steps to ward off these fears; they spend their time and energy on the telephone, writing notes, instant-messaging instead of doing homework, expending energy to be seen in the "right" places. There is a sense of desperateness that infuses the emotional intensity already there, something that parents find difficult to understand.

Adolescents have a healthy fear of the unknown, but they will mask it so adults have difficulty recognizing what is really going on. They are filled with unfamiliar feelings, thoughts, and challenges. Everything is changing, and everything is unpredictable. They often feel terribly alone and alien in a world that used to feel familiar to them.

But they don't exhibit fear toward areas where *we* think they should display caution: drugs, drinking, risky behavior. The major issues for kids are not the issues we would expect; many times their issues revolve around the pressure they perceive from the adult world, pressure to succeed, to get good grades, to obey and follow the rules. They perceive this pressure to be so great, they sometimes they even justify cheating to achieve the end result.

How can we support them in facing their fears? By understanding their reality as best we can. By appreciating that we will get mixed messages. By having the courage and confidence to provide boundaries and a safety net, even when they are pushing to make their own decisions. We need to do the best we can to apply appropriate pressure and aim for a healthy balance.

For some parents, the difficulty lies in allowing enough freedom for our children to make mistakes. Although it feels terrifying, parents need to let their teenagers take risks. It is sometimes hard to trust them based on the behavior we see, and yet we want to prepare them to make good decisions when we are not there. How else will they learn, but to try? Some of their most important lessons will come from their mistakes, and it is important for them to learn that they will survive a mistake.

The amount and timing of new freedoms and responsibilities should be negotiated differently in each household, and finding the balance that works for you may not be easy. But teenagers must gradually learn to face their fears, accept their responsibilities, and make good choices. We must understand those fears, and what drives them, as best we can. And we must offer them support for their development as they cross safely into adulthood.

This exercise is best when done with others. It can be an effective way to begin your first meeting, if you choose to join a parenting discussion group.

First, complete the list on the left. Develop a list of adjectives that describe teenagers. Then, complete the list on the right. Develop a list of decisions or issues teenagers are likely to face (see examples).

Compare your two lists. Are kids that fit the description in list #1 likely to be able to face the realities in list #2? How can you support them? How does this reality make you feel?   Riera[35]

List #1—Descriptors

challenging

self-conscious

moody

highly emotional

private

confused

insights

inconsistent

observant

risk takers

opinionated

maturity

social

List #2—Decisions, Issues

type of friends they want

sexual activity

risky behaviors

peer pressure

academic success

perfectionist

what social niche

ISSUES TO EXAMINE AND DISCUSS

Refer to

1. Using your letter/exercise on page 12 as a reference, identify what you hope to get out of this program. You need not share the letter/exercise unless you choose to. — 12

2. The brainstorming exercise on page 38 provides an excellent way to begin a group discussion about adolescent development. — 38

3. What changes do you see in the following areas? Pick two or three areas that feel particularly relevant to you and discuss with your child's other parent: — 18-37
    a) Passion – In what new areas is your child passionate?
    b) The shift to abstract thinking
    c) "Imaginary audience syndrome" and extreme self-consciousness
    d) Contrasts between teens' behavior at home and away from home
    e) Physical changes – How much have they grown?
    f) Evidence of you or your spouse having fallen off the pedestal
    g) Your teenager's choice of clothes, haircut, etc.
    h) Interests in religious or spiritual exploration
    i) Willingness to accept parental input and advice
    j) Self-confidence
    k) The need for approval from their peers
    l) Friends – Are his current friends different from before? In what way?
    m) Fears – What is your teenager afraid of? How do you know?

4. How might parents help their children develop the capacity to see shades of gray, rather than everything in black and white terms? — —

5. Listen to the words of the songs your children are drawn to. What are they saying? Is this a vehicle through which you can gain understanding of their struggles, their issues, their world? What songs from your adolescence speak of the search for identity? Look at examples of music from both generations. — 28

6. How might parents manage the process of "falling off the pedestal" so they are less likely to feel the pain of that awkward rejection by their teenager? — 34

7. Discuss the concept of surface structure work vs. deep structure work. Does this seem to make sense in your case? Can you think of examples of what was probably tension releasing behavior? — 32

8. How might you support the child who defines herself too much from the outside? — 29

9. What did you learn about friends and teenage fears that is new or enlightening? Does this help to explain some recent behavior? — 36-37

10. Discuss the opening scenario. — 15

 Download a special "Tips" sheet for this chapter from the "Tools for Groups" section at www.PleaseStoptheRollercoaster.com.

➡️ *TAKE-AWAYS*

What are my "take-aways" from this chapter?

_____

_____

_____

_____

_____

_____

_____

_____

_____

What specific things am I going to do differently as a result of what I've learned?

_____

_____

_____

_____

_____

_____

_____

_____

_____

ZITS

2

A scenario

Those days when he was still in elementary school look pretty good in hindsight. Now you hardly recognize this boy as the person you've been raising. All of a sudden, his bedroom is a pit. He has taken his bed frame off, and the mattress is right on the floor. Clothes are no longer put into drawers; they are piled on the floor— clean and dirty alike! The curfew you both had agreed upon is gradually being stretched by 15 minute increments. You know he is challenging you intentionally. And when you talk about homework, your home turns into a war zone. He acts as though you have no right to ask about what is happening in his life. You feel like he doesn't respect you, like you are losing your authority.

How do you feel about your authority being threatened?

Chapter Two: Overview and objectives

As your adolescent begins to pull away and you see signs of her growing independence, you may become aware that your role and relationship is changing. This process is important to examine because your ability to manage your emotions during these changes will have an impact on your teenager's experience. Parents benefit from the thoughtful consideration about how our role changes while our children prepare to leave home. What kind of a relationship do you want to have as your child grows through middle and high school? How might you help him be prepared for what lies after high school? What kind of parenting style will help him be ready? You and your child stand to benefit if you are thoughtful and intentional about this process.

Objectives

In this chapter you will:

- Explore your changing role as parent of an adolescent. How is this different than it was when your child was young? How does your role evolve over the next decade as you become parent of an adult?

- Identify what might need to change in your behavior to support these changes in your role.

- Explore and discuss the contradictions you and your teenager face everyday.

- Examine the behavioral elements that comprise authoritative parenting. How does this change in the teenage years?

- Gain some insight into the important relationships of mother/son, mother/daughter, father/son, and father/daughter.

> *"Parents of teenagers have an odd role. They fight to control their teenagers, but with inadequate weapons. And after a few years of heated but at best only partially successful battling, they give the control over to their children anyway. The idea, is to give them time to mature."*
>
> *Anthony Wolf*[1]

Chapter Two: Instructions

Reader Instructions

How to get the most out of this chapter:

- Read the entire second chapter; you may want to highlight the areas that strike a chord with you.

- Complete the exercises on pages 51, 53, 55, 56 and 66.

- Study the model for authoritative parenting on pages 56 and 57. Plot your parenting style on the three dimensions. If possible, discuss these dimensions with your spouse or another significant person involved in raising your teenager. Ask that person to plot herself or himself. Plot your parents.

- Examine the issues and questions on page 67. Discuss the most relevant questions with a friend, spouse or in your parenting discussion group, if you have one.

- Be sure to write down your "take-aways." These insights will help you translate your intentions into actions.

If you have a parenting discussion group:

Group Recommendations/ Reminders

- Begin by asking how you were able to apply what you learned at the last meeting as you put your "take-aways" into action.

- Ask each group member to identify which of the issues on page 67 they wish to discuss.

- The facilitator for the meeting can guide the group discussion to ensure that the issues of greatest interest to group members are examined and explored, and that all group members participate.

- See page 11 for more recommendations for group leaders.

 Be sure to access supplementary and current information on this topic at www.PleaseStoptheRollercoaster.com.

A sense of perspective

No doubt about it; today's kids are different.

*Parents today need confidence. You **are** the right person for the job.*

W hat we see in this generation of teenagers sometimes alarms us and often confuses us. They truly are different than we were as a generation. And we, as parents, are truly very different than our parents were. It is a different ballgame today. How is it different? Why is it different?

Engaged parents treat our children differently, for one. We tune in to them and listen to them. We work to earn our children's respect through our strength of character. These fundamental changes in attitude may well represent an evolutionary step, and, in fact, may prepare our children to be better parents themselves.

Anthony Wolf, author of *Get Out of My Life, but First Could You Drive Me and Cheryl to the Mall?*, feels that our parents instilled a certain element of fear in us as a basic component of maintaining control and power. We were expected to conform because they "said so." Authority was autocratic; we were just one generation removed from the "children are to be seen and not heard" philosophy. In most homes, respecting parents was just expected, not earned. What did this teach us? It taught that parents have inherent power over their children, that intimidation is an appropriate tool, that fear and resentment are a part of the child-parent dynamic.[2] We also learned what we *didn't* want to bring to our roles when we became parents.

How much freedom is the right amount? When do we step in? When do we let go?

But we get confused. Confused by finding the right balance between freedom and control. We understand, appreciate even, the adolescent's cry for freedom. And sometimes we give them too much freedom in an effort to do right by them. It is easy to misunderstand our children's pleas for freedom and independence. It is challenging to maintain close contact when they are pulling away with intense verbal ferocity. When teens act in ways with which we are not entirely comfortable, we are not sure whether we should intercede or not. And, thinking that the adolescent desire for space is a natural part of growing up, we too often leave them alone. For some parents it's not through neglect that they allow their kids this sought after space, but it's more a matter of wanting to do the right thing, which they often think is letting the kids do their own thing.

Parenting behavior at the opposite end of the spectrum is currently called "helicopter parenting" which references parents who hover too closely. This, too, is tempting behavior, driven by love and a desire to help, in a world fraught with danger, challenge and competition for

A sense of perspective (cont.)

Their world provides endless and intense stimuli. As they embark on their search for identity, they are faced with an assortment of lifestyle choices that can be overwhelming.

opportunities. It's easy for parents to hover too closely, or allow an abundance of freedom in an effort to do the right thing. The challenge for parents is in finding the right balance between the two. This is tricky to achieve, requires constant monitoring and adjustment, and yet it must remain parents' goal. Kids that have too much space become too disconnected from parents to be safe; they miss important opportunities for guidance and support and are expected to manage issues for which they are not developmentally prepared. However, teens who are over-supported are denied opportunities to gain independence, stretch, learn on their own and risk failure—all vital experiences that provide essential lessons.

Adolescence used to be a place between childhood and adulthood. Kids of all types pushed the rules, but the extent of the dangers were less severe as they sneaked cigarettes, beer, or engaged in some intense kissing in the back seat. Today, guns and knives are brought into schools, and death by shooting is a real and present danger. Schools practice lockdowns in preparation for a response to life-threatening situations for the student body. The outside world, with all of its ugliness and danger, has invaded the world of adolescents forever. Their world contains an array of issues that includes oral sex, easily attainable drugs of alarming purity, AIDS, actual weapons, and true threats of violence … combined with worries about today's math exam, tonight's basketball game, their missing math book, and their friend's dating issues, all in the same day.

Applying our standards just doesn't work because what we worry about, they take in stride.

Old standards do not apply. The experiences of home, school, expectations, safety, values, sexuality, violence, communication, extra curricular activities, money, spare time, friendship, stress—are all vastly different than the experiences we had. As teenagers search for identity they do so in an unpredictable world which assaults them with a confusing assortment of stimuli and choices.

We gain much by putting ourselves into their shoes and understanding their perspective. This will enable us to do the best job we can in guiding our kids to a mature and healthy adulthood.

Our changing roles

At some level, I have always known that I was raising my kids only to see them leave home. As they change before my eyes, I'm reminded that our time with them is temporary and precious.

But it's only recently that I really thought about the way my role changes as they get closer to leaving home. My job description actually changes, and I'd better be on top of the changes that are required of me as we go through this growth and separation.

As my teenagers grow into independence, we struggle over control. I've exercised control for decisions and actually managed their lives for a very long time. Clearly, they have gradually gained control over more and more decisions as they have grown older, but this issue of control is central to our relationship. As they ready themselves to move away, I must make sure they are ready to take the helm and to make good decisions. Will they be prepared for the responsibilities ahead?

To face this question squarely and honestly requires me to examine both the skills my teenagers need to develop as they mature into adults, and what needs to change within my role to help them acquire these skills. By definition, the parenting role I've loved since their birth is redefined, re-scripted. And profound changes like this are not without pain...for both of us.

Again, Stephen Covey's advice to "begin with the end in mind" plays well in our discussion about parents' roles. If we want our teenagers to be competent, confident in their abilities, and able to display good judgment, we must give them the opportunities to learn and test these areas as they grow. Understanding this gives a different spin to the topic around which most disagreements take place—control. As we find the right balance for our family, as we gradually give them more rein, we parents are wise to remind ourselves of the end we're looking to achieve.

Dad, I want you to raise me *showing* me some kind of love, not just caring about health and success in school. You never talk to me about deep, personal things. You never tried to get closer to me and I don't like you for that.[4]

Adam, 14

Our changing roles (cont.)

Two driving forces in the adolescent's life are sexuality and control. He is focused on moving out and moving on. He is focused on moving away from the family ties and into the world of his peers. These drives are normal, and healthy, in our society. Our job is to make sure he is safe and prepared to handle a world that is frequently overwhelming to him and full of opportunity, excitement, enticement, and harm. Our job is to help him learn and grow in ways, and at a pace, that feels right to us and to him, which will at times be very different. It will be a dynamic ride as we negotiate this development.

In a way, you could say our roles are evolving from that of managers to that of mentors. Without getting into issues of semantics around mentorship, let's look at what it means, this spirit of mentorship. It provides some relevant guidelines for examining the ways our roles change.

Mentors function as teachers and coaches to create learning opportunities and to challenge their protégés to develop to full potential. Mentors are facilitators; they aid in a process of discovery. They provide role modeling, personal support, friendship, and counseling. Does this describe the relationship you hope to have with your children as they grow through their teenage years and move on?

E

"Despite dramatic changes in adolescents, their families, their relationships, and the surrounding environment, the basic functions of parents really change very little from childhood to adolescence. It is the strategies for carrying out these functions that can, do, and must change significantly."

A. Rae Simpson, *Raising Teens: A Synthesis of Research and a Foundation for Action*, 40

Raising Teens: A Synthesis of Research and a Foundation for Action, was authored by A. Rae Simpson, Ph.D. in conjunction with the Project on the Parenting of Adolescents and the Center for Health Communication at the Harvard School of Public Health. This comprehensive "synthesis of research" provides insight and data from many sources, along with recommendations for actions.

Our changing roles (cont.)

As a mentor: [5]

- You rarely have any real control—at best you are able to influence, educate, and facilitate development.

- Your goal is for your child to become "self-correcting" and responsible for himself.

- You are most effective when you are close enough to know your child intimately but remain objective and not too involved in areas that she must own.

- To be most effective, you must pay attention to the rational, explicit discussion, as well as the relationship and the emotional level.

- Be clear about your own assumptions, style, and needs; being conscious of this will enable you to apply your point of view appropriately, and not apply it when it does not help the situation.

- Your new job is about meeting your child where she is in her view of the world and helping her to grow in her own way, not forcing her to subscribe to your expectations.

- You need to ask good questions. "Have you thought about this?" "Would you consider that?" Your style should be non-confrontational.

- In addition to allowing natural consequences to apply, your child should be taught to take responsibility for, and resolve, conflicts that arise.

Danny, 17

Mom, if you would support me in my interests instead of discouraging me maybe we would have a better relationship. [6]

Our changing roles (cont.)

Have you thought about the types of skills it takes to parent during adolescence? *Families First* is an organization in the Boston area that offers education in parenting. Linda Braun, former Executive Director of *Families First,*[7] offers an interesting insight: Perhaps the skills involved in parenting are the *exact opposite* of the leadership skills that are so often valued in the adult world. Effective parenting may involve "following skills" as opposed to "leadership skills."

The leadership skills that make you successful in the outside world may actually inhibit your success as a parent. Instead of giving direction, inspiring action, and exhibiting leadership, the parent who allows his teenager to learn from her own actions, decisions, and mistakes is likely to have facilitated the learning of life lessons that will stick.

What does it take to assist your teenager to become "self-correcting"? To learn to take responsibility for her actions? To develop her sense of confidence in her own abilities and to make the judgment calls she will be required to make? Ms. Braun suggests, "Following, not leading one's children, involves a complicated set of skills: figuring out your child's needs, understanding your own needs, and being able to untangle your agenda from your child's. You must then have the wisdom to know how best to balance those agendas so that children learn what they need to know, without either parent or child feeling overpowered or bossed."

The distinction between "leadership skills" and "following skills" intrigues me. As I "follow" my teenager I try to reinforce his or her attempts at time management and organization. I gently reinforce the positive decisions and successes, while facilitating the corrective measures necessary when things are out of synch. *"I'm worried that working all day each Sunday deprives you of necessary study time. Might you work our some alternative arrangements?"*

Following skills. It's a different perspective on our job as parent. It's worth examining.

What "following skills" do you exhibit that support your child's independence and growth? In what ways might you do a more effective job in enhancing her growth?

Parenting levels: a model

Carolyn Moore Newberger is a psychologist and faculty member of the Harvard Medical School. She has developed a model[8] identifying four levels of parenting that provides a framework for examining our roles as parents and can serve to inspire and sensitize us to these role-related issues. This model is for your review and discussion; it will be referred to in several other sessions.

Level One: ***ME FIRST***   →   Parent only views the child and the relationship through an adult lens, without regard to the child's point of view. The parent's role is organized around the parent's wants and needs.

Level Two: ***FOLLOW THE RULES***   →   Hard and fast rules, derived from one's tradition, culture, or authority, determine what is a "good" parent and a "good" child. The child is viewed through this lens, and the parental role is organized around these socially-defined notions of correct practices and responsibilities.

Level Three: ***WE ARE INDIVIDUALS***   →   The child is viewed as a unique individual with special needs and potentiality. The parent understands the child's world from his point of view and strives to meet his needs. The parental role is organized around identifying and meeting the needs of this child rather than as the fulfillment of predetermined role obligations. This assumes the adult also views himself as a unique individual.

Level Four: ***LIVING AND GROWING TOGETHER***   →   At this level, the adult appreciates the child's individuality, as in Level Three, but the context is different: the adult and child are in a mutual and reciprocal relationship that continually develops and changes. The parent, as well as the child, grows in his role, and the parent recognizes that the relationship and the role are built not only on meeting the child's needs but also on finding ways of balancing his or her own needs and the child's, so that each can be responsibly met.

Parenting levels: a model (cont.)

I found this model to be unique in it's ability to recognize and validate my experience…that I'm going through significant growth and changes too! In its most positive sense, Level Four parenting not only helps to articulate a goal for me, it gives me a framework for recognizing and appreciating that I'm growing and evolving. As I learn more about my adolescent children and how I want to prepare them for adulthood, I find that I must examine myself, my beliefs and issues, and my roles.

That this timing coincides with my mid-life years is no accident. Many parents feel the intense changes associated with mid-life at the same time as they face the intense challenges of raising teenagers. In fact, Laurence Steinberg's book *Crossing Paths: How Your Child's Adolescence Triggers Your Own Crisis,* states that "the child's passage into adolescence reverberates throughout the entire household",[9] frequently triggering major changes for parents. I prefer not to focus on this stage in my life as a personal "crisis," but as an important growth phase. And recognizing that I am growing along with my teenagers feels like a statement that empowers me. It gives me a hope and a vision for a relationship that values me as well as my children. And it provides a framework that we will look toward in our future: a relationship that continues to evolve, as we do, with our children.

Can you think of examples in which you exhibit behavior on all four levels of parenting? What does Level Four parenting mean to you?

It's a contradictory world

The contradictions just don't stop. Think about the mixed messages you get from your teens. Think about the mixed messages they get from you. It's a confusing whirl for all of us. Take a look at these opposite, yet common, messages:

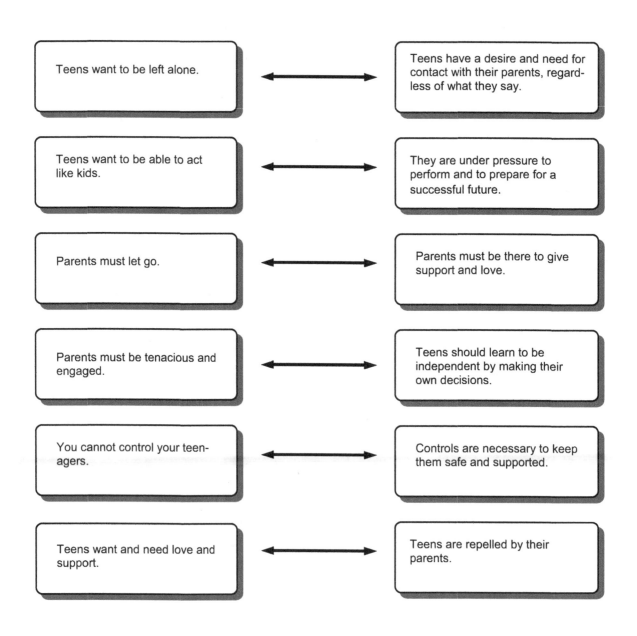

It's a contradictory world (cont.)

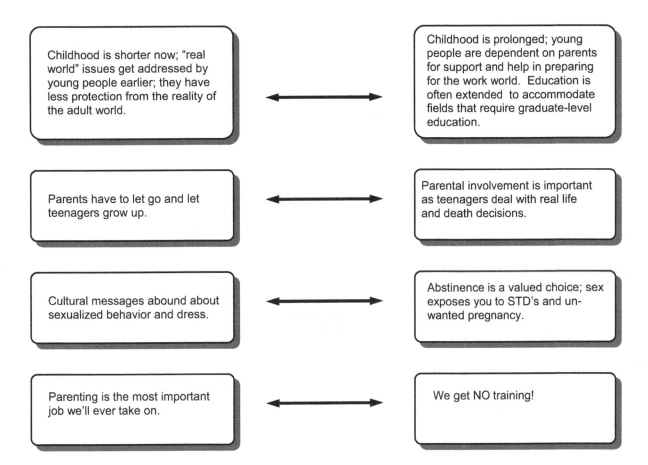

Childhood is shorter now; "real world" issues get addressed by young people earlier; they have less protection from the reality of the adult world.

⟷

Childhood is prolonged; young people are dependent on parents for support and help in preparing for the work world. Education is often extended to accommodate fields that require graduate-level education.

Parents have to let go and let teenagers grow up.

⟷

Parental involvement is important as teenagers deal with real life and death decisions.

Cultural messages abound about sexualized behavior and dress.

⟷

Abstinence is a valued choice; sex exposes you to STD's and un-wanted pregnancy.

Parenting is the most important job we'll ever take on.

⟷

We get NO training!

What other contradictions can you think of? How do these examples make you feel? How do you think your teenager feels about these contradictions?

The Authoritative Parenting Model

Years of research in the field of adolescent development and child psychology have yielded data about what comprises "effective parenting." While many researchers have studied this, Laurence Steinberg's *Beyond the Classroom* provides an excellent summary from which I've drawn the material below. He points out that the results of 50 years of research is quite consistent: "children develop in more healthy ways when their parents are relatively more accepting, relatively firmer and relatively more supportive of the child's developing sense of autonomy."[10] Parents' behavior can be viewed in terms of three dimensions:

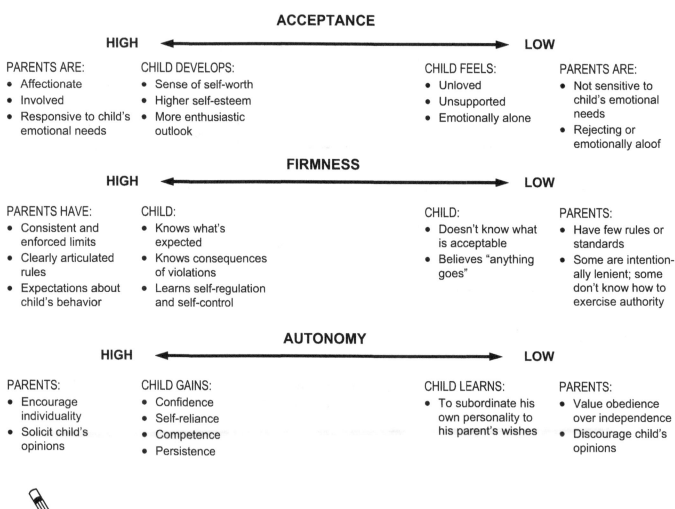

ACCEPTANCE

HIGH ←——————————————→ LOW

PARENTS ARE:
• Affectionate
• Involved
• Responsive to child's emotional needs

CHILD DEVELOPS:
• Sense of self-worth
• Higher self-esteem
• More enthusiastic outlook

CHILD FEELS:
• Unloved
• Unsupported
• Emotionally alone

PARENTS ARE:
• Not sensitive to child's emotional needs
• Rejecting or emotionally aloof

FIRMNESS

HIGH ←——————————————→ LOW

PARENTS HAVE:
• Consistent and enforced limits
• Clearly articulated rules
• Expectations about child's behavior

CHILD:
• Knows what's expected
• Knows consequences of violations
• Learns self-regulation and self-control

CHILD:
• Doesn't know what is acceptable
• Believes "anything goes"

PARENTS:
• Have few rules or standards
• Some are intentionally lenient; some don't know how to exercise authority

AUTONOMY

HIGH ←——————————————→ LOW

PARENTS:
• Encourage individuality
• Solicit child's opinions

CHILD GAINS:
• Confidence
• Self-reliance
• Competence
• Persistence

CHILD LEARNS:
• To subordinate his own personality to his parent's wishes

PARENTS:
• Value obedience over independence
• Discourage child's opinions

Plot yourself, your spouse, and your parents on each dimension on this chart.

The Authoritative Parenting Model (cont.)

The style used by most parents is measurable, to a relative degree, on the three dimensions described on the previous page. Parents who tend to be low in firmness, but high in acceptance and autonomy are generally called "permissive" parents. Those who are low in acceptance and autonomy but high in firmness are labeled "authoritarian." Parents who are relatively high in all three dimensions are labeled "authoritative." The authoritative style of parenting has been associated with many positive outcomes: social confidence and competence, moral development, self-control, resiliency, and optimism. Additionally, this approach has been associated with risk prevention and lower rates of depression, anxiety, delinquent activity, and susceptibility to negative peer pressure.[11]

What kind of parent are you? When push comes to shove and you are forced to choose between various responses, your parenting style becomes evident.

PERMISSIVE PARENTS	AUTHORITATIVE PARENTS	AUTHORITARIAN PARENTS
GOAL: Happiness	GOAL: Maturity	GOAL: Obedience
Permissive parents believe they are to facilitate their child's growth by supporting the child's natural inclinations. Their focus is on making sure the child is happy and her needs gratified.	Authoritative parents emphasize self-direction. They are focused on helping the child become personally and socially responsible. They do this by guiding the child toward proper behavior and nurturing his developing sense of judgment	Authoritarian parents believe they must control the child's impulses. They feel the child must learn to obey and respect authority, above all else.
Acceptance: HIGH Firmness: LOW Autonomy: HIGH	Acceptance: HIGH Firmness: HIGH Autonomy: HIGH	Acceptance: LOW Firmness: HIGH Autonomy: LOW

The model above[12] describes about 70% of parents in America today, with most parents being permissive, authoritative, or authoritarian. While the model indicates that the authoritative style offers the most benefits for children, the tragedy is that 25% to 30% of parents are so disengaged from their teenager's life they don't fit into this model at all. Parental disengagement is a very good predictor of problem behavior: alcohol and drug abuse, delinquency and violence, suicide, and sexual precocity.[13] According to several national studies, only 50% of parents know their child's friends; only 50% know what their kids do after school or when they are out in the evening; only 33% know how their teenagers are spending their spare time or their money.[14]

The research indicates that authoritative parenting yields the best results. Within the context of your family's beliefs and values, this can provide a guideline for your engagement, goals, and behavior.

Are You in the Way?

Wise parents let things unfold
with as little interference as possible.
They remain out of the way,
not calling attention to themselves.
Their children discover
the natural harmony of things,
and work out their conflicts
in ways that establish true peace.

When parents interfere,
and constantly meddle in their children's lives,
the natural order is forgotten.
Conflicts are escalated,
learning is curtailed,
and confusion reigns.

There are certainly times when we should guide.
We naturally want to protect our children,
and teach them what we have learned.
But it is best when we let that guidance
be as unobtrusive,
and gentle as possible.
Forcing lessons on our children
may get the immediate results we want.
But our children may be left without discernment,
unable to build internal strength of character.
What are your children in the midst of learning now?
Are you in the way?

From *The Parent's Tao Te Ching, a New Interpretation*
by William Martin

Changing relationships

Exploring the nature of our family relationships can be deep and rewarding work. Literature for centuries has tried to give light to such understanding, and yet each of us, in our own way and time, will make our personal discoveries. We'll look here at our relationships in practical and easy-to-understand terms.

Boys and their mothers   One reason mothers have such a difficult time understanding our sons is because we are, in some very fundamental ways, very different. That's obvious, of course, but it helps to understand the nature of the differences, and how that plays out every day. Our experiences are very different, and our way of processing them is different. Wolf, and others, provide some understanding of this dynamic which allows us to better understand our relationship with our adolescent sons.

E

> Particularly troubling from the perspective of the mother is that her previously open, talkative, very huggable boy disappears absolutely and is replaced by a young man who seems to radiate an aloofness that, if anything, makes her feel scorned. The situation can create real problems. Hurt by her son's aloofness and feeling rejected, a mother may aggressively communicate her hurt to her son, which is the worst thing she can do....
>
> Anthony Wolf, *Get Out of My Life, but First Could You Drive Me and Cheryl to the Mall?*, 29

Wolf, and many other experts, offer that one reason for this withdrawal is due to the boy's developing sexuality. Not being a psychologist, I find the topic of my son's developing sexuality, and how it affects his behavior, a little foreign. Do you? But Wolf certainly describes my feelings of rejection very accurately. We parents must understand that our developing sons need some distance from us. The trick becomes, then, dealing with my feelings, which are at times hurt and confused, while at the same time successfully providing the support to my boy that I want to provide. I find it really difficult at times to act like the adult that I am, and yet I know that I must.

William Pollack provides a piece of information that really sheds light on boys' behavior. Has your son come flying into the house after a day at school angry, and refusing to talk? Sometimes, when a boy is hurting, he finds it extremely difficult to talk. Pollack calls this the "timed-silence syndrome." What can happen is that a well-intentioned mom can try to press her son to talk about his problem, which may only make him more angry...and so he retreats

Changing relationships (cont.)

behind a closed door. As he retreats to be alone, he may hurt his mom's feelings by his gruffness. After he has had some time to sit with his pain he may be ready to come out and talk about it—but his approach might be so subtle that his mother could easily miss it! " When the boy comes back to her and makes a cautious overture, indicating he might want to talk, she may miss his subtle cues, particularly if she's still bothered by the previous rebuff, angry that her son was rude, frustrated that she doesn't know how to help him. In fact, his initial gruff "Leave me alone" may simply be an indication of how badly he's hurting and may really be an indirect call to his mother to be there for him—but later."[15]

But, no matter how bad things feel at times, do not underestimate the importance of the mother-son relationship. Psychologists will say that the emotional connection between a man and his mother is likely to be the most deeply rooted connection of his life. Through the mother-son relationship boys gain strength, emotionally, psychologically and in many other ways. Mothers give their sons the courage to explore their world; from the beginning of the relationship moms provide the "home base" to which he will always come back.

Mothers sometimes wonder if they should "cut the apron strings" as a way to help their boy mature. They wonder if a close relationship with a teenage boy will negatively influence their son's sexual development. The experts say "no," and "no." In fact, a close relationship with mom makes boys stronger. Mothers help boys develop their masculinity. And mothers can help boys integrate and value their emotional lives, balancing feelings that can be overwhelming and confusing at this time of dynamic adolescent development.

Expressing affection is one of the most meaningful ways to keep the connection strong, and yet this can present some challenges as old behaviors may feel less comfortable. Moms who have spent years putting their sons to bed may be rejected at the door. The hug and kiss goodbye as he runs out for the bus may be a thing of the past. "What does this mean?" we wonder. It requires us to renegotiate our turf, and to understand his messages even when they are contradictory. Remember this: it's vital to continue to express our affection; he needs to be reminded of your unconditional love no matter how unloving he may appear.

A mother-son relationship is a dynamic and changing affair. The desire to provide the safe warmth and deep connection is offset by his growing need to step out and explore more independence. This pattern is set early in the relationship, and as his independence grows mothers may struggle to find a new sense of balance. What presents challenges to many mothers is our feelings of rejection as our sons develop a new sense of self in their adolescence. While we may strive to change our expectations, and while we understand in our heads that his new behavior toward us may be "normal," we often cannot deny that it hurts. Changing such a fundamentally significant relationship may come with a bit of pain.

Changing relationships (cont.)

Boys and their fathers   Fathers and sons have a special relationship, and it is fundamentally different than that between mothers and sons. Fathers do things differently than mothers; they behave differently, respond differently and help their sons develop a different kind of emotional expression. Dads help boys begin to develop the ability to deal with, manage, recognize and express specific emotions and feelings through different means than mothers..

States Eli Newberger in *The Men They Will Become*: "Boys need to become more familiar with feelings and with the vocabulary of feelings if only to be men of excellent character. This 'emotional literacy' will make them better fathers, and better husbands and professionals, too."[16]

Fathers are apt to interact differently with their boys; they are likely to share their involvement around an activity. Women, who are more likely to want to talk, may find themselves underestimating the value this holds to men.

E

"Dad play" . . . leads to important *emotional mastery skills.* As a father coaxes a son to cope with interactions that test his limits and stretch him emotionally, the boy starts to feel empowered to effect change in his environment by analyzing what he is feeling and then communicating these feelings to his parents and others. . . . To put it simply: that roughhousing between father and son that may make mom cringe is actually the rudimentary beginning of a boy's management of his aggression and his ability to substitute emotional mastery and mutual cooperation for violent interaction.

William Pollack, *Real Boys*, 115

Pollack shares additional information about fathers and sons; when fathers are actively involved in their sons' lives the boys are:[17]
- Less aggressive
- Less overly competitive
- Better able to express feelings of vulnerability and sadness
- Higher in self-esteem
- Lower in incidence of depression
- Lower in social delinquency

Additionally, Pollack reports a connection between boys who excelled in high school and college, and fathers who provided social and emotional support during their sons' first ten years of life. Furthermore, the sons' career success was also influenced positively when fathers continued nurturing through their sons' adolescence."[18]

Fathers and sons connect when working side by side; they join their worlds by engaging together in an activity that may be work focused, sports oriented... or any other activity. Fathers *show they care* through this action-oriented connection; it's actually a way in which they *nurture* their sons, and it's very important to understand and support these activities.

Changing relationships (cont.)

Girls and their mothers   This important relationship has been the subject of many books over many years. As a mother, I feel deeply connected with both my children, and I'm fortunate to have both a son and a daughter. And, although it would be inaccurate to say that I feel closer to my daughter than my son, there are important things that we share as women. I can understand many of her experiences and feelings better than I can my son's; it's as though we speak with same *language*, which is precisely where I feel disconnected with not just my son, but sometimes with men in general.

Cohen-Sandler and Silver (*"I'm Not Mad, I Just Hate You!"*) comment on why mothers might have a more intense experience than fathers with their child's adolescent voyage. Because women often serve as the emotional caretakers within the family, they feel an increased burden during their child's adolescence, especially their daughter's adolescence. In addition, mothers are sometimes affected by unresolved issues with their own mothers and fathers, regrets, glories, mistakes, and hurts. A mother may closely and intensely identify with her daughter's experiences, and although father can sympathize with a daughter's experience, mother senses that she actually *feels* what her daughter is feeling.[19]

A daughter's development is all very personal to a mom. You cannot get around the fact that her development has a profound affect on you. You've spent her life caring for her, so there is an impact on you when your daughter communicates that she no longer needs your help.

Many mothers have felt the painful scrutiny from their adolescent daughters, and know how difficult—impossible perhaps, it is to measure up. Cohen-Sandler and Silver help to uncover and identify the essence of the dynamic when they say "the adolescent uses her mother as the standard to which she both aspires and struggles against." They go on to explain, "You are the vehicle through which your daughter tests out her shaky opinions and practices expressing her thoughts...she will likely instigate fights and herd you into battles, poking, prodding, and provoking you so she can ultimately hear your reasoning."[20]

Your daughter is involved in an important developmental task: establishing her positions, uncovering her tastes, and establishing her identity. That she does it in relation to her mother is part of the very nature of this complex relationship. That there may be pain during this process for mothers speaks to the significance of the relationship. "It is true that sometimes girls provoke arguments not to refine their belief systems but simply to take out their frustration and anger on their most available and prized targets, their mothers."[21]

Changing relationships (cont.)

In their book *Girl in the Mirror*, Nancy Snyderman and Peg Streep offer a more optimistic and upbeat attitude than frequently seen. In their book's jacket they suggest you view the adolescent years not as something to be "gotten through" but as an opportunity to "foster social, emotional, and intellectual growth" as well as to "forge new connections between us and our daughters." They criticize the messages in many popular books (all of which I've quoted in *Please Stop the Rollercoaster!*) such as *"I'm Not Mad, I Just Hate You!": A New Understanding of Mother-Daughter Conflict; Get Out of My Life, but First Could You Drive Me and Cheryl to the Mall?; Surviving Ophelia: Mothers Share Wisdom in Navigating the Tumultuous Teenage Years* for encouraging us to see adolescent girls as "either troublesome or troubled." They raise an interesting question: "how much of what goes on between mothers and daughters in the adolescent years is fed or even created by cultural assumptions? Are we working with models for behavior—ours and our daughters'—that will enrich our daughters' experiences through these years, or make us better mentors and guides?"[22] Must girls separate from mother for healthy growth to occur? Is it time to challenge this cultural assumption?

Terri Apter, in her book titled *Altered Loves*, elaborates on this point, suggesting the separation process for girls is quite different than for boys. "The interesting story is how a girl develops within her family. Having, in general, less distinct self-boundaries than a boy, she negotiates her individuation differently. To emerge as a self, distinct from other family members (particularly her mother), she does not cut herself off from them. Her individuality matures with a constant reference to them."[23]

Snyderman and Streep have a point; and it will be made again in this book in a different context in Chapter 7. If we focus on the challenges and stresses of this stage in our relationships, we'll surely find plenty to stew over. But, in fact, most teenagers manage this stage in their life without experiencing any significant problems. So, is our cultural portrayal of adolescent girls fair and appropriate? Do the models we use and the expectations we express support, or undermine, our efforts?

Changing relationships (cont.)

Girls and their fathers   Fathers and daughters—what a special relationship this can be! What is the nature of this relationship? How does it change during adolescence? How does this relationship differ from the mother-daughter relationship?

E

> A father's love can make or break a girl. Just as there is no way to understate the importance of a mother in a girl's life, there is no way to understate a father's. He is the hero of her childhood and often a wall she pushes against in adolescence. He is both the rule-maker, laying out laws of discipline and competence, and the rule-breaker, helping his daughter take risks, push the envelope, and explore uncharted worlds . . ..
>
> Michael Gurian, *The Wonder of Girls: Understanding the Hidden Nature of our Daughters*, 156

Fathers demonstrate and teach different things to their daughters than mothers do; psychologists will point out that daughters learn what to expect from men in terms of love relationships and respect. Joe Kelly in *Dads and Daughters* says "We can send our daughters down their life roads with clear and healthy expectations for men, or leave our daughters lost in tangled underbrush, confused about what to accept from men. They will probably be drawn toward men who choose paths similar to the ones we tread as men and fathers."[24]

While the professionals call the relationship with Dad almost a "dress rehearsal" for future heterosexual relationships, Kelly also emphasizes the importance of listening to daughters. He calls a girl's voice the "most valuable and most threatened resource she has." While recognizing that listening may be difficult to men who, by nature have a different way of processing information and are accustomed to being "fixers," it is essential as part of validating her experience. Trusting in her ability to solve problems, and her strength and ability to learn from mistakes, Dads can change this dynamic for the better. Validating girls' experiences and feelings is essential. As Kelly says, "If Dad doesn't hear what I'm feeling, maybe what I'm feeling and what I'm going through is not important."[25] Indeed, her own sense of worth may be what is on the line as a father learns to listen and respect her feelings.

Fathers frequently interact with their daughters in a different manner than mothers do. Where mothers tend to calm, sooth, and support, fathers tend to interact in more active ways, stimulating the child. Psychologists will point out that children learn self-regulation from the mother's soothing touch, and from the father's stimulation children learn to initiate activity.

Changing relationships (cont.)

A daughter may find her relationship with her father to be a safe haven at times during adolescence; she may be able to maintain a warm relationship and accept support and guidance *because of* their inherent differences. Experts agree it is because a girl closely identifies with her mother that she must struggle to dis-identify with her as she establishes her own identity. Mother poses a threat to her daughter's developing autonomy. Wolf notes that "the attachment to their mother is stronger than the one to their father, and therefore the adolescent mandate requires that much more negativism in order to deny that tie with the mother."[26] So it is precisely here that the relationship with Dad may be a special blessing—because the identification is not so intense, daughter doesn't have to work so hard to disassociate.

It is not always that way, however. Some mom's find themselves trying to help bridge the gap between battling fathers and daughters. What is the appropriate role for a mother to play when this type of battling goes on? How might the situation be helped? These are difficult questions to answer.

Some fathers distance themselves from their daughters during adolescence—just when their presence is essential and their role is key. In a way it is understandable that a father would feel uncomfortable with his daughter's extreme attention to her looks, her social life, her music, her need to conform within her social structure. Fathers may feel shut out, and not at all sure what to do about it. And of course a daughter's increasingly womanly body, impossible to ignore, can make a father uncomfortable.

Unfortunately, if a dad chooses to withdraw, he disengages at the worst possible time, just as she is on the cusp of major developmental growth.

Girls need their fathers reassurance; they gain important confidence from this relationship, and the benefits derived from his unique way and point of view offer much to girls at this stage in their development.

Changing relationships (cont.)

Mothers and fathers   Families with strong and respectful communication between the parents have significant advantages. When that is not present, teenagers find ways of playing one parent off the other, and the kids frequently suffer from the confusion of mixed messages. I've seen kids get lost in the chasm that sometimes separates adults—an unacceptable consequence. It isn't always easy to achieve, but parents need to be conscious of good communication between them and ensure they send consistent messages to the children.

E

In the best scenarios, fathers and mothers—whether they are married to each other or not—embrace the idea that they have different yet equally valuable parenting styles: they talk about their differences, listen to and respect each other's concerns, make compromises where possible, agree "to win some and to lose some," and try to work as a team.

Evelyn Bassoff, Ph.D, *Cherishing Our Daughters,* 39

E

It's just as essential that fathers spend some of their time *supporting* their wives and children by being physically and emotionally present as it is that their wives facilitate their husbands' learning how to take care of a newborn and how to parent a young child. Men need to accept that wives can mentor them in nurturing skills. At the same time, wives need to recognize that male ways of parenting can be a valuable complement to mothering.

William Pollack, *Real Boys,* 123

What new insights have you gained from reading these segments about family dynamics? How does this information help you? What will you share with your spouse?

ISSUES TO EXAMINE AND DISCUSS

<u>**Refer to**</u>

1. Imagine what you would love your relationship to be like when your child leaves home after high school graduation. Imagine what you would love your relationship to be like when your child is an adult. How will that differ from what it is now? How will you need to change?

2. Think about specific ways in which you have already changed your style from manager to mentor. What are you still trying to manage in your teen's life? Is it still appropriate for you to do this? Identify ways this shift from manager to mentor will continue to manifest as your teen grows.

    50

3. Refer to the parenting levels on page 52, and think of examples that you have seen, or demonstrated yourself, of parenting on Levels One, Two, and Three. What might you have to change in your style to live in Level Four parenting on a regular basis? What is significant about Level Four?

    52

4. What are your thoughts about the "It's a Contradictory World" section? Brainstorm additional contradictions and ways of managing them.

    54-55

5. Review the model for authoritative parenting. What did you learn about the parenting style with which you were raised? Does cultural heritage affect the way this model can be applied? Which style most accurately applies to you?

    56-57

6. How do you respond to the poem "Are You in the Way?"

    58

7. What did you learn in the section on family relationships? Name 3 points that were particularly interesting or that offer an explanation for behavior you didn't understand previously. Discuss.

    59-66

8. What is your response to the scenario given at the beginning of this session?

    43

➤ *TAKE-AWAYS*

What are my "take-aways" from this chapter?

_____

_____

_____

_____

_____

_____

_____

_____

_____

What specific things am I going to do differently as a result of what I've learned?

_____

_____

_____

_____

_____

_____

_____

_____

_____

ZITS

© Zits Partnership. Reprinted with Special Permission of King Features Syndicate.

Improving Communication

3

A scenario

The days when your son would fly off of the bus and through the front door to show you what "fun things" he had done in school that day are long gone. Now that he is 14, you feel lucky on the days when you get anything more than a grunt when he walks through the door. His usual answer to any question is either "fine" or "nothing." His shutting down, and therefore shutting you out, is frustrating to you. When you suspect something might be bothering him and ask about it, he abruptly closes the door on any possible communication. You want to know more about his experiences at school and with friends, and you wish he would spend more time just talking with you. But you also want to respect his privacy and need for "space."

How would you approach this situation with your child? Would you take some action to encourage communication, or would you "leave him alone" and hope he decides to talk to you at some point?

Chapter Three: Overview and objectives

Communication...such an important topic! So much of our success in any relationship depends on good communication. We are aware of its importance, but not always able to see how we can improve our communication. In this chapter our focus shifts to the communication in your family and how you can impact it positively. By highlighting some of the obstacles that frequently get in the way, we hope to sensitize you to communication in all of its forms. We'll share some strategies that will help you to enhance your family's communication environment. Setting limits and disciplining teenagers fall into this chapter as well.

Objectives

In this chapter you will:

- Take a brief look at what good communication looks like in a family setting.

- Learn about communication by highlighting obstacles and examining elements that are inherent in good communication.

- Study several different strategies to enhance communication with your adolescent.

- Examine the recommendations of two authors with regard to setting limits and consequences.

> *"Frustrating parents, teens want to be with them except when they don't, teens want their help except when they don't, and teens behave in excitingly more mature ways— except when they don't. . . . Throughout, they need parents to remain available, taking the emotional high ground by providing opportunities for closeness that teens can sometimes accept and sometimes reject."* A. Rae Simpson[1]

Chapter Three: Instructions

Reader Instructions

How to get the most out of this chapter:

- There is a lot of very concrete information in this chapter so we encourage you to take your time with it and be sure to prepare the exercises. By creating your own guidelines (page 75) you will be offering important advice for yourself. There are many worthwhile exercises that will heighten your observations and self-analysis on pages 76, 77, 78, 79, 81, 87, and 88. The discussion of disciplining teens is explored in exercises on pages 92 and 93; share some advice on 96.

- Examine the issues and questions on page 97. Discuss the most relevant questions with a friend, spouse, or in your parenting discussion group, if you have one.

- Be sure to write down your "take-aways." These insights will help you translate your intentions into actions.

If you have a parenting discussion group:

Group Recommendations/ Reminders

- Begin by asking how you were able to apply what you learned at the last meeting as you put your "take-aways" into action.

- Ask each group member to identify which of the issues on page 97 they wish to discuss.

- The facilitator for the meeting can guide the group discussion to ensure that the issues of greatest interest to group members are examined and explored, and that all group members participate.

- See page 11 for more recommendations for group leaders.

 Be sure to access supplementary and current information on this topic at www.PleaseStoptheRollercoaster.com.

Communication

As adults, we need to be prepared to take on more than our fair share of the responsibility in making communication successful, and mutually fulfilling, with our kids.

Communication is one of the most discussed, examined, and stressed about issues between parents and teens. Do we currently enjoy honest and open communication? Precious few parents say "yes" to that question. What are we doing wrong? You've heard the complaints: "Sara will talk and laugh with her friends on the phone, but when she comes down to dinner, she clams right up." "My daughter communicates with me—at the top of her lungs!" "I don't know what is going on in my son's life because he won't talk to me!" Obviously, there are calm and positive moments to counteract the challenging ones, but chances are, this is an area that can improve.

Like a river flowing through an ever changing landscape, sometimes calm and serene, other times churning and out of control, our communication within our family unit is responsive to the environment and situation present at the time. And communication ebbs and flows, responding to the changes in all of us as our family grows dynamically.

Most parents want the "key" to open the door to good communication. Would that it be so simple! As is the case in making most relationships successful, there is work involved here: thoughtful, objective, adult, unselfish work.

Don't forget that a significant amount of communication comes in forms other than through words. Tone of voice, body language, attentiveness, eye contact—all of these more subtle ways of communicating carry more weight than you may realize.

Communication is a two way street, and it is truly more about listening than about speaking. Listening has many different levels to it. Although exact numbers vary according to the particular study, the figures are all similar in their overall message; words are just a small part of communication.

As adults, we have learned to take in communication in all of its forms without even thinking about it. But to *intentionally tune in* to the various types of messages more closely may open up volumes of information to you and bring a new level of understanding. It is worthwhile to consciously sensitize yourself to communication forms that may not come as naturally to you. It requires openness on your part.

Communication (cont.)

Being attentive to body language can give us important information.

My son had tickets to attend a concert by his favorite band. He had invited many friends, but due to the fact that it was a mid-week evening shortly after the beginning of the school year, nobody was available. His desperation was palpable. He was only a high school freshman at the time, and I had offered to drive him and a friend. I was willing to entertain myself elsewhere during the concert to provide the necessary transportation home. But, as he was coming up empty with available companions, it looked like I was the lucky winner of a concert ticket. I knew he was uncomfortable going with me, but I was trying to make the best of it. It wasn't until we were in the car driving south on the highway and he lowered the window next to the passenger seat, *practically hanging out of it*, that I realized just how painful it was for him to be going to this concert with his mom. His body language spoke volumes and gave me a great deal of information about his level of discomfort, and, consequently, about my approach.

There may have been times you've been criticized for being a poor communicator in one way or another; perhaps others have noticed you're not a good listener or that you're not as observant as you could be. Perhaps you've given mixed signals that were confusing to others. Think about where your communication may be deficient. Be as honest and specific as you can be. Then think about a specific situation with your child when this deficiency came between the two of you. Now, write *two* guidelines for yourself to remember to overcome this deficiency.

(A guideline might be: *"listen completely before I respond,"* or *"don't assume I understood what she said; ask questions to clarify."*)

1.)

2.)

Communication (cont.)

It is helpful to give some consideration to what good communication looks like. By breaking it down, you may be able to identify both what you do well and areas that can use improvement. Although there are many areas where your communication style may be perfect for your family, there is always room for improvement.

Good communication consists of the following things:

Give and take   Good communication goes in both directions. As we focus on facilitating growth in our children, we need to ask ourselves if our communication style is helping to foster their development. Are you supporting his originality and helping him develop confidence in himself and his ideas? Are you providing an open environment for her to share her thoughts? Your teenager's thoughts and points of view may be different from yours. Do you support her originality? We know his ideas will change over time during adolescence; do you provide an environment that enables him to experiment with his new and changing ideas? Who better than you to listen to her thoughts and points of view? Are you *listening*? Or, as parents, are you doing too much of the talking? Many parents spend more time sharing their own wisdom than listening to the developing thoughts of the next generation. Do you have the right balance between teaching and learning? Think about spending less time on your podium and more time being an active listener, supporting a developing mind.

How often are you working harder to push your point than to understand hers?

Elaine, 14

"Tell me about yourself and your mistakes so I don't feel so tiny in your presence."[2]

Communication (cont.)

Respect and honesty   Sharing honest, forthright, respectful attitudes towards our children as they are growing yields the same return as they get older. Chances are there will be bumps in the road during adolescence, but you will be much better prepared to handle these if your teenager is confident in receiving a basic level of respect from you. Honesty and respect in a family dynamic create an environment for positive communication as children reach young adulthood.

How would your teenager answer this question: Do your parents treat you with respect? Try to answer the question yourself. Then test your answer by asking your teenager to answer it, too.

Trust   Can he count on you? When you say you'll do something, are you true to your word? When she confides in you can she count on your word of confidentiality? Can he count on you not to embarrass him in front of his peers?

In *The Other 90%*, Robert K. Cooper states that "trust advances one brief interaction at a time. Each human point of contact either opens or closes a door." He suggests there are three specific actions that you can take that will positively impact your ability to increase trust through your communication.[3] They are:

• *Breathe before you speak.* It slows the world down a bit, it allows you to increase empathy, patience and curiosity. It gives you an opportunity to focus on making eye contact.

• *Be clear about time.* If you have limited time to spend at a particular moment it's good to let your child know that up front. But reassure her that if she needs more time you'll arrange for it. Your commitment to make more time when necessary makes your child feel valued; rushing through your communication with your kids all too often undermines the relationship.

• *Sit down rather than stand.* Not only does communication that occurs when sitting down feel more sincere, it is particularly important to get on eye level with kids. It can increase the trust you're trying to build.

Communication (cont.)

Without basic trust there can be little meaningful communication. Can your child count on you unconditionally? How would she answer this question? Test your answer by asking your teenager to answer it, too.

Humor   Opportunities to laugh together, and even to laugh at yourself, may be one of the most helpful gifts in finding the way to open the doors of communication. Look for opportunities for light heartedness and humor. Appropriately applied (this is key!), they create an atmosphere where love and openness can shine through, even if other communication feels strained. Sharing humor with children increases their comfort in the relationship and may be one of the very best ways to enhance an atmosphere of sharing.

Do you go out of your way to find humor and to share it in your family setting? Is it appropriately applied? Develop some ideas as to how you might find more levity at home if that will enhance your home atmosphere.

Obstacles to communication

It will help to identify and examine common obstacles to communication. Once uncovered, we have something to get our arms around so that we can make the changes we desire. Dr. Thomas Gordon, who authored a program called Parent Effectiveness Training (PET), has identified 12 non-productive verbal responses that have become known as the "dirty dozen." These responses, which are too frequently used by parents, undermine productive and positive communication. They are largely self-explanatory. Which ones are you likely to catch yourself engaging in from time to time?[4]

ordering	arguing	diagnosing
threatening	criticizing	sympathizing
moralizing	praising	probing
advising	ridiculing	withdrawing

Pick the two non-productive responses that you're most likely to use. How does this behavior on your part undermine good communication with your teen?
Why do you suppose "praising" and "diagnosing" are on this list?

In *Raising Resilient Children,* Brooks and Goldstein identify three obstacles to communication.[5] They are:

- *We practice what we have lived.* We may naturally fall into the patterns of communication that we experienced as we grew up. We have to consciously work at creating the type of communication we want for our family.

- *Anger clouds effective communication.* When we're angry it's unlikely we'll listen or communicate effectively.

- *We sometimes believe that our children's goal is to wear us down.* Our teenagers are likely to test us and the limits we try to enforce. But if we take this personally rather then accept it at face value we run the risk of negatively coloring all our communication.

Obstacles to communication (cont.)

Filters, distractions, and more   Our list of obstacles to communication grows even longer. We have many distractions during our normal every day life; the telephone rings, the TV is on, family members and friends have needs and wants—you are most likely very adept at juggling all of these things regularly. Notice these distractions so you can deliberately eliminate them when necessary. Also, try to tune in to the more subtle forms of your communication as you make your way through the day. What does your body language say as your child converses with you? Are you facing him or engaged elsewhere? Distractions can be physical in nature (is the TV on in the background?), or they can be internal, resulting from what is going on inside of our heads.

The filters through which we gather information from the world around us come from a combination of our long term and short term mindset. Your long term mindset has been developed over time, and results from your past history, experiences, values, and upbringing. Your current mindset will be the result of recent experiences and current information. Without knowing it, you are listening through these filters; to expose them will enable you to examine whether they are enhancing or damaging your listening capabilities with your teenager.

Some common immediate filters include:[6]

- *Your expectations* Your expectations can create a self-fulfilling prophesy. Your child arrives home after curfew and you've been worried sick and getting angrier by the minute. If you're expecting trouble or deceit, you'll be pretty sure to find it, no matter how innocent the reason for her delayed arrival.

- *Your mood and state of mind* If you present a positive and pleasant air about you, those in your presence are likely to be affected. And you are likely to hear others in a way that is congruent with your mood.

- *Your relationship* It is hardest to be objective with those we are closest with. Parents, in particular, find it challenging to be objective. Be aware of how your lack of objectivity may hinder your ability to really listen. This becomes particularly interesting to tune in to because our adolescents are maturing all the time, and sometimes we respond to them in a way that isn't congruent with their current level of maturity.

- *Background "noise"* This can come in the form of either mental distractions or real physical distractions. The mental distractions are more likely to be affecting your ability to listen without you being aware of it. Perhaps you've had a particularly tough day at the office, or you're worried about something; this can have a big impact on your ability to listen well. Try and clear your mind, even if it's just for a few minutes, so that you can focus on giving her the attention she deserves.

Obstacles to communication (cont.)

To give you a hand at clarifying your major obstacles to communication, here is a model that can help you tune in to the quality of your listening. In *Listening: The Forgotten Skill,* Madelyn Burley-Allen identifies three levels of listening.[7]

- *Level 1:* Empathetic listening is when the listener is paying attention to what is being said both verbally and non verbally. It requires the listener to suspend her own thoughts and feelings, and to pay attention only to the speaker and his communication, including his body language and expression of feelings. It is about listening from the heart.

- *Level 2:* At this level the listener hears the words but does not go deeper than that. The listening is all logical, there is little emotional connection; the focus is on content not feelings. The speaker can believe he is being heard, however, because visual cues may indicate so; however, miscommunication is not uncommon at this level.

- *Level 3:* Here, the listener is following the conversation but is really planning her response. She is not focused on listening to content or the emotions underlying the communication. Sometimes the listener makes it obvious that she is not engaged, or she may appear to be listening while her mind is really elsewhere.

Tune in to your quality of listening as you converse with your teenager. You will probably find that you engage at all three levels regularly; obviously the more time you spend listening at level one the better your communication will be.

Do this exercise for five days in a row: tune in to yourself during three conversations with your teenager each day. Identify if you're listening at level 1, 2 or 3. If you're at level 2 or 3 identify what is preventing you from listening at level 1. Try to name the filter or distraction specifically. Keep a list of the distractions or filters that interfere with your ability to listen completely to your teen.

Strategies and techniques

We're going to examine several popular strategies for improving communication. These come from a variety of sources; some may be new to you, some may be old hat. Communication is a basic human dynamic, and yet it is one we must consciously work at to improve, whether we're at home with loved ones, in the workplace, or in any other situation with people.

Strategy #1: "Seek first to understand, then to be understood."[8]

Stephen Covey offers what, for me, is the very best advice. If you approach all communication with your teenagers from the point of view of first understanding *them*, you can avoid what usually undermines good communication. Following what is one of Covey's "habits of highly effective people" puts you in the position of *first listening*, a good place to start! It requires your attention to be placed on your child, not on yourself and your opinion. It demonstrates to your child the importance you give to her and her point of view. And it makes you slow down, allowing you time to listen and give a considered response. When faced with a disagreement, anger over misbehavior, when worried sick about a teenager who is not home at the designated time, applying this principle works wonders. And, frankly, it saves embarrassment over your own possible misbehavior.

Covey also brings to the parenting discussion another concept that has outstanding applications when considering communication with teenagers. Covey speaks about what he calls the "emotional bank account."[9] The emotional bank account is the amount of trust that has built up between two people. I "make deposits" into my daughter's emotional bank account by expressing thoughtfulness, kindness, courtesy, honesty, etc. I "make withdrawals" from her account by overreacting, treating her with disrespect, ignoring her, betraying her trust.

Let's think about how to apply this in every day life. The parents who have ample opportunity to spend time with their kids doing fun things, sharing sports, or other activities, are making deposits by sharing experiences and by being tuned in. Parents who have kids who are involved in many activities away from home, or who prefer spending time behind their

Don't insist, "It's time to have a serious talk." Talk to me about serious things but don't make a Big Deal about it.[10]

Sam, 17

Strategies and techniques (cont.)

closed doors, will have to work extra hard, and it is for them that this concept is so important. When given a few short minutes to communicate with your teenager, it is best if those few short minutes aren't just spent harping on her about chores, homework, etc. When communication is limited to the withdrawal side of the account, it takes a toll. Overdrafts have serious consequences in a relationship. Being conscious about your deposits makes you focus on positives in your relationship with your teen; the benefits of which are invaluable. Raising the concept of the emotional bank account to your *conscious* level, so you can be *intentional* about making deposits, may be all it takes to improve communication between you and your teenager.

Strategy #2: Active Listening

Do you know someone who makes you feel as though you've truly been *listened to*? It's a special feeling when you are heard, and it has inherent value and tremendous power.

Many times in conversations, others are thinking about their response rather than what you are saying. You probably do it to others unconsciously, from time to time. Active listening is a discipline that can be applied in many settings, certainly not just with our children. You may have been exposed to this concept in the workplace, or in working with a professional counselor or therapist. Although it may not have been named, this "language of acceptance" is widely used and easily learned.

Active listening can open doors in your communication with your teenager because its premise is that the listener offers no judgment, only an honest intent to truly hear what is being said. It requires you to monitor the filters that impede good communication. Your filters can take many forms: preconceptions, expectations, opinions, and more. Active listening will help you tune in to and possibly "turn off" the filters that are in effect during conversations with your teenager. Active listening also requires you to become conscious of the non-verbal communication that is taking place; notice the tone of voice and body language. What does it mean? What is your child saying non-verbally?

The objective in active listening is to get into the shoes of your child, to completely understand what she is saying *from her vantage point*. In order to do this, you must suspend judgment and be completely open and able to show empathy for her. It is essential to listen both for *content* (what is being said) and *intent* (what is "between the lines" and what is not being said).

Strategies and techniques (cont.)

Here are five techniques[11] that you can apply to your active listening strategy. Become conscious of times that you can appropriately apply them and gently try it. Active listening can become a habit and will enhance your communication with your teenager.

Technique		Examples
Reflect / Paraphrase	Rephrase by using your own words to confirm your understanding of what has been said.	Teen: *"Mom, you never let me do anything!"* Parent: *"You're upset with me because you think I don't give you enough freedom."*
Perception Check	Deepen your ability to provide support and empathy by checking out your own belief about what your child feels or thinks.	Teen: *"I'm not a little kid anymore! You can't control my life!"* Parent: *"It sounds like you think I'm trying to keep too much control over you. Is that the way you feel?"*
Summarize	Pull the important facts, thoughts, or ideas together.	*"Let me make sure I understand what it is you're asking. You want to go to Tom's house and spend the night, but his parents are not going to be there. Help me understand why you feel this will work and be safe."*
Open-Ended Questions	Probe for further information by asking questions that require more than a yes or no answer.	*"How important is this to you?"* *"What do you want to happen?"* *"What are you thinking of doing about it?"*
Body Language	Increase the comfort level for your child by consciously using your body (eyes, torso, arms) in a way that is congruent with your words.	• Use eye contact • Lean forward • Open your stance • Nod understanding

Strategies and techniques (cont.)

**Please Don't Say Anything,
Just Listen**

Listen

When I ask you to listen to me,
And you start giving me advice
You have not done what I asked.
When I ask you to listen to me,
And you begin to tell me why I
shouldn't feel that way,
You are trampling on my feelings.
When I ask you to listen to me,
And you feel you have to do
something to solve my problems,
You have failed me, strange
as that may seem.
Listen: All that I ask is that you listen,
Not talk or do – just hear me.
When you do something for me
That I need to do for myself,
you contribute to my fear
and to my feelings of inadequacy.
But when you accept as a simple fact
That I do what I feel,
no matter how irrational,
Then I can quit trying to
convince you
And go about the business
Of understanding what's behind
my feelings.
So please listen and just hear me.

And if you want to talk,
Wait a minute for your turn –
and I'll listen to you.

- Anonymous

Strategies and techniques (cont.)

Strategy #3: "The Relationship Approach"

This point of view is based on a book called *Parent/Teen Breakthrough: The Relationship Approach*, by Mira Kirshenbaum. Its point is simple, and it merits discussion.

The principle is simply this: "Work only at improving your relationship with your teenager. If you think something will improve your relationship, do it; if not, don't".[12] Some people refer to this as "relational parenting."

Our "control" over our teenagers is an illusion, and a negative one that undermines their development. Kirshenbaum promotes the concept that if we continue to "manage" the lives of our teenagers, we are delaying their ability to become self-reliant, which is the end result that we all desire. In order to develop their own identity they need to take risks, experiment, and learn who they are. So parents trying to gain control create the problem, not the solution, and they even exacerbate the problem by creating resistance, which creates more problems.

When you focus your attention on the *quality* of your relationship, you focus on the ways you can provide a positive influence and create an atmosphere of sharing, trust, and open communication while giving the teenager the control and the responsibility for themselves that allows them to grow independent. Kirshenbaum writes, "Your relationship with your teenager is the only thing you have control over, and there it is, in your face every day. You can evaluate it, assess it, influence it, and see how it is, every day."[13]

Relationship Approach Principles:
- Ask questions; use active listening.
- Say how you feel using "I" sentences.
- Ask for what you want directly and specifically.
- Expect to negotiate; you will work out solutions together.
- Provide information; it is the basis on which your teen will make good decisions.
- Ask permission when you want to provide parental advice.
- Don't make rules. Make agreements.

Whether or not this approach feels right to you, you can likely see some merit in it. And it certainly puts our focus on an important place—our relationship. It's worthy of some serious thought.

Strategies and techniques (cont.)

E

Here is an example of the relationship approach in action. Your 15-year-old wants to stay out way past her curfew for a special party.

Using the relationship approach you:

1) **Ask questions and get more information**. *"What's happening that is making this party go so late?"* (When you know more about the situation, you can understand each other better.)

2) **Say how you feel.** *"I feel that is awfully late for you. I'm feeling that you're growing up too fast."* (When you share your feelings it makes your teen understand you better, get closer to you as you behave more like a human being and less like a parent.)

3) **Ask for what you want directly.** *"It would really mean a lot to me if you would come home by midnight. Would you do that for me?"* (You are not pulling rank, but are treating your kid with respect.)

4) **You can try to work out a solution together.** *"One a.m. seems really late; let's see if we can agree on a time that would feel fair to both of us."* (When people solve problems together, they feel better about each other.)

Mira Kirshenbaum and Charles Foster, *Parent/Teen Breakthrough: The Relationship Approach,* 77

What are the merits of the "relationship approach?" What would change in your behavior if you were to actively employ this strategy?

Strategies and techniques (cont.)

Notice 3 conversations with your teenager this week. Tune into your emotional filters or distractions that are activated at the time. Identify them and write them down. How did they influence your communication?

Think of a conversation you had with your teen that did not go well. Using one of the strategies discussed in this session, outline a better way to have this conversation.

Strategies and techniques (cont.)

As a student of human behavior, I find it interesting to apply lessons and observations from one part of my life to another. For instance, there are times I learn something in a business environment that has applications at home and vise-versa—certainly you have the same experience from your various roles. It's great to share those observations with our teenagers for many reasons, one of which is that is helps to bring your world alive to them. Here is a useful piece of information gained in a recent organizational development workshop that has tremendous relevance to our discussion of communication with teenagers:

E

A business colleague who specializes in organizational development has expertise facilitating conversations that deal with communication breakdowns. This is a tricky kind of conversation to handle with your teenager, but as you may have occasion to use this, there is merit in examining the strategies that can improve your chances of success.

When trying to understand why there is a breakdown between you and your teenager, examine *trust* closely. Trust is made up of three elements:
- sincerity
- reliability
- competence

If trust is the issue, ask yourself these questions:
- Is the breakdown due to a lack of sincerity? On whose part?
- Is it due to a lack of reliability? How might that be addressed?
- Is it resulting from a lack of competence? Does your teenager have the knowledge, experience, and skills necessary for the situation? The two of you may not agree on the assessment of competence, but identifying what experience, skills, and knowledge are at issue, and evaluating them in a conversation, may lead to greater understanding, respect, and ultimately, trust.

Trust is a big issue between parents and teenagers and you may be able to get a better handle on correcting what's wrong if you can more closely identify the underlying cause.

Another useful insight that can be applied to a breakdown with a teenager is to examine the types of **responses** you have as options. When there is a communication breakdown you can respond in one of two ways:
- with an emotional response, or
- with a problem-solving response.

There are times when both may feel appropriate, but it will help to understand what is at stake when you make your choice. To respond emotionally satisfies a need that you may have, but it probably won't positively influence your teen's position and may shut him down. If you begin with an emotional response, you will probably not get to the problem-solving conversation at the same time; you will have to come back later to accomplish that—if the damage done from the emotional response is not irreparable. But if you begin problem solving, there is room to express your emotions at the end of the conversation—and you may find that your need to express those emotions has diminished greatly after you've discussed how to solve the problem.

Source: Thomas C. Matera[14]

Strategies and techniques (cont.)

Intuition - recognize the important role it plays   In our culture, intuition frequently isn't regarded with much respect. But in the area of parenting, it is an essential tool. We read our family members by observing their body language, their tone of voice, their words, and by our intuition. It is our "sixth sense," and I urge you to bring it above ground and enhance your intuitive capabilities consciously. Tuned in parents already recognize the value of intuition; how many times have you had a conversation with the pediatrician telling her, "I know that she has an infection, even if the test results are negative." And you're right, most of the time.

There are numerous ways to enhance this important sense, and there are some wonderful books, tapes, and Web sites on the subject. One of my favorite books is Belleruth Naparstek's *Your Sixth Sense*. Also, Lynn Robinson also has done some interesting work and written several books on intuition; visit her website at www.LynnRobinson.com.

For another fascinating discussion of this topic, visit Robert K. Cooper's book, *The Other 90%*. In it he describes the *three brains* humans are endowed with: in the gut, in the heart, and in the head. He claims the neurological networks of the heart and gut respond more quickly to experiences than the brain in the head. When you over-rely on your head, you're setting yourself up for extra struggles because you're working without being balanced by the gut and the heart. He encourages human beings to consciously tune in to the perceptions and impressions of all three of our brains, because that is the way we become fully informed.[15]

Stephen, 15

Hey, Mom, you seem to think I should tell you everything that's happening in my life. I won't, ever. Get over it. Believe me, if I absolutely need to tell you you'll be the first to know.[16]

Negotiation and setting limits

Any discussion between parents of teenagers will get around to discipline, control, and negotiating the setting of limits. This is dicey turf for many of us. Parents who are completely comfortable with their stand, and who don't revisit it regularly, worry me. Although I envy their confidence, the reality is the ground is constantly shifting as our kids get older, and it's important to be letting out the rein—gradually and with consideration. Both flexibility and firmness are important; parents who maintain an inappropriate level of control are handicapping their kids from important learning opportunities. On the other hand, those who take the easy way out apply little or no control (many parents fall into this category), and that is at least equally harmful.

Nobody said parenting was easy!

E

Throughout a person's growth, infancy through adulthood, structure and limits need to evolve to reflect each developmental stage. For instance, you wouldn't negotiate with a one-year-old about bedtime. Nor would you insist that your seventeen-year-old be in bed by 9:00 pm. every night. These are not developmentally appropriate limits. Ideally, limits and structure form the foundation of the stable platform that adolescents use to launch themselves into adulthood. Realize that these rules include not only the actual guideline, but also the consistent enforcement and follow-through. Consistency between words and action is crucial, because no matter what you say about limits, it is what you do that truly matters. . . . In fact, consistency is so important that in some instances consistent "bad" parenting is better than extreme inconsistency between "bad" and "good" parenting.

Michael Riera, *Uncommon Sense for Parents with Teenagers*, 73-74

Important things to remember when setting rules:

- Words are important, but there is no substitute for action—your *behavior* is what carries the most weight.

- Problems arise when kids get mixed or muddled messages from their parents. Sometimes they are looking for limits and they are given more space. Parents need to be very sensitive to not give mixed messages and be consistent, clear, and appropriate.

- When you set rules, make sure they are in sync with your values and that you are willing, and able, to enforce them.

- It is appropriate to negotiate with teenagers.

- Rules should be clear and clearly stated; however, there are times it may make more sense to enforce them in spirit than to the exact letter.

Negotiation and setting limits (cont.)

Wolf explains that parents can empower themselves by recognizing that adolescents may sometimes obey the intent, or spirit, of the rules even if they choose not to obey them to the letter. This means that parents' rules are, in fact, working.[17]

Why negotiate?   It's important to recognize that it is through negotiation kids learn to develop autonomy and to take responsibility for themselves. Gradually they have more say, more input on decisions that affect them. This is appropriate and an important part of their developmental process.

At some point, many parents face a certain amount of sneaking around on the part of their teenagers as they begin to test limits. Riera maintains that parents often head in one of two directions: becoming over-rigid or over-flexible. Over-rigid parents expect the trash to be taken out at the moment the parent says so. Over-flexible parents may never mention the garbage at all, but instead take it out themselves thinking that it is not worth arguing over anyway. Riera suggests that both are "equally disastrous to the adolescent's development" as they are maturing and learning to accept responsibility. According to Riera, kids need to be able to negotiate and take stands responsibly. This process should be important to parents because "the negotiated limits and structure are your greatest sources of accurate feedback about your teenager's current level of maturity."[18]

Another reason why it is important to include teens up front in negotiation and decision making is because if you don't, they may agree to anything just to get the conversation over with. If kids know they have no influence over a decision, you may actually be setting them up for a rule infraction or lie. Everyone is likely to be happier and safer with clear negotiation and communication up front.

How do you negotiate in your house? Do you allow your teenager to have input into the rules and limits? How do you enforce them? Are you consistent? Does your teenager know what to expect from you and your spouse?

Negotiation and setting limits (cont.)

Natural consequences   If your teenager elects not to spend time studying for her Spanish test, the natural consequence might be that she doesn't do well on the exam. If she stays up until the wee hours of the morning at a friend's sleep-over, she may be too tired to function well the next day. A parent does not have to enforce any punishment in those cases, perhaps; there are natural consequences that will take place on their own.

Once your adolescent is well into his teen years, natural consequences may be the best kind of influence that you have. The benefit of this is that it takes the parent out of the position of "enforcer" of rules and puts the responsibility directly on the teenager's shoulders. The reality is, anyway, as your child gets older, parents have less and less direct control, and the teenager knows it. By relying on natural consequences you are allowing him to accept responsibility for his actions and non-actions, and you are simply supporting the law of cause and effect.[19]

E

> The essence of firm strong parenting is the ability to make rules, unpopular though they may be, and keep them in place, regardless of the reaction that such rules may provoke. Now that the rule is firmly in place, the next step is up to the teenager.
>
> Anthony Wolf, *Get Out of My Life, but First Could You Drive Me and Cheryl to the Mall?*, 95

What examples can you think of from your adolescence when the lessons you learned came from natural consequences? Did these lessons have a lasting value? How might you apply this to your teenager?

Negotiation and setting limits (cont.)

Lying Unfortunately, lying is something parents of teenagers may face. It's not one of the behaviors that tends to endear teens to their parents; however to gain some understanding on the issue can arm you and help you prepare your response.

According to Ava Siegler (*The Essential Guide to the New Adolescence),* teenagers lie when they feel there is no room to tell the truth, or when the truth would be totally unacceptable to their parents. She claims that lies tend to fall into two categories:

- *defensive lies* which are intended to protect their newly formed sense of self, to protect their privacy and secrets and to protect others: "I don't know who was smoking in the driveway."
- *inflating lies* which are intended to promote their status in the community: "My boyfriend gave me this bracelet."[20]

Wolf suggests that parents focus on the situation that the teen lied about and deal with the situation, rather than focus on the lie itself.

Help your teenagers comply Some experts emphasize that it may be helpful to brainstorm with your teenager to help him develop strategies to live within the boundaries you've established. It's one thing to "lay down the law", but if, realistically, it will be difficult for him to live within these boundaries, you will both benefit by discussing openly the nature of the disagreement. This dialogue will also help you to better understand what is happening in his world, and helping him figure out ways to live within your rule system can go a long way toward ensuring that will happen.

The bottom line For parents, the bottom line is to find a place of balance—where you are gradually giving over responsibility and the natural consequences for that responsibility, to the teenager. Negotiating your way through this growth process is unlikely to be elegant or without stress. That's when it becomes the most important to be thoughtful about your position, your stance. It is a strong parent who is willing to examine her position, to accept input, and make changes when appropriate.

Several experts refer to the concept of setting your sights for "the north star," for only by knowing your ultimate objectives and goals will you be equipped to manage the storms along the way. Sometimes the storms are violent and the currents strong; it is your strength and ability to focus on your destination and goals that will keep you on course.

Natural consequences apply to parents as well as teenagers. Parents will learn from the actions that we take; we will learn what works and what doesn't. As we examine this ever-changing, ever-developing relationship we can apply what we learn, and get better as we grow.

Negotiation and setting limits (cont.)

Parents won't be perfect. What's important is that we do our very best, and continually strive to learn and be better. Remember Level Four parenting in Session 2? We're learning and growing too. And we're guaranteed to make mistakes. I heard one parenting education expert say that if parents "did it right" 40% of the time we're doing well!

One of the most important things for parents to remember is to approach this "job" with a positive attitude, and to assume a firm, but upbeat manner. If teenagers can push their parents around, the results can be harmful for the very people we are trying to protect—the teens themselves. Wolf talks about "bullying," the tactic that teens may employ when trying to push their parents into submission. While he points out that "being a strong parent does not mean than one cannot reverse a decision"[21], it does mean that parents shouldn't cave in to bullying.

E

Children of parents who cannot be bullied will also argue, and they too will push—but not nearly so hard, because they have learned that it won't work with their parents. How does a child know whether a change resulted from her bullying or from a parent's independent decision? In any given instance she may not. But over time, over repeated instances, children learn whether theirs are parents who make decisions based on what they think is best or on what they think their children will accept without a tantrum.

Anthony Wolf, *Get Out of My Life, but First Could You Drive Me and Cheryl to the Mall?*, 63-64

Communication: sharing ideas

We parents have been having conversations about our kids, and sharing techniques that work since our kids were born. And thank heavens for the sharing, because it is one of the best ways we gain information and insight! Let me share a few ideas that others have generously shared with me:

- The following technique was used by one friend of mine when direct communication was just too uncomfortable for her daughter. The mom ended up writing down what she needed to say in a spiral notebook and left it for her daughter to read. Her daughter spontaneously wrote a reply, in the same notebook, and left it for her mom to read. They used this notebook for some personal and important communication, conversations that were just too touchy for the daughter to have directly. They ended up using the same notebook for these personal conversations over several years, yet they never actually mentioned them in conversation. The technique was satisfactory to both of them, however, and allowed them to cover some sensitive ground.

- One family friend has a technique that helps to ease the family into dinner table conversation: each person takes a turn telling three things that happened to them that day.

Share one "best practice" with your group that you use (or have heard of) to enhance communication in your home.

ISSUES TO EXAMINE AND DISCUSS

<u>**Refer to**</u>

1. Take another look at your personal guidelines for communication. Share with another person why remembering these guidelines will be important to you.

    75

2. What did you learn by doing the exercises on page 88? What filters did you identify that affected your conversations? How can you diminish the effect these filters have on your communication?

    79-88

3. Which of the communication strategies discussed feels more appropriate to try with your teen? Pick one that resonates with you, and commit to putting it into practice this week.

    82-90

4. What is your reaction to the concept of "relational parenting"? Discuss.

    86-87

5. Do you agree with the three components of trust? How might you use this information?

    89

6. How has your intuition helped you? Can you learn to use it consciously? How?

    90

7. How do you handle rule infractions at your house? What is your response to the inevitable testing of limits?

8. Examine the difference between natural consequences and punishment (e.g. grounding your teenager). Think of examples of when each might be appropriate.

9. Share with a friend or your group, if you have one, some ideas for improving communication with your teenagers. Be sure to write down the ideas you may want to use at home!

10. What do you think of the opening scenario?

    71

 Clearly there are additional topics to cover in topic area of communication, such as internet communication, etc...and you'll find this material on the website. You'll even find a self-guided course you may take in the articles area. If you are an educator, you'll also find materials of interest in the "Parent Involvement" section, as improving communication between parents and secondary schools is an area of focus for us.

TAKE-AWAYS

What are my "take-aways" from this chapter?

_____

_____

_____

_____

_____

_____

_____

_____

What specific things am I going to do differently as a result of what I've learned?

_____

_____

_____

_____

_____

_____

_____

_____

_____

ZITS

Friends, Culture, and Risky Behavior

A scenario

You've been aware that your daughter hasn't been spending as much time lately with her usual group of friends. Not daring to say much, you tune in and watch and listen. Hoping to encourage her, you suggest that she invite some friends over on Friday night. As the doorbell begins to ring you realize you're meeting numerous kids you don't know. "What is happening here?" you wonder. The evening appears to go without a hitch, however, and the kids who took time to speak with you in the kitchen seemed pleasant and articulate.

Monday evening you get a call from the parents of one of your daughter's friends. He has been caught with a small pipe in his pocket. He told his parents that it belongs to your daughter.

How do you respond? How can you read what is happening in your child's social life? How can you determine if this is mere experimentation or if she is really using drugs?

Chapter Four: Overview and objectives

Friendship can be one of the best, and one of the most difficult, experiences in the life of a teenager. Many friendships come; some remain, others painfully go. Through it all, teenagers remain almost hypnotized to the power of peer approval. At times, it seems to be the center of their lives. In this chapter we will examine the importance of friends, the central role they play in our children's lives, and the realities of peer pressure and cultural influences. In addition, we'll look at some of the risk behaviors in which too many of our children engage, and the important ways in which our behavior affects theirs.

Objectives

In this chapter, you will:

- Learn about the importance, developmentally, for teenagers to form healthy friendships.

- Explore the strong influence peers and peer pressure have on teenagers.

- Examine and discuss the positives and negatives our kids are exposed to in our culture.

- Examine a brief overview of the most commonly seen risk behaviors and the role parents can play in keeping kids safe.

- Make sure you've established your position in regards to alcohol, drugs, and sexual activity and communicated it to your teenager.

> *"...because I had freedom, I felt I was able to talk to my parents about the choices I made and nothing was undiscussable from sex to drugs. This way there were no secrets."*
>
> M, 20-22, in college
> "Young adult" respondent to survey reported in
> *Parenting Teenagers: The Agony and The Ecstasy*
> www.PleaseStoptheRollercoaster.com

Chapter Four: Instructions

***Reader
Instructions***

How to get the most out of this chapter:

- Read all of Chapter 4; you may want to highlight the areas that strike a chord with you.

- The exercises in the first half of this chapter, on pages 105, 106, 110, 111, 115, ask you to take a close look at friends, and cultural influences. The exercises on pages 118, 121, 123, 124, 125, 132, 134, and 135 ask you to examine some tough questions about possible risk behavior and where you stand as a parent.

- Examine the issues and questions on page 136. Discuss the most relevant questions with a friend, spouse, or in your parenting discussion group, if you have one.

- Be sure to write down your "take-aways." These insights will help you translate your intentions into actions.

If you have a parenting discussion group:

***Group
Recommendations/
Reminders***

- Begin by asking how you were able to apply what you learned at the last meeting as you put your "take-aways" into action.

- Ask each group member to identify which of the issues on page 136 they wish to discuss.

- The facilitator for the meeting can guide the group discussion to ensure that the issues of greatest interest to group members are examined and explored, and that all group members participate.

- See page 11 for more recommendations for group leaders.

 **Be sure to access supplementary and current information on this topic at
www.PleaseStoptheRollercoaster.com.**

Friends

*During adolescence
friends, not family, take
center stage.*

It's hard for a parent to feel that her influence is diminishing with her child, especially in comparison to the influence of her child's friends. Though we may miss being the center of their world, the forming of friendships is a vital part of healthy development. According to Michael Riera, "Close friendships take the pressure off the family, encouraging the adolescent to leave childhood behind and move gracefully into the adult world."[1] As teens move into adulthood and build lives of their own, they will have to focus more on non-family members in work and other relationships. Before we begin to discuss the challenges that go along with this often painful realization, let's get a feel for what good and positive results come when teenagers form healthy friendships.

Teenagers benefit from friendships in many ways:

- They learn to be less self-centered.

- They learn about themselves through interactions with friends.

- They experiment with new behaviors.

- They learn how to accept friends' flaws.

- They learn what kinds of friends they want, and what kind of a friend they want to be.

- Friendships can provide a mirror of themselves.

- They learn skills such as empathy, support, honesty, and trust.

*Managing the dynamics
of friendships gives kids
experiences and
knowledge that will
serve them throughout
their lives.*

Accept the fact that I am growing up and I need
to explore the world with and without you. Put
some of your fears behind you and let me take
chances that are healthy for me. I can't always be
right by your side and under your wing. I need to
learn how to be a good leader to myself. [2]

Trisha, 16

104

Friends (cont.)

Strong family ties and support serve to bolster the teen as she ventures out into the world of her peers.

They still need us—desperately   Developmentally, it makes sense that teens would seek assurance and acceptance from peers above all as they seek to form their own identities. However, we must be careful not to misread these cues and either assume teens want nothing to do with us anymore or force our views about "appropriate" friends on them. Eli Newberger, author of *The Men They Will Become,* states: "It would be a grave mistake to read adolescence as the withering of need for strong relationships with the family. To the contrary, a strong family relationship can give an adolescent the self-assurance he needs to cope with all of the challenges of identity formation, including the welding of important peer friendships and winning acceptance in cliques and crowds."[3] Although it may seem that our teens don't "need" us as much as they used to, the truth is, as they navigate the sometimes difficult waters of peer pressure, they need our support to help them stay afloat.

Avoiding the temptation to judge   As detrimental as it can be to wrongly assume that teenagers do not need parents during this time, it is also a mistake to try and control their friendship choices. By attempting to project our own choices onto our children, we risk burning any bridges of trust and openness already established. In fact, pushing too hard may just push your child closer to the disapproved-of friend. It may be difficult to withhold judgment about a friend of theirs we think we don't like, but unless we feel our teens are at risk, we may be better served by taking a more trusting, empowering approach. Another benefit to taking this approach is that if for some reason a friendship ends painfully, our teenager will be more likely to feel comfortable openly discussing her feelings if she does not have to worry about the "I told you so" element of the conversation.

Have you noticed your teenager's focus shift from family to friends? How does that make you feel?

Friends (cont.)

On the other side of that coin, parents need to play it cautiously when they befriend one of their child's friends. It is my experience that parents can overplay the importance of their own relationship with their child's friends, when what may serve their child is demonstration of their loyalty. Not everyone shares this experience, or point of view, but my memory is a painful one. I had just broken up with a long term boyfriend and was preparing to return home from college for summer vacation. When my mother put her own relationship with this young man above my aching heart and extended to him an open invitation for a visit, I felt betrayed and diminished. It was a poor decision on her part when what I so badly needed was someone in my court, a good place for a mother to be.

Have you ever felt that your teen was at risk due to certain friendships? How did you handle the situation?

Are you able to refrain from judging your teenager's choice in friends? Are you able to give your teenager the "reflecting space" necessary to make decisions? If not, how can you adjust your parenting style to allow for this?

Peer pressure

How peers put the "pressure" on   The desire to fit in can be overwhelming—and overwhelmingly painful—for teens. Clothes, language, friends, cars, music, movies, likes and dislikes...they feel judged and measured in every aspect of their lives. As much as teens seem to be forging their independence by pulling away from family influences, they are actually being controlled more than ever by the powerful influence of their peers. Kids are most susceptible to peer pressure from the ages of 12-16.[4] The fears of being singled out, excluded, and ignored by friends are daunting and real. In fact, loneliness has been called "the single most important organizing factor of the adolescent and adult."[5] For many young people, their behavior results from their desire and need to be a part of the group, so they conform and show loyalty through their actions.

However, being a member of a group can be a wonderful and positive thing for kids. They can enjoy, and gain confidence from their sense of belonging while they explore individual interests and uncertainties. Not all peer pressure is negative pressure. Peers can keep kids off drugs and committed to school.

At various stages of adolescence, friendships and relationships can begin and end quickly, sometimes within days, and the effects of this emotional rollercoaster are often painful. But as they grow into upper levels of high school, deeper, lasting friendships are sought and forged.

The influences of their social circle   Let's take a closer look at adolescents and this thing we call peer pressure. Laurence Steinberg and his colleagues conducted extensive research into the lives of adolescents and their families. *Beyond the Classroom* discusses much of their findings and provides excellent and actionable insight for adults to learn from and use. The model and information below comes from his work.[6]

An adolescent's social circle typically includes one or two best friends, and a small group, or clique, of six to ten friends. Crowds, though less obvious in their influence, play a very important role, as you will read.

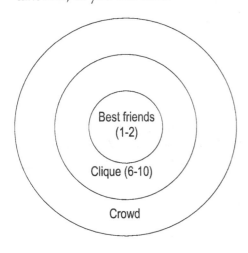

Best friends and cliques tend to influence teenagers in three ways:

1) Modeling ("Everyone is doing it.")
2) Rewards and punishment ("You're not going to wear *that!*")
3) Direct pressure ("Come on—just try this cigarette.")

Peer pressure (cont.)

Various versions of the "crowd" populate high schools across America. They are visible as the "jocks," "brains," "partiers," "druggies," or whatever current culture wants to call them. Influence from the crowd may be less obvious to adults because it is more subtle than the peer pressure used by best friends and cliques. The crowd is a group of like-minded kids who share attitudes, interests, and activities. The kids in the same crowd do not necessarily know each other, but they share norms and standards and adhere to these. These standards become internalized to the degree that teens do not feel they are responding to peer pressure; rather, that they are expressing themselves.[7]

Teens are influenced by their friends and by their school environment which can lead to both desirable and undesirable behavior. Teen "popularity" influences behavior and has been linked to increased substance abuse. Recent (2007) research from the National Center on Addiction and Substance Abuse at Columbia University (CASA) indicates that "popular" teens who attend schools where drugs are present are five times likelier to have a reputation for using illegal drugs and three times more likely to have a reputation for drinking a lot.[8]

How does pressure from peers differ from parental pressure? Kids tend to share the same basic morals and values as their parents; it is only when parental influence is perceived as negative or deficient that kids are more responsive to their peers in this regard.[9] By high school, friends are more influential than parents in terms of drug use and day to day school performance (class attendance, time spent on homework, attentiveness, grades).[10]

The world through their lens An important reminder for parents is that groups of teenagers see the world by their own set of rules—not ours. And the environment that persists at their school helps them to develop this set of rules and expectations for their behavior. The CASA research shows a strong correlation between levels of drug activity in schools and individual usage. Teens are more likely to act in similar ways to the peers they witness. Brain development and emotional maturity are also factors in this phenomenon. Teens are more likely to engage in risky behaviors without thinking the consequences through.

Whatever behavior is common to a group of kids feels normal to them. So whether they say, "Let's light up a joint," or "Let's go study together," they are not thinking about what parents think or what trouble they are likely to get into. Patricia Hersch states: "Whether the adult world sees the lifestyle as positive or negative is not the standard the kids are using."[11]

E

The incidence of minor crime rises in early teenage years, remains high in the middle stage, and declines toward the end of adolescence. The curve of data reflects the waxing and waning of peer influence. First, as they spend more time with peers, they may succumb to peer pressure. In later adolescence, they become more selective about their friends.

Eli Newberger, *The Men They Will Become*, 257, 258

Our culture

We could talk for days about the culture in which we are raising our children. This can be a highly emotional topic, as parents often complain that our culture seems to work against them. My own research about parents' attitudes underscores this. One Dad speaks for many when he said in my survey "Most of society seems to be giving diametrically opposed messages to the ones I am giving my kids. The outside message, from films and TV and music and the media, seems to be 'have sex, drink and take drugs, resort to violence to solve disputes, treat partners badly, and never confide in your parents. Oh, and driving fast is cool too.'"

Parents complain about many aspects of our culture, and indeed, there is much to focus on there. But it is not all negative. For a sense of fairness, and also a sense of accuracy, our discussion should include what is positive about our culture. Let's look at both sides. Begin by working on the exercise on the next page. Think, for example, about the attributes and elements in our culture in regards to our kids' dress: perhaps you, like me, are uncomfortable with the tight, low cut tops and ever-so-tight pants our girls wear. Then think about the positive elements of their way of dress: perhaps I'm aging myself here when I share that I was in junior high school before girls were allowed to wear pants to school! The freedom our girls have to dress appropriately for bad weather, for gym days—for everything, is liberating, indeed. Spend some time thinking about both the positives and negatives on the list in the exercise; discuss it with your spouse, kids, and friends. If it seems difficult to find positive attributes of our culture, that makes a statement about how important this is to review!

In my research I obtained surveys from over 380 current parents of teenagers, (the resulting report, titled "PARENTING TEENAGERS: The Agony and The Ecstasy" is available for downloading at www.PleaseStoptheRollercoaster.com) and I was struck by the intensity of their feelings and complaints about our culture. This is clearly a big issue for parents. Some deeply felt comments include: "The hardest part about parenting teenagers today is maintaining the values in our house despite the daily deluge of inappropriate messages." And another woman said "Teenagers have unlimited access to information and communication. I feel like a dog chasing a tail. I feel powerless and totally out of control. I cannot possibly keep up with the constant barrage of messages they receive. Of course, this is the backdrop to my constant fear that they will use drugs and engage in unhealthy and unsafe sexual activity."

I can understand how parents sometimes feel overpowered by the culture. It is not easy to run interference or keep tabs on the images and messages our teenagers receive. In the final analysis , though, we must inoculate our kids, and teach them to thrive regardless of cultural messages and norms with which you—or they—don't agree. HOME...this is where the battle line is drawn. This is where families must counter the negative aspects of our culture every day. But be wary of using heavy handed tactics in this battle as they can work against you. You can only fight this battle when there is communication between you and your teen...so your battlefield tactics must include subtlety, gentle dialogue and compromise as your teens learn to make good choices in this fast moving world.

Our culture (cont.)

Here is a partial list of ways through which culture is expressed. Identify significant aspects of our culture that have a direct affect on you and your family. List both positive and negative attributes. Add additional categories if you like. Prepare on your own and then brainstorm as a group.

	POSITIVE ATTRIBUTES	NEGATIVE ATTRIBUTES
Dress		
Work ethic and expectations		
Achievement and rewards		
Rituals and celebrations		
Communications: how you get and share information		
Racial and ethnic diversity		
Cross-cultural relationships		
Jargon and use of language		
Food and eating		
Day to day responsibilities		
Family closeness and care		
Educational opportunities		
Freedom to make personal choices		
Money and how it is spent		

Our culture (cont.)

Is the media the only "enemy?" The power of the media presents a daunting challenge for parents. Messages that objectify women or glorify violence and sexuality are particularly abhorrent. Some messages are much more subtle. Advertisers work hard to sell cigarettes, clothing, music, alcohol, food, and other products to our children. And they succeed in influencing their wants, desires, dreams, values and expenditures. Take a walk through readily available cable channels with your teen and view the messages they consume regularly about sexual conduct, social behavior, materialism, alcohol and drug consumption, violence, relationships and honesty. Computer games, internet sites, magazines, even billboards on the sides of city buses communicate powerful messages that influence us all.

Although it can be difficult developmentally for teenagers to understand the complexity of these media messages, we must make an attempt to raise their awareness around these issues. If we choose not to, the roles, behavior and values of our boys and girls may become scripted by Madison Avenue and television writers rather than based on the values and beliefs we want to instill and perpetuate.

But the media isn't solely responsible for all the cultural challenges we face in parenting our teens. In some situations, we can see the enemy in the mirror. Few will deny the focus on materialism present in kids today, who desire, demand even, the latest cell phone, electronic gadget or designer label. What's interesting to note is that numerous studies link material focus and indulgence with depression—and both are increasing in certain quarters. Yet parents continue to indulge their children's endless wants and desires. Why? Dan Kindlon in *Too Much of a Good Thing* notes that an alarming trend in parenting today is the blurring of the line between "parent" and "friend." Parents are reluctant to deny their teens the items in demand for fear of losing their child's love, or making the child feel left out in her peer group. So parents, too, are subject to cultural expectations and norms even when they actually undermine the experiences, the resilience, the self-esteem and long-term success of our children. Some parents must learn to make tough calls, and get comfortable with saying "no."

Are you aware of the television programs, video games, music, and movies your teenager is seeing/hearing? Have you ever tried to open up a dialog about these influences? If so, what was the result? If not, how might you try doing so?

Our culture (cont.)

Cultural pressure today in some middle class communities has raised the level of stress and competition to new heights. The competition to get into Ivy level colleges is undeniably intense, but parents who unceasingly push their teens with an "Ivy or bust" mentality risk undermining their teen's self esteem and confidence should they not make the grade. Some children are so pressured by parents' unwavering focus on "excellence-only" they become unwilling to try their hand at new activities. Parents' best intentions can produce behavior that undermines their desired outcomes.

Today we refer to "helicopter parents," a term that describes parents who hover too closely. This cultural phenomenon may result from what initially are good intentions to protect our kids in a society that feels challenging and frightening, to assist children to develop and compete in a culture short on enough opportunity for everyone, and to defend and support kids who are not developmentally equipped to make their own way. But children of helicopter parents learn that they don't have with it takes to succeed; rather than becoming empowered they become more reliant.

Our culture can support parents, and at the same time it can be the source of added pressure, criticism and input that serves to increase parents' worries, lack of confidence and confusion. Parents, you'll have some important choices to make relative to your own behavior as you raise your teenagers. Informed and thoughtful parents will learn to resist cultural pressure to behave in a way that is counterproductive to raising healthy, competent teens.

Our culture and girls There is a developing body of research and writing that seeks to illuminate the challenges girls face growing up in our culture. Resulting from overt and covert pressure, girls sometimes face contradictory expectations... and it's easy for parents to inadvertently be part of the problem.

Mary Pipher believes girls are evaluated in society based on appearance, while being caught in an onslaught of what she calls "double binds: achieve, but not too much; be polite, but be yourself; be feminine and adult; be aware of our cultural heritage, but don't comment on its sexism." She writes about the common response of girls who react to cultural pressure by conforming, and in the process drive underground their authentic selves.[12]

Rachel Simmons and Rosalind Wiseman have brought the issue of female aggression and girl bullying out under public scrutiny with their best-selling books *Odd Girl Out* and *Queen Bees & Wannabes*. Their examination of female relationships yields important new insight into the way teen girls relate to one another. Simmons' work describes a "hidden culture of girls' aggression in which bullying is epidemic, distinctive and destructive."[13] It is because our culture does not allow girls to express open conflict that their expression of anger goes underground into under-the-radar-screen acts of backbiting, exclusion, rumor-passing and name calling.

Simmons refers to the significant research of Carol Gilligan which indicates that girls and women are more focused on relationships than males, relationships playing a more significant

Our culture (cont.)

role in girls' development. It is for this reason, coupled with the fact that girls are socially scripted to *not* express conflict, that conflict is expressed in more covert ways and within intimate relationships. Girls are expected to be nice above all else; in fact they want to be nice and have many friends, a drive that compels many to accept covert bullying while still valuing and seeking the perpetrator's friendship. The articulation of unacceptable feelings, of anger, hurt, and loneliness is not tolerated in a society where girls are expected to be nice and friendly to all. So, while striving to maintain position and relationships, they will "attack within tightly knit networks of friends, making aggression harder to identify and intensifying the damage to the victims."[14]

The role of parents to correct this teaching is essential, but it can only be done by parents who are willing to do the work of examining and challenging culturally scripted roles, expectations and values. Joe Kelly of *Dads and Daughters* says, "If you are silent about the things your kids hear from media and culture, then those things gain an authority that they do not deserve. Your silence can leave your daughter feeling adrift and uncertain. The way to clear up the confusion is to speak up about how your personal and family values compare to values in the media." [15]

Ultimately we can teach our girls to be empowered by choices available to them, and we must understand the importance of our role in helping them to see these choices. This requires effort and time from enlightened parents who are willing to take personal risks to question the cultural influences to which we all are exposed.

Our culture and boys And boys? How does our culture affect them? We get some thought-provoking, and sometimes conflicting messages on this topic.

There are numerous experts that decry a "crisis" situation with boys in this country. Some experts point out facts that should worry us as to how boys fare as compared to girls:
- more boys are in special education classes,
- more boys drop out of high school,
- more boys are subject to disciplinary actions,
- fewer boys take the SAT,
- fewer boys graduate from college,
- more boys are prescribed mood-managing drugs,
- suicide rates are higher for boys,
- more boys than girls are incarcerated in prisons.

In the important educational arena we see that many times classrooms and curricula are not designed for the active learner, expecting boys—and girls—to sit in conventional classrooms for hours at a time preparing to spew forth correct answers on high-stakes standardized tests.

William Pollack (*Real Boys*), Michael Gurian (*The Wonder of Boys*), Michael Thompson and Dan Kindlon (*Raising Cain: Protecting the Emotional Life of Boys*) all highlight issues around a

Our culture (cont.)

culture that is doing harm to our boys as we raise them. They make some important points. William Pollack points out that our society has developed cultural norms that may harm boys psychologically as we expect them to separate from their mothers prematurely. He criticizes a culture that pushes boys from the nest too early, expecting them to achieve independence before they are ready. He says "We expect them to step outside the family too abruptly, with too little preparation for what lies in store, too little emotional support, not enough opportunity to express their feelings… We believe that disconnection is important, even essential, for a boy to 'make the break' and become a man. We do not expect the same of our girls…" Significantly, Pollack asserts that this forces boys to feel ashamed of their feelings of vulnerability and teaches them to mask their emotions and their authentic selves. The result is boys who must act tough, "like a man," and who are ultimately disconnected from their emotional lives.[16]

While we consider how this may or may not describe the way each of us raises our sons, we cannot deny some of the previously shared facts. But a new look at some data points in a 2007 *Time* Magazine piece offers yet another view, and suggests that the boys-in-crisis discussion has been influenced by those with political agendas. They report that some trends have turned around, and boys' achievements are improving in several key areas: drug use, juvenile crime rates, high school drinking, teen pregnancy and unprotected sex, to name a few.[17]

Importantly, see what we can learn about boys when we take a longer view: the *Time* article asserts that over the course of history sociologists have claimed a boy/men "crisis" numerous times, ultimately inspiring, in response, the creation of the Boy Scouts, the Olympic movement and football. Look at what these movements have in common: active, physically focused, hands-on action-oriented activities…all of which speak to the natural ways many boys learn.

Parents today have made some changes that benefit our boys, and our girls, for that matter. In the 1960's parents spent about 13 hours a week on child-focused activities, and by 1985 it had dropped to 11 hours per week. But a 2005 study found parents spending 20 hours a week focused on family.[18] These are positive changes that are reflected in some positive trends.

What may matter the most to caring parents raising boys is what happens within the family and in your son's educational experiences. Are you raising your boys with expectations and opportunities to express a full range of emotions or are certain expressions devalued? Are educational opportunities matched up with his learning style, recognizing that many boys respond best in an active, hands-on environment? Are we subjecting our sons to double standards that force them to shove their feelings underground?

Hand-wringing aside, we benefit from the discussions raised in the boys-in-crisis literature as we become more tuned in to the types of values and teachings that may be harmful to our sons. Let the sociologists argue the broad points. Be thoughtful, intentional and careful about the messages and behavioral examples you teach your sons in the meantime.

Our culture (cont.)

An optimistic view The generation of teenagers born between 1977 and 1994 is widely referred to as the "millennials." 70 million strong, they represent the biggest population boom since their parents, the baby boomers, came on the American scene. The truths about this generation are often different than popular images would have you believe, and there is much to be optimistic and excited about! Neil Howe and William Strauss , in *Millennials Rising* share some facts that will leave you hopeful. Millennials are:[19]

- **upbeat and optimistic:** Nine in ten describe themselves as "happy," "confident" and "positive."

- **cooperative team players:** community service has seen unprecedented focus from this group, and they believe they will do the most to help the environment over the next twenty-five years.

- **in agreement with their parents' values,** and nine in ten say they "trust" and "feel close to" their parents.

- **clean living:** abortion and pregnancy rates are down from when boomer parents were teens; alcohol consumption and drug use is down, as are many violence statistics.

- **academically successful:** with rising aptitude test scores, higher scores on college boards, and more teens taking AP tests, record attendances at colleges make the "cream of the crop" larger than ever.

Is limiting your child's exposure to American culture an appropriate way to prepare him for adulthood? Why or why not? Can you impose limitations while helping him prepare to manage himself on his own? How?

We've just touched upon the influences and issues our culture imposes on our young people. I urge you to spend a good amount of time discussing it in depth and developing strategies and creative ideas for the approach that feels right for you and your family.

Risky behavior

Lectures about teenage "risky behavior" fill auditoriums with anxious parents. Aware of the consequences of such behavior, loving parents are hungry for information. Risky behavior comes in many forms: abuse of alcohol, drugs—illegal and prescription, inhalants, eating disorders, driving unsafely, smoking, sexual activity....and this isn't a comprehensive list. If you are dealing with a teenager who is engaging in risky behavior you may need the help of a qualified expert in the area—and there are many of them. This session will not be a comprehensive information source for parents to learn the latest statistics or current trends; what we will explore and discuss here is adult behavior. How does our behavior influence and affect the risk behavior of our teenagers? What can we do? What does engagement look like in this area?

We will focus our discussion on the most common concerns of parents: alcohol, drugs, and sexual activity; there is much data about how parents can have a positive impact on these behaviors. Again, if your child is involved with something that really concerns you, seek professional help.

We are looking at this important topic to learn the following:
- What are realistic expectations for parents to have of our teenagers...and how likely is it we'll be facing these issues?
- What actions can parents take that make a difference?
- What decisions must parents make? Where must parents take a stand?

What parents do matters....a lot   In fact, what teenagers perceive about your involvement and actions has a significant effect on their behavior. Your actions matter. Engaged parenting. We'll get specific as to what it means in this context.

Numerous studies have shown a link between teenagers' perception of their parents monitoring them and their engagement in risk behavior. Teens who perceive less parental monitoring are more likely to consume more alcohol, use marijuana more often, have multiple sexual partners, not use any contraception, test positive for a sexually transmitted disease, have a history of arrests and engage in fights.[20]

There is no uniform definition of "parental monitoring," but there is general agreement on two of its elements: parental knowledge of who their child is with, and the knowledge by parents of where the child is when she is not at home or in school.

Recent research conducted by CASA reveals that there is a disconnect between parents' behavior, expectations and monitoring at teen parties. 80% of parents believe that neither alcohol nor marijuana are usually available at parties their teens attend, but 50% of teen attendees say these substances are present. Teens who say that parents are not present at the parties they attend are 16 times more likely to say alcohol is available, 15 times more likely to say illegal and prescription drugs are available and 29% more likely to say marijuana is available, compared to teens who say parents are always present at the parties they attend.[21]

Risky behavior (cont.)

While there are other factors that are associated with teenagers engaging in risky behavior*, for this discussion we will focus on the family and home environment. Family-focused factors such as family connectedness, parent-child communication, parental modeling, and parenting style influence teenagers' participation in, or rejection of, risky behavior.

Family dinner as proxy for parental engagement: CASA regularly explores the interconnection between parental engagement and teen behavior, as well as other influencing factors on drug and alcohol use. As a way to measure and demonstrate family engagement they view the number of dinners a family shares during a week.[22] Teens who have infrequent family dinners (two or fewer a week) are twice as likely to smoke daily and get drunk monthly, compared to teens who have frequent family dinners (at least five per week.) Teens who have infrequent family dinners (<2 per week) are:

- More that twice as likely to have tried cigarettes;
- One and a half times likelier to have tried alcohol;
- Twice as likely to have tried marijuana; and
- More than twice as likely to say future drug use is very or somewhat likely.

In addition to lower levels of risky behavior, there is a direct and positive correlation between increased levels of parental engagement and improved relationships between teenagers and parents. Compared to parents who say their families have dinners together frequently, those who have infrequent family dinners are:[23]

- Five times likelier to say they have a fair or poor relationship with their teen;
- One and a half times more likely to say they know the parents of their teens friends not very well or not at all;
- More than twice as likely to say they do not know the names of their teen's teachers;
- Twice as likely to say that parents deserve not very much blame or no blame at all when a teenager uses illegal drugs.

Teens who have frequent family dinners are likelier to get better grades in school. Higher academic performance is also associated with lower levels of risky behavior.

Even families who are suffering through times of tension or poor communication fare better than those with little or no connection, so keeping to regular family time and family meals is very important. If at times you feel your teen is pushing you away or doesn't want to spend time with your family, research indicates that this does not represent your teen's long term view. In previous research CASA has been able to demonstrate that parents who are "hands-on" vs "hands-off" have better relationships with their teens, *as reported by the teens....by wide margins!*[24] Match this point up with the Authoritative Parenting Model on page 56, and you'll see how these recommendations map to one another. Parents who express affection and provide boundaries are creating an atmosphere where parent-teen relationships are solid, and kids are less likely to get involved with risky behavior.

*some other factors include family dynamics, friends' substance use, and school and neighborhood environments; these factors tend to cluster together.

Risky behavior (cont.)

How often does your family sit down for dinner together? If you have difficulty increasing the frequency because of schedule conflicts, how else might you get quality family time together? Are your dinners usually pleasant or full of discord and tension? How might you move the more challenging interactions to another venue?

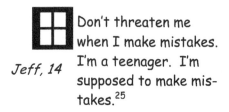

Don't threaten me when I make mistakes. I'm a teenager. I'm supposed to make mistakes.[25]

Jeff, 14

You should give me a curfew. You're so liberal all I have to do is call before I come home, whether it's 10 o'clock or 2 in the morning. You should be more strict.[26]

Lisa, 18

How do you not see me? I am not the perfect soul you picture in your mind. I am not the angel that won't drink or lie or be mean. Do you really know what I am doing? And if you did would you still trust me? I drink, but I don't do drugs. But I don't know whether that's okay with you. Talk to me. I want to be able to tell you everything I do and not have your eyes turn down in disappointment.[27]

Katie, 17

Risky behavior– alcohol and drugs

Alcohol—the drug of choice for many of today's teens
Let's look at the facts:
Kids are likely to try alcohol.[28]
- By the time they reach 12th grade, over 72% of American students have tried alcohol.
- Over 45% of high school seniors have used alcohol during the past month.

However, fewer kids drink today than when we were teenagers.
- 2006 figures show that alcohol use overall among 8th through 12th graders has been showing an overall downward trend since 1991.
- However, approximately 30% of 12th graders report they've been drunk in the past 30 days. This figure remains fairly steady from 1991—2006.[29]

Figures about binge drinking (defined as 5 or more drinks in a row), a perennial cause for concern, seem to be showing positive trends:[30]
- There is a decline in binge drinking in recent years,
- Perceived risk and disapproval toward binge drinking have increased, suggesting that such drinking (and very likely the drunk-driving behavior often associated with it) became increasingly unacceptable in the peer group.

School environment plays a part in "popular" teens drinking:
- Among drug-free schools, 32% of popular teens drank, while 57% of popular teens drank at drug-infested schools. [31]

The substance abuse gender gap has closed.[32]
- Girls 12 to 17 are at equal or higher substance abuse risk compared to boys of the same age.

E

"My husband and I both made the decision long ago that family came first and that being a part of our teens' lives was the most important thing we could do for them. We both worked, but always found the time to be with them when they needed it the most. We took family vacations a few times a year...we always knew where they were and who they were with. By letting them know that we were always watching what they were doing, they had a sense of security and knowledge that we cared and that is the most important thing that you can do as a parent. Many parents are misguided with the notion that they need to give their teens freedom and stay out of their lives. We made sure that we were a big part of it."

"Veteran" parent respondent in our survey titled
Parenting Teenagers: The Agony and The Ecstasy
Full report is downloadable at www.PleaseStoptheRollercoaster.com

Risky behavior– alcohol and drugs (cont.)

Alcohol use at a young age is significant   Seventh graders who experiment with alcohol should concern you. Studies have shown that teenagers who begin drinking before age 15 are four times as likely to become dependent on alcohol as those who start drinking at age 21.[33] According to other studies, kids who start drinking early are also 10 times likelier to be involved in a fight after consuming alcohol, seven times likelier to be involved in a car accident and 12 times likelier to be injured.[34]

Obviously, when your children get to high school and are driving, parents and teenagers have additional concerns to manage in regards to alcohol use. Alcohol use impacts the engagement in other risky behaviors (such as sexual activity,) and is linked to behavioral problems such as stealing, fighting, and skipping school. All of these considerations will need to be examined when establishing your position on teenage drinking.

If almost 75% of high school graduates have tried alcohol, it might be unrealistic to expect your child to abstain completely. Many experts say that experimentation is a part of the normal teenage experience. However, if we, in being "realistic" expect our kids to try alcohol, are we not in some way giving them tacit approval? Are we virtually guaranteeing that experimentation? CASA research shows that teens whose parents believe it is very likely that their teen will try drugs in the future have substance abuse risk scores that are almost three times greater than those of teens whose parents believe their child will never use drugs.[35] Our expectations have an influence on our kids' experimentation.

A conversation that took place in my kitchen brought this to light for me in a dramatic way. A fifty year old family friend (with a colorful past) had dropped by and the conversation got around to the challenges of raising teenagers. She sympathized with our parental challenges by saying "When I think about what I did back then it's amazing I'm alive!" Significantly, however, it was the giggles and the "between the lines" communication that she expressed that left an impact on me. Her memories were fun ones! She communicated a positive association with the behavior she now recognizes as dangerous.

What kind of messages are we giving our kids when we speak about our experiences growing up? Do we express, in subtle or direct ways, all the fun we had during our wayward teenage experiences? Might there be danger in this approach? I believe we could be communicating a tacit expectation that teenagers are *supposed* to be wild—it's a "right of passage," if they care to imbibe.

That said, the high social acceptability and use of alcohol makes prevention difficult. Perhaps a more realistic goal is to curb alcohol misuse rather than preventing any use.

Risky behavior– alcohol and drugs (cont.)

When reminiscing about your teenage years, do you mention the "wild times" that you may have had? Do your kids hear you talking about those wild and fun times in your past? What kind of message do they take away from that? Are risks included in these discussions?

Many specialists remind anxious parents that curiosity and experimentation are normal during adolescence. Not all kids who experiment are, or become, addicts. It's important for parents to keep a perspective on this.

That said, however, it's worthwhile to explore the issues that drive chemical use. "Why?" is an important question to ask if your teenager is using drugs. Experts will tell you that chemical use in teenagers may signal issues that need addressing, not just by the teenager but sometimes by the entire family unit. It can be a cry for help. It is likely to involve issues that go beyond just the teenager. It isn't always fun to stop and honestly examine the current state of family relationships. This is when getting expert input and help can be important.

Is it possible that an adolescent is intentionally behaving rebelliously to make a statement? To gain attention? What is missing in this child's life? Sometimes focusing on family relationships, respecting and including teenage friends, may create enough change to make a chemical abuse problem fade away.

Obviously, there can be many other influences that drive this type of dangerous behavior, but families and family relationships can play an important role in creating the situation, and in helping to solve it. If you suspect something is amiss don't waste precious time—address it with the help of qualified professionals.

Risky behavior– alcohol and drugs (cont.)

Drinking at home   The way you treat alcohol in your home undoubtedly has an affect on your child's use of it. In *The Idiot's Guide to Parenting a Teenager* Kate Kelly[36] offers the following suggestions:

- Evaluate how your family uses alcohol and consider the message this behavior conveys to your children. Do you drink daily? For relaxation? To socialize? Is drinking a part of celebrations or holidays?
- Don't ask your teenager to prepare a drink for you or bring you one.
- Be deliberate and intentional in whether you introduce alcohol to your child in your home, or not. Consider the pros and cons for your family as there are arguments on both sides of this issue. Some parents feel that by introducing kids to alcohol at home they help to remove some of the mystique while keeping their teenagers safe. Others feel that, in addition to the legal issues, this sends a very bad message. Either way, Kelly points out that most alcoholic drinks are an acquired taste and there are advantages in not helping your child learn to like them.
- Lock your liquor cabinet. Unsuspecting parents are usually amazed at how much teenage alcohol is acquired from the family stash.

The issue of age   Experts do not agree as to whether the drinking age of 21 helps or hurts. Yet another "sticky wicket" on this path of parenting! It deserves a bit of your consideration as it may come up in discussions with your child. Here are some of the issues: Although it is undeniable that highway accidents are down since the drinking age went back to 21 in all states, there are those who believe that a drinking age of 21 exacerbates the very problem it's trying to solve. Some have noted the "prohibitionist mind-set" actually causes young people to drink furtively, quickly, and dangerously– and behind closed doors away from adult supervision. In fact, on some college campuses administration officials support the lowering of the drinking age so that the activity can be monitored. As reported in *Time,* "The 21-year drinking age has not reduced drinking on campuses, it has probably increased it," said the former president of Middlebury College, in Vermont. "Society expects us to graduate students who have been educated to drink responsibly. But society has severely circumscribed our ability to do that."[37] Since leaving Middlebury, John McCardell has launched an organization called "Choose Responsibility" to lower drinking ages in conjunction with heavy education and regulation for 18 to 20 year olds. But don't make the mistake of thinking this is only a college problem; colleges complain that they inherit the drinking behaviors their students learned in high school.

Risky behavior– alcohol and drugs (cont.)

What do you think about the 21-year-old limit for alcohol consumption? Do you favor allowing your teenager to drink in certain circumstances at an earlier age? In what circumstances? Under what conditions?

In some high schools, students who participate in extra-curricular activities must sign an agreement promising abstinence from harmful substances. What is your school's policy on drinking? Is it enforced equally?

E

Your Liability: Here's what you should know about the legal aspects of serving liquor to minors:

- You can serve your own minor children in your home.
- You are responsible for any illegal behavior of your minor child, whether she has been under the influence of alcohol or not.
- Any person who delivers, sells, or gives liquor to a minor is liable to be punished under the law.
- If you serve minor children (other than your own) in your home, you can be held liable for any resulting problems

Kate Kelly, *The Complete Idiot's Guide to Parenting a Teenager*, 207

Does your town have a "zero tolerance" policy on teenage drinking? What does that mean? What are the likely consequences should your child be caught drinking?

Risky behavior– alcohol and drugs (cont.)

Some facts about alcohol:

- One third of American adults don't drink at all and many Americans are drinking less and less. Per capita alcohol consumption has been steadily declining.
- Teenagers are more affected by alcohol than adults.
- Girls are more affected by alcohol than boys.
- A third of all high school seniors say that they drink more than five drinks in a row in one sitting at least twice a month.
- Teenagers drink 35% of all wine coolers because they like their fruity, non-alcoholic taste and because they believe that wine coolers don't contain much alcohol; overall, they drink more beer because it's cheap and easy to get.
- The majority of teens who use illegal drugs first use alcohol and those who begin using alcohol at an early age have a higher tendency to be current users of alcohol, tobacco or marijuana than do those who start drinking when they are older.

National Council on Alcoholism and Drug Dependence, Inc.

What is your stand on your teen drinking? Is your teenager clear on your stand? Are you prepared to enforce it? When or under what conditions might it change?

Risky behavior– alcohol and drugs (cont.)

What to tell your kids about your experiences, and possible experimentation, can present a challenge to parents. Many parents are aware that being honest with their teenagers is extremely important, yet complete and full disclosure could carry with it potential consequences. How should parents answer the inevitable question: *"What did you do, Mom?"*

Experts do feel there are ways to effectively cover both needs—that of honesty and of conveying an anti-drug or drinking message. Here are some suggestions:[38]

- Be sure not to glamorize your youthful pursuits if they included behavior you'd rather not see duplicated by your teenager.
- Rather than confessing details about all of your activities, you can talk about your friends back then and interject your current opinion. For instance you might say "Back then a lot of people used marijuana, but that was before much was known about it. Today we know much more about the dangers of the drug, and the marijuana that is available today is far more potent and dangerous."
- Remember that there is a big difference between experimentation and regular use. You might say "Yes, I tried drinking a few times in high school because my friends did, but I stopped because I quickly saw it was dangerous and not productive in any way. But just because I tried it a couple of times, that doesn't mean I'm giving you permission to do so. There is nothing to be gained, and a lot that you risk when drinking or using drugs."
- Ask your teenager questions about her views on the subject. Once you know her thoughts you'll be better prepared to respond to her questions in way that will help her, and satisfy her need for information.

Only you know if there might be risk involved in telling your kids what you did in your teen years. If there might be risk involved, identify the pros and cons of being completely honest. Speak with others and brainstorm as a group about why—and how—you might find an appropriate way to best address this topic.

Risky behavior– alcohol and drugs (cont.)

Our conversation about drug use will focus on what you need to know so that you are informed about current day realities. Who is using drugs today and what are the chances you will be confronted with your child's involvement?

Overall, according to printed government data, rates of drug use are associated with age. The age group in which drug use is the most prevalent is the 18 to 20-year-olds (22.3%). Ranked second are the 21 to 25-year-olds, (18.7%) third are the 16 to 17-year olds (17.0%), with 14 to 15-year- olds in the group ranked fifth (8.9%).

The drugs used in the past month vary dependent on the age group:[39]

12-13 year olds	**14– 15 year olds**	**16-17 year olds**
Prescription* (1.7%)	Marijuana (5.9%)	Marijuana (13.6%)
Inhalants (1.5%)	Prescription* (2.8%)	Prescription* (5.4%)
Marijuana (0.9%)	Inhalants (1.2%)	Hallucinogens (1.7%)
		Cocaine (1.2%)
		Inhalants (1.0%)

*prescription-type drugs used nonmedically

All in all, drug use has decreased over the last several decades. In 1979 14% of the U.S. population (age 12 and older) reported using an illicit drug during the past month, with that figure bottoming out at slightly below 6% in 1993. Usage figures have increased since 1993 to 8.3% in 2006.[40]

Looking at data that is specific to junior high and high school students gives us a picture of what parents are likely to face. The National Institute on Drug Abuse publishes a study each year called "Monitoring the Future." This captures usage statistics and measures trends annually across the population of 8th graders, 10th graders, and seniors in high school. The 2004 study surveyed more than 49,000 students in 406 schools across the nation.

On the next page, you can see that after alcohol, marijuana usage is the most common. Inhalants present a common problem across all the age groups, particularly the younger kids. Among older high school students tranquilizers, hallucinogens, and cocaine are popular. The figures vary widely as to use over their lifetime or in the last 30 days.

Risky behavior– alcohol and drugs (cont.)

National Institute on Drug Abuse Youth Trends 2006[41]

% usage	8th graders	10th graders	12th graders
Any drug—lifetime	20.9	36.1	48.2
last month	8.1	16.8	21.5
Marijuana*—lifetime	15.7	31.8	42.3
last month	6.5	14.2	18.3
Inhalants—lifetime	16.1	13.3	11.1
last month	4.1	2.3	1.5
Hallucinogens– lft.	3.4	6.1	8.3
last month	0.9	1.5	1.5
Cocaine—lifetime	3.4	4.8	8.5
last month	1.0	1.5	2.5
Amphetamines-lft.	7.3	11.2	12.4
last month	2.1	3.5	3.7
Tranquilizers—lft.	4.3	7.2	10.3
last month	1.3	2.4	2.7
Steroids—lifetime	1.6	1.8	2.7
last month	0.5	0.6	1.1
Ecstasy—lifetime	2.5	4.5	6.5
last month	0.7	1.2	1.3
Alcohol—lifetime	40.5	61.5	72.7
last month	17.2	33.8	45.3

*includes marijuana and hashish
"Lifetime" refers to usage at least once during the respondent's lifetime. "Last month" refers to usage during the month preceding responding to the survey.

I had an interesting experience at a concert that I attended with my son. At this particular venue they had beer on sale, and the authorities were impeccable about applying rules: one beer per person, everyone was carded, etc. However, in the seating section where the audience danced and enjoyed the music, the smell of marijuana was thick and pungent. This can be a common experience at concerts—how do you prepare your kids for this situation?

Risky behavior– alcohol and drugs (cont.)

Perception vs. reality   There is a phenomenon that is taking place in some circles about which you need to take note. Kids' perception about their peers' participation in some of these risky behaviors may be very different than actual usage numbers. Health educators who are tuned in to students' perceptions share that there can be a sizable disparity between the "actual" usage numbers and kids' perceptions. Kids estimate high. Think about the implication of this: if teenagers [erroneously] perceive their peers are engaging in risky activities, their perception of "peer pressure" may be based on inaccurate assumptions. So, arming them with a more accurate understanding of what their peers are *really* doing may help keep them safe.

The bottom line   The chances are pretty good that you will be faced with your teenager's use of drugs or alcohol. He may experiment once, or dance with real problem behavior. Think through this issue in advance—it will help you if you are not caught off guard.

Make sure your actions and reactions give the message you want to give. It helps to understand the difference between simple curiosity and problem behavior, and what might be behind the latter. Sometimes drug and alcohol use is symptomatic of developmental issues and personal conflicts, making professional intervention appropriate. But, many times it is the simple result of teenage curiosity and that feeling of invincibility that many teens have.

E

You may be thinking that alcohol and drug experimentation is a terrible thing. However, in real life it is not this cut-and-dried. Many teenagers are able to experiment with drugs and alcohol without becoming dependent, and in a manner that doesn't impede their ability to grow and mature. Research by Jonathon Shedler and Jack Block showed that adolescents who experimented moderately with drugs (no more than one time per month and usually just marijuana) were psychologically healthier than those who abused drugs (more than one time per month) *and* those who abstained from drugs altogether. This is not to say that drug experimentation is either good or recommended; rather, it indicates that drug abuses are the symptoms of deeper problems....In this study, which followed the same 101 boys and girls over fifteen years, those who were psychologically the healthiest as children were the same ones who just moderately experimented with drugs as teenagers. This, I believe, puts drug experimentation into a more differentiated framework. While moderate experimentation is not necessarily good, it is also not necessarily a sign of a deep psychological crisis. On the other hand, more than a casual experimentation is cause for deep concern, not only as a problem in itself, but also as a sign of deeper problems. This research clearly shows that drug or alcohol use can itself be the cover to deeper issues.

Michael Riera, *Uncommon Sense for Parents with Teenagers*, 96-97

Catching your teenager once with drugs isn't necessarily a time to panic, but it should be a wake up call for some thoughtful parental involvement and discussion.

Risky behavior– sexual activity

Is talking openly about the sexual activity of teenagers a difficult topic for you? Having realistic discussions about sexual activity, expectations, and education is the only way to keep our kids safe.

You, undoubtedly, have values you wish to share with your children. Have you done that in regards to their sexual activity? Have they heard your views on the subject? Have you heard theirs? Is this a conversation that you find difficult to have? Many parents find it a difficult subject to broach, but finding a way to do it is essential. Studies vary as to where young people get their information about sex, but most say that kids get most of their information from other kids. Others say that the main source of information for children and teens about sexual behavior is from the media—what they see on television, in movies and in magazines.

Is this where you want your kids receiving their training? Don't leave the conversation to someone else—you're the parent, and you have the biggest influence of all. Remember, their world is different than the one we negotiated in our teenage years; they face very severe consequences of unprotected sex. In addition to the obvious issues around values and pregnancy, the dangers of today's sexually transmitted diseases can be life threatening.

Again, our objective is to provide a framework of information so that you can have realistic expectations of your teenagers, and so that you will be informed as to the role you play in educating them. I hope you will have an informative and honest discussion in your group on this topic and learn from one another. We will provide some statistics, discuss some trends and what's behind them. But the bottom line is this: you will need to decide what information you will facilitate (and participate in) getting into your kids' hands. Don't abdicate your responsibility—give this issue serious thought and make conscious choices about your actions.

Current data:

The Kaiser Family Foundation is one of the leading organizations reporting on sexual activity. They find:[42]

- The number of 9-12th graders who report engaging in sexual intercourse has declined in the last decade.
- Among teens who are sexually active, rates of contraceptive use have increased.
- U.S. teen pregnancy rates have decreased a significant 28% between 1990 and 2000.
- Fewer than half of all 9 -12 grade students report having had sexual intercourse, reflecting a decline from 53% to 47% during the last decade.
- Males are more likely than females to report having had sexual intercourse.
- Median age at first intercourse is 16.9 years for boys and 17.4 years for girls.

Risky behavior– sexual activity (cont.)

More data, facts and trends[43]
Contraception:
- 98% of teens aged 15 - 19 who have had sex report using at least one method of birth control. Most commonly used are condoms (94%) and birth control pills (61%).
- Condom use has increased over the past decade.
- "Protecting against HIV," "protecting against other STDs "and "pregnancy prevention" are the primary factors in choosing to use birth control.

However:
- 34% of young women become pregnant at least once before the age of 20.
- While the teen pregnancy rate in the U.S. has declined, it remains very high compared to other industrialized nations and about double the rate in England.
- Approximately 4 million teens contract a sexually transmitted disease; compared to adults 10—19 year olds are at higher risk for acquiring STDs .

Abstinence:
- Among teens aged 15—17 who have never had sexual intercourse, their reasons were: "concern about pregnancy" (94%); "influence of HIV/AIDS" (92%); "other STDs" (92%); and "feeling too young," (91%).
- A recent study of four separate abstinence programs, conducted for the Department of Health and Human Services found no evidence that the programs delayed the start of sexual activity among teens.

Sex and substance abuse:
- Among sexually active 9-12th graders, 25% report using drugs or alcohol during their most recent sexual encounter.
- Among 15-17 year olds, 51% say they are concerned they might "do more" if they are using drugs or alcohol.

Sex and age discrepancy between partners:
- The younger a girl is when she has sex for the first time, the greater the age difference is likely to be between her and her partner.
- Teen girls with older male partners are more likely to be sexually active, less likely to use contraceptives, and more likely to face an unintended pregnancy.

E

The extent to which parents are involved and the manner in which they are involved in their children's lives are critical factors in the prevention of high-risk sexual activity. Children whose parents talk with them about sexual matters or provide sexuality education or contraception information at home are more likely than others to postpone sexual activity. And when these adolescents become sexually active, they have fewer sexual partners and are more likely to use contraceptives and condoms than young people who do not discuss sexual matters with their parents, and therefore are at reduced risk for pregnancy, HIV and other sexually transmitted diseases.

Family Planning Perspectives, March 2001, v33, i2, 52

Risky behavior– sexual activity (cont.)

Kids are doing more, younger   A study was released in 2000 that caused an uproar by suggesting that young teenagers are engaging in oral sex—possibly as a way of remaining virgins in this age of abstinence education. Although hardly a new activity, some parents have found it shocking that their teens may engage in such behavior. Researchers have been following the trend, and Kaiser reports that 49% of teen males 15-19 said they had received oral sex, and 39% that they had given oral sex.[44] These figures approximately mirror other data, such as that from the Centers for Disease Control and Prevention.

Current experts point to a new definition of "intimacy" for today's younger generation. Whether it's oral sex or "friends with benefits," a casual attitude toward sex concerns many experts. Sabrina Weill, a former editor in chief at *Seventeen Magazine* and the author of *The Real Truth About Teens & Sex* says that this casual attitude toward sex reflects teens' confusion. And, she says, they are "exploring dangerous territory without a map."

Most parents don't need data points to tell them that casual relationships that are focused on sex are relatively unsatisfying—to say the least. Yet the role models that teenagers see on television and in movies often indicate casual sex is the norm. Herein lies a major opportunity for parents to influence and teach teenagers about the joys of intimacy, and the responsibility inherent in mature relationships...yet this is an opportunity that many parents ignore.

My research shows a big disconnect between parents and teens on the subject of sex. The twenty-year olds that I surveyed and report on in *Parenting Teenagers: The Agony and The Ecstasy** indicate that parents have not communicated well on this topic. One 20 year old said of her parents "We discuss a lot of topics, but sex has been the one topic that we never really discussed." Another who says she "engaged in risky sexual activity with her boyfriend," points out the importance of discussions that go beyond the basics: "...no one had ever really talked to me about the EMOTIONAL effects of sex. I knew all about STDs and pregnancy and how that happens, but I had no idea what would happen to me psychologically."

Health and sexuality educators are expected to teach about AIDS, condoms, and general sexual health, but discussions that address the emotional aspects are left up to parents. And who would you like to have these values-based discussions with your teenagers? Even if it's awkward or uncomfortable for you, this is essential territory for you to cover.

Deborah Roffman's excellent book *"Sex and Sensibility; The Thinking Parent's Guide to Talking Sense About Sex"* is filled with her years of experience as a certified Sexuality and Family Life Educator and parent. She says children and adolescents have five core needs. The needs don't change over your years of child-rearing, but the topics covered certainly will. They are:[45]

*report is available at www.PleaseStoptheRollercoaster.com

Risky behavior– sexual activity (cont.)

- **Affirmation:** Children and adolescents need adults to recognize and validate their particular stage of sexual development.

- **Information giving:** Children and adolescents need factual knowledge and concepts about sexuality, presented in on-going and age-appropriate ways.

- **Values Clarification:** Children and adolescents need adults to share their parental values and to clarify and interpret competing values and values systems in the surrounding culture.

- **Limit setting:** Children and adolescents need adults to create a healthy and safe environment by stating and reinforcing age-appropriate rules and limits.

- **Anticipatory guidance:** Children and adolescents need adults to help them learn how to avoid or handle potential harmful situations, and to prepare them for times when they will need to rely on themselves to make responsible and healthy choices.

It's best to have many short discussions rather than one "big talk." Do your best to make this a comfortable topic, it's okay to bring it into conversation on a regular basis. This tells your teenager that she can talk with you about her questions and feelings—and they are bound to be there!

And, according to the experts, when you think the time is right, you're probably two years too late. So don't delay. It's never too late to begin.

> What messages do you communicate to your child about expectations, and appropriate activities? Do you do this enough?

How do teenagers view the information they receive from television? The Kaiser Family Foundation gives us insight from a national survey they conducted showing:[46]

- Nearly three out of four teens think sex on TV influences the sexual behaviors of kids their age "somewhat" or "a lot"; but just one in four think it influences *their own* behavior.
- Many teens say they have learned something helpful about sexual decision-making from TV. Six in ten say they have learned about how to say no to a sexual situation that makes them uncomfortable.

Risky behavior– sexual activity (cont.)

How are we preparing our kids to handle tough situations?   Again, the parental conversation is essential to prepare our children. Both girls and boys need to develop specific skills to enable them to handle themselves. I was overwhelmed with grief when the daughter of a friend was the subject of a date rape. The dangers of drinking at parties is greatly exacerbated with the "date rape" drug, a pill that can be slipped into a girl's drink that not only makes her compliant, but wipes out her short term memory. The story that was the final straw for me was of a girl who was at an un-chaperoned party, didn't like what was going on, and went into the room to retrieve her coat so she could leave. But a boy whom she knew followed her into the room and raped her. Upon hearing this I enrolled my daughter, an eighth grader at the time, in a self defense course, with the result that we are both more confident in her capability to protect herself. One lecturer that I heard emphasized an important point—that girls need to practice saying "NO!" It isn't enough to know in their head what their course of action should be—they need to *hear themselves* say the words and actually practice it.

E

> When we asked teens about specific sexual situations they might have faced…a troubling picture emerges. Among teens who have been in an intimate situation, almost half (47%) have done something, or felt pressure to do something, they didn't feel they were ready to do. Teen girls are more likely than teen boys to have had these experiences (55% vs. 40%). Specifically, teen girls are twice as likely as teen boys to have been in a situation when someone was pressuring them to do more sexually than they felt comfortable doing (28% vs. 13%), to admit having actually done something sexual they did not feel comfortable doing (31% vs. 16%), and to have been in a relationship that was moving too fast sexually (33% vs. 15%).
>
> Kaiser Family Foundation

Abstinence education vs. sex education? Are our teens' interests being served?
Abstinence is a respected option for many teenagers. It's becoming increasingly clear that more and more teenagers have made a conscious decision to delay intercourse. While this is an encouraging trend, it cannot be expected to be the only answer for our teenagers. Education remains important. A report from the Kaiser Family Foundation points out a serious gap exists between what teens think they know about contraception and what they really know. They demonstrate "dangerous misperceptions" about which methods are effective for disease prevention versus pregnancy.[47] The experts who favor sex education, as opposed to abstinence-only education claim the risk teens run is that when they do have sex, those who have not received adequate education are less likely to use proper protection.

Risky behavior– sexual activity (cont.)

Sexual development is normal   All of this discussion about contraception, sexual activity, etc. tends to mask a fact that is frequently forgotten by parents: sexual development is a normal part of growing up. Some experts feel that we undermine our kids' healthy sexual development by not validating it and focusing only on the risks involved in sexual activity.

Regarding boys:

Today we find a predominant wish that adolescents would practice sexual abstinence, but that if they can't hold to that goal, they should at least avoid contracting sexually transmitted diseases, and avoid causing pregnancies. These concerns are undeniably important...what is missing in this approach is an acknowledgement or acceptance of the adolescent drive for pleasure....

Adolescent discussions and media presentations need infusions of knowledge and insight that parents and teachers could effectively provide if they were willing to accept and honor, rather than to attempt to deny or proscribe or shame or riddle with fear, the adolescent's sexual drive.

Eli Newberger, *The Men They Will Become,* 260-261

Regarding girls:

We do not teach girls that they are entitled to their own sexual desire or sexual pleasure, that "good" and "nice" girls have sexual feelings, too. We teach girls to be the objects of others' sexual longings.... Unlike being violent, becoming a sexual person is a normal part of growing up. We do not talk with adolescents about physically and emotionally safe ways to explore their developing sexuality; we just tell them not to "do it."

Deborah L. Tolman, Frontline Web site, *The Lost Children of Rockdale County*

What actions and discussions might you take to support the healthy and normal sexual development of your teenager?

Risky behavior– sexual activity (cont.)

The bottom line.....*talk*. Don't allow your child's sexuality to be a taboo subject. And to think that your kids will remain inactive sexually because you've kept the facts from them is naïve.

E

> Research has shown repeatedly that, over the long term, comprehensive sex education does not "cause" adolescents to have sex, and that abstinence education does not prevent them from having sex. For those who do have sex, comprehensive sex education is associated with an increased use of contraception and condoms, while students who have had abstinence education who subsequently become sexually active are much less likely to take these precautions.
>
> Deborah L. Tolman, Frontline Web site, *The Lost Children of Rockdale County*

E

> Informal sex talks with your teen shouldn't center on "sexual plumbing" facts and scare tactics. Your talks should focus more on the emotional and social factors of teenage sex and sexuality, as well as your own values regarding sex within a committed, caring and mature relationship.
>
> FamilyEducation.com *Let's Talk About Sex*

Your kids may make it hard on you, but don't be put off. Many professionals will tell you that the teens are listening to every word, and every message you deliver on the subject, even if they act embarrassed and uninterested. Say it anyway; they'll probably appreciate the advice in the long run.

You've taken a stand on alcohol and drugs; is there a stand to take in regards to your child's sexual activity? How much say do we have in their sex lives? What is your role here? How will it differ depending on the age of your child?

ISSUES TO EXAMINE AND DISCUSS

Refer to

1. How might you handle the situation when you feel uncomfortable with your teenager's choice of friends? How has your child's choice of friends been a reflection on him, his self-esteem, and level of maturity?

   104-108

2. Think back to your teenage years. Can you remember when friends' opinions became more important than those of your family? How would you describe this shift?

   —

3. If you have a discussion group, begin your discussion about our culture with the exercise on page 110, or try this with a friend. Brainstorm the positive and negative aspects of our culture in the categories given. Add additional categories that are relevant for you. Discuss how parents can mitigate the negative influences.

   109-112

4. What is your response to Pipher's view of our culture's impact on girls? How about Pollack's discussion of the "Boy Code?"

   113-114

5. nnnnnnnnnnnnnnnnnnnnnnnn

   117

6. What should you tell your kids about your exploits and adventures in growing up? Should you be truthful if your exploits included experimentation with drugs and alcohol? Discuss with peers, your spouse and/or discussion group possible approaches that give the message you want to give.

   125

7. *Discuss the fact that the 40–44 age group shows an increase in drug use. How might you handle the situation if one of your child's friends allow drug use in their home? How might you find this out?*

   126

8. What is your position on teenage drinking? Are there any conditions under which you would support it? Discuss this with your spouse, your peers and others to challenge ideas and clarify positions.

   119-124

9 Identify your expectations and the options available to you when determining consequences for misbehavior around drug and alcohol use.

   —

10. What resources are available in your community for information on contraception and related medical issues. Will you share these with your teenager? What are the pros and cons?

   129-135

Special note: For those of you in a discussion group, preparation for Chapter 5 is different than for any other chapter. It involves other members of your family and may require some advance planning. Don't wait until the last minute to prepare, as many people tell me this is their favorite chapter!

 There are two copies of the Personal Style Inventory on pages 253 and 257, if you need more you can download them from our website.

TAKE-AWAYS

What are my "take-aways" from this chapter?

_____

_____

_____

_____

_____

_____

_____

_____

_____

What specific things am I going to do differently as a result of what I've learned?

_____

_____

_____

_____

_____

_____

_____

_____

_____

ZITS

5

A scenario

Very early Sunday morning, you wake to the sound of the phone ringing. First, it is the mother of one of your son's best friends, and while you are on the line with her you receive a call from the police station. Your sixteen-year-old son was sleeping at this friend's house, and you now learn that the two boys snuck out during the night and sprayed graffiti on a local bridge, were caught by the police, and were now being held in custody.

Speaking with your son at the police station, you are amazed at his lack of understanding for what he did. "Did you think about the consequences of this before you did it?" you ask. He answers that no, it just seemed like fun at the time. "Did you think about what would happen if you got caught?" you wonder. No, he says, one of his friends came up with the idea, and the rest just went along with it.

You are frustrated and furious that this person who looks like an adult has the reasoning capability of a child. Why can't he think through the consequences of his actions? What is going on inside his head when he is faced with making these kinds of decisions?

Chapter Five: Overview and objectives

You will be exposed to some fascinating ways of viewing yourself and your teenager in this chapter. Examining your own personality type, character, and temperament using a well documented and popular assessment model, will undoubtedly bring to light new insights about yourself. Applying the same process to your children and other family members can be very enlightening and can allow you to appreciate and understand each other differently. In addition, we will share with you the latest research in the brain development and sleep patterns of adolescents, which will also shed some light on teenage behavior. The more you know, the better equipped you are to be the best parent you can be.

Objectives

In this chapter you will:

- Understand the personality type, character, and temperament of each member of your family by using an assessment instrument.

- Examine the results and how they can be used to improve communication and appreciation of each other within the family dynamic.

- Explore how your own personality traits may enhance or detract from a conscious, healthy parenting relationship with your teenager.

- Understand the behavioral implications of the latest research into adolescent brain development.

- Learn about normal sleep patterns in teens.

> *"We must allow our children to become actually what they are potentially; in other words, we must let nature take its course by giving our children ample room to grow into their true, mature character."*
>
> David Keirsey[1]

Chapter Five: Instructions

Attention: If you are in a discussion group you will need extra time to prepare this assignment. Do not wait until the last minute!

Reader Instructions

How to get the most out of this chapter:

- Read the chapter through page 145. Take the Personal Style Inventory on pages 253-259 in the Appendix, referring to the instructions on page 145. Score using the scoring sheet, also in the Appendix. Fill your profile in on the worksheet on page 147.

- Have all willing family members take the assessment and add their information to the worksheet on page 147. Now learn about your family member's profiles using the information on pages 146 through 157.

- Complete the exercises on pages 148, 149, 150, 151, 157, and 160. Discuss your insights with family members who participated in this process. Using the recommendations on page 152, discuss with family members specific ways that communication can be improved upon. Let them know how you prefer to be communicated with.

- Be sure to write down your "take-aways." These insights will help you translate your intentions into actions.

If you have a parenting discussion group:

Group Recommendations/ Reminders

- Begin by asking how you were able to apply what you learned at the last meeting as you put your "take-aways" into action.

- Ask each group member to identify which of the issues on page 162 they wish to discuss.

- The facilitator for the meeting can guide the group discussion to ensure that the issues of greatest interest to group members are examined and explored, and that all group members participate.

- See page 11 for more recommendations for group leaders.

 Be sure to access the "Tools for Groups" area on our website www.PleaseStoptheRollercoaster.com.

Personality type, character, and temperament

According to the Greek myth, a young sculptor named Pygmalion, disenchanted by the women of Cyprus, sought to create a statue of the ideal woman. He worked tirelessly for months, molding and forming with frenzy and compulsion, until he had in fact created the most beautiful figure of a woman ever conceived through art. Pygmalion quickly fell in love with his perfect creation, kissing and caressing the figure for hours on end. Of course, the delicate stone figure could not love him back, so Pygmalion soon became desperate and unhappy. He had set out to create his perfect mate, but instead, he created only his own sadness and frustration.

In our attempt to be good and responsible parents, we sometimes confuse "good parenting" with "controlling behavior." It is vitally important for us to recognize the difference and change our behaviors if necessary. The healthy emotional development of our teenager is at stake. When we fall into Pygmalion-like parenting, we are thinking more about who we'd *like* our children to be instead of who they actually *are*.

*Learning about person-
ality type is an enlight-
ening way of gaining
information about one-
self and our family
members, so that we
may apply new, more
positive methods to our
parenting style.*

It is helpful to understand how character, personality type, and temperament help to shape our teens. If we gain an understanding of our child's character, type, and temperament, and those of ourselves and other family members, we can maximize communication techniques to enhance each person's style. And, rather than trying to mold our child into the person we think she ought to be, we can help her grow into her own unique person, building on her natural style and strengths.

In exploring personality type we are accessing the work of Carl Jung. We will work with the four dimensions that make up one's personality type in his model. The four dimensions indicate one's preference, or natural style, in four significant areas:

- **Where you get your energy** (the *extroversion/introversion dimension*)

- **How you take in information** (the *sensing/intuiting dimension*)

- **How you make decisions** (the *thinking/feeling dimension*)

- **How you relate to the world around you** (the *judging/perceiving dimension*)

The strength of your preference in each dimension helps to determine your personality type.

Personality type, character, and temperament (cont.)

The theory behind this work comes from the work of C.J. Jung, a Swiss-born psychiatrist who died in 1961. There has been much written about Jungian type as it is applicable in many areas where humans interact.

People with the same psychological type share a common set of characteristics, but they remain uniquely different due to both their upbringing and their set of experiences as they are growing up. This framework, while it enhances understanding and communication, also enables you to not just tolerate differences, but to appreciate them.

Some of you may be feeling a little worried about this topic already. Don't be put off by the scholarly look of this effort—this really can be fun, and we have simplified the process tremendously. My parenting group found this to be one of our *most enlightening* topics, as we uncovered and named what it was that had puzzled us about some of our family relationships. You may get the most concrete information of this whole program from this session. And with a little concentration it really shouldn't take very much time.

Although there are many different types of assessments, many feel that measuring personality type and temperament is one way that is particularly appropriate in the context of improving communication and understanding within families. In order to make it understandable and the material useful for you, we have simplified the discussion. And, hopefully, as you apply this introduction of the concepts to your family members, you'll ignite a desire to learn more about this. There are many resources available; for a start see the resources noted on page 147. Shortly you will use the instrument that has been included in the appendix of this book, and each participant in your family should take and score their instrument separately. (See instructions on page 145.)

As you create your profiles you can open up a new world of understanding, communication, and support for one another. Are you ready to begin?

Personality type, character, and temperament (cont.)

Type in action   One of my friends, Nancy, an "intuitive extrovert," tells about growing up with a mother who is her exact opposite. Of course, it wasn't until she was grown (and familiar with this framework) that she realized why they had such a challenging dynamic: her mom wanted her to do projects that some children would love—sewing, cooking, playing with puzzles, etc. But Nancy, an intuitive, was imaginative, loving creative, fantasy filled projects. To her, sewing and working with puzzles was far too concrete and consequently, utter drudgery. Her mom, thinking she was doing her best for her child, wanted Nancy to get her head out of the clouds! Interestingly enough, as Nancy grew older she grew closer with her dad (also an "intuitive") as she realized how much they had in common. Their idea of a good time now is concocting plots for fantasy novels!

Why understand "types"?   Businesses, government, family practitioners, and schools are just some of the groups who have benefited from "type-watching." This is a scientifically validated approach that enables one to attach "names" to types of people to enhance their ability to improve communication. It is a "judgment-free psychological system" as Kroeger and Thuesen say in *Type Talk,* and it is "a way of explaining 'normal' rather than 'abnormal' psychology. It allows us to celebrate differences; in fact it highlights differences."[2] Understanding the type of another person gives you a reference point and useful information about their behavior. And it helps you understand your own preferences and behavior, too.

Try to understand that just because I'm different from you doesn't mean I'm bad. I don't know how I got into this family but I'm trying my best not to upset you.[3]

Stewart, 16

Author's note: You may find yourself with a family member who resists this assessment process. Some people feel it is intrusive and don't like the idea of being "labeled." In truth, the process fosters understanding and increases your ability to appreciate other people's uniqueness. You should avoid labeling at all costs. But don't turn this exercise into a battle; a friend of mine had a teenager who simply refused to take this assessment—period. That deserves to be respected.

Personality type, character, and temperament (cont.)

After reading the tips below, have each member of your family take the ***Personal Style Inventory*** in the Appendix of this book. Read the instructions carefully. Two copies are provided; however you may need to make additional copies (or download copies from our website) for all your family members.

After taking the instrument, score all of the results using the scoring sheet in the Appendix. Again, be sure to read the instructions carefully. Then apply the results following the instructions on the next several pages.

A few comments and tips about this assessment process:

- Don't stress over the instrument and the questions. Try to answer using your first "gut" instinct; don't over-think your answers and make it a big deal. You can actually skew the results that way. You should only take about 10 minutes to complete the instrument.

- You are being assessed on four dimensions of your personality. This instrument cannot fully capture you—indeed, no assessment can. Keep in mind there are no right or wrong ways of being—therefore there are no right or wrong answers.

- Parents with younger teens may find them struggling with the questions in the assessment instrument. Do what you can to help them by providing examples or paraphrasing.

- You will end up with a "profile" that consists of 4 letters, one from each of the four dimensions. For instance, ESFJ or INFP, etc.

- Notice when you score the results what the actual numbers are. The higher the actual number, the more intense your preference in that area. If the two numbers are close, you fall closer to the mid-point on the continuum, meaning that preference is less intense, and may actually be situational.

- There are 16 possible variations in the profiles, and you may find it instructive to learn more about your style. Reference any one of the many books available on the subject to read more detailed information. Several books that I use are mentioned on the worksheet on page 147.

 Additional copies of the Personal Style Inventory are available in the "Tools for Groups" area at www.PleaseStoptheRollercoaster.com.

The Four Preferences[4]

Where You Get Your Energy

E ——————————+—————————— **I**

Extroversion
Sociable, talkative
Life's generalists
Do first, reflect later
Excited by variety and action
Think out loud
May be easily distracted

Introversion
Internal, thoughtful, reserved
Need time for privacy
Life's specialists
Wait and watch before doing
Retreat from too much stimulation
Energized by ideas

How You Take in Information

S ——————————+—————————— **N**

Sensing
Experience oriented
Realistic, practical
Notices details
Remembers facts
Wants clear directions
Works at a steady pace

Intuition
Future oriented
Imaginative and creative
Works with bursts of energy
Sees possibilities, fantasy
Dislikes routine

How You Make Decisions

T ——————————+—————————— **F**

Thinking
Objective, analytical, logical
Focuses on policy, laws, justice
Wants consistent standards
Not naturally empathetic
Values competence and
individual achievement

Feeling
Sensitive and empathetic
Diplomatic, expressive
Sensitive to tension between others
Takes criticism personally
Needs physical contact, affection
Avoids confrontation and conflict

How You Relate to the World (Lifestyle)

J ——————————+—————————— **P**

Judging
Results, not process oriented
Decisive, wants closure
Wants to know the rules
Dislikes change
Likes order and structure
Productive and responsible

Perceiving
Open ended, tentative
Adaptive, flexible
Enjoys the unexpected
Dislikes decision making
Spontaneous and impulsive
Cheerful and fun

My personality type is:	E/I	S/N	T/F	J/P

The personality type of others in my family:	E/I	S/N	T/F	J/P	*I am different from this person in the following dimensions:*	*I am like this person in the following dimensions:*
NAME _____						
NAME _____						
NAME _____						
NAME _____						

Learning about personality type can shed light on your preferences and can give insight into your behavior. It can also serve to enlighten you about the preferences and behavior of others, increasing your ability to understand them and communicate better with them. It would be misusing this information, however, to "label" and to use it as an excuse for certain behavior.

Additional Resources

Books: (see bibliography)
    Please Understand Me*
    Nurture by Nature*
    Type Talk
    The Developing Child
        * Includes complete descriptions of the 16 personality types

Web site:
    www.keirsey.com

The E/I Dimension

Children who prefer Extroversion (E)

♦ Like variety and action

♦ Learn better if given opportunities to talk about the information they are learning

♦ Demonstrate energy and enthusiasm for activities

♦ Are stimulated by and respond well to activities in the environment

♦ May be easily distracted

♦ May act before they think

♦ Are usually friendly, talkative, and easy to get to know

♦ Become energized when they interact with others

♦ May say things before thinking them through

♦ Have a shorter "wait time" between questions and answers than introverts

Children who prefer Introversion (I)

♦ Enjoy individual or small group activities

♦ Are energized by ideas

♦ Think before they act

♦ Carefully form ideas before talking about them

♦ Usually wait for others to make the first move

♦ Like to observe things before trying them

♦ May not share their thoughts and feelings with others

♦ Need time for privacy

♦ Dislike interruptions

♦ Pause before answering questions and have a longer "wait time" between questions and answers than extroverts

♦ Can ignore distractions

♦ May seem reserved and quiet

Are you and your child on the same side of the E/I scale, or are you opposites?

How does your child express her E or I traits? Think of concrete examples.

How do you support this expression? Do you understand her style or has it been puzzling to you?

How do you like to interact with people? Is it the same way your child does? Think of examples. How are you and your child alike? Different?

Give an example of a time when the basic differences in your styles led to a conflict or misunderstanding.

How can you use your new understanding in ways that will support your child and enhance your rapport?

The S/N Dimension

Children who prefer Sensing (S)

- Like precise directions
- Prefer using skills they've already learned
- Focus on the present
- Work at a steady pace
- Prefer step-by-step learning; using a sequential series of steps
- Rely on experience for learning rather than on what they read
- Are likely to have a good recall for details
- Draw on proven methods to solve current problems
- Want facts and examples to describe issues and mistrust vague ideas
- Focus on what actually is

Children who prefer Intuition (N)

- Need opportunities to be original
- Like tasks that require imagination
- Enjoy learning new skills more than mastering familiar ones
- Dislike routines
- Work in bursts of energy with slower, less productive periods in between
- Focus on the future
- May skip over facts or get them wrong
- Spend so much time on the design stage of a project that, when finished, it often falls short of expectations
- Need variety
- Have a seemingly sporadic, random approach to learning
- Like to imagine what could be

Additional Points:

- Both sensing and intuitive children take in information through the five senses but process it differently.
- Both types are creative, but the sensing child begins working with the details and builds to a theme, while the intuitive child begins with a theme and adds details later.
- Intuitive children need help actualizing their design, while sensing children need help planning their designs.

What type is your child on the S/N dimension? Where are you on the continuum?

Think of specific S or N examples that describe the way you two are alike or different.

How do you show support for your child's S or N style?

How does this knowledge about your child enhance your understanding of him?

How can you express this understanding in new ways?

The T/F Dimension

Children who prefer Thinking (T)

♦ Value individual achievement

♦ Need to know why things are done

♦ May find ideas or things more interesting than people

♦ Need opportunities to demonstrate competence

♦ Are concerned with truth and justice based on principles

♦ Spontaneously analyze the flaws in ideas, things, or people

♦ Need to know the criteria for grades and evaluations

♦ Try to prove their points logically

♦ In younger grades may enjoy talking with teachers more than with peers

♦ May have difficulty accepting nonspecific praise

Children who prefer Feeling (F)

♦ Need feedback and praise about their performance

♦ Avoid confrontation and conflict

♦ Are skilled at understanding other people

♦ Spontaneously appreciate the good in people

♦ View things from a personal perspective

♦ Are concerned about relationships and harmony

♦ Enjoy pleasing people, even in seemingly unimportant matters

♦ Enjoy subjects that concern people and need to know how decisions affect people

♦ Have difficulty accepting criticism and can find sarcasm and ridicule devastating

Additional Point: Two thirds of American males are Ts, and two thirds of American females are Fs. This fact helps to reinforce gender stereotypes and expectations.

Where do the people in your home fall on the T/F dimension?

Do you have any female Ts or male Fs? In what ways are their attributes different than what is expected of them based on their gender?

Think of examples of interactions that demonstrate their T or F traits. Is this style in synch with others in the home? Is it in conflict with others?

How might you provide additional support to your child based on this new information about the way he/she make decisions?

The J/P Dimension

Children who prefer Judging (J)

♦ Prefer expectations for tasks to be defined clearly

♦ Like to get things settled and to get work done

♦ Prefer completing one project before beginning another and can become stressed by too many unfinished projects

♦ Don't usually appreciate surprises

♦ Need predictability and can find frequent changes upsetting

♦ Like to make decisions

♦ Want to do things the "right" way and try to make things happen the way they're "supposed to"

♦ Work best when assignments can be planned and the plan can be followed

♦ Work well if tasks are paced, become frustrated with incomplete assignments when deadlines loom near

♦ Do not like to mix work and play but would rather work hard first then play

♦ Value the finished product rather than the process of doing something

Children who prefer Perceiving (P)

♦ Act spontaneously

♦ Like freedom to move and become bored with too much desk work

♦ Are cheerful and bring fun and laughter to the world

♦ Enjoy the process of doing something more than the finished product

♦ Work and play simultaneously and try to make work fun

♦ Enjoy the unplanned and the unexpected

♦ Adapt well to change

♦ May start too many projects at once and have difficulty finishing them

♦ Let work accumulate and then accomplish a lot with a last-minute flurry of activity

♦ May turn in assignments late as a result of poor planning or time management

♦ Work better against a deadline

Additional point: The contrasts between the Js and Ps in the parent-child relationship can be the most frustrating to understand. The Judgers like to be decisive, responsible, and to live by the rules. Contrast this to the Perceivers who are flexible, tentative, and impulsive; the differences are a set up for challenges in a family environment.

Are you and your adolescent on opposite or same sides of this dimension?

How does this manifest itself behaviorally in your home? In school?

How can your increased understanding of this dynamic be used to improve your communication style with your child?

Improve your communications by being deliberate in your approach when talking with....

EXTROVERTS

- Show energy and enthusiasm
- Respond promptly without long pauses
- Anticipate "thinking out loud" and allow it
- Communicate openly
- Focus on people and things—the external world

INTROVERTS

- Include time to get to know each other and develop trust
- Encourage responses with occasional questions to uncover their thoughts
- Don't overwhelm with questions
- Have one-on-one activities
- Don't assume lack of interest. Allow time to think and process information

SENSING TYPES

- Show evidence (facts, details, examples)
- Be practical and realistic
- Have a well thought out plan with details worked out
- Show how your suggestion is a continuation, rather than a radical change
- Be direct
- Show the steps involved

INTUITING TYPES

- Present the big picture or main idea first
- Don't give lots of details before being asked
- Describe the challenges, possibilities, and differences your ideas will bring
- Highlight future benefits
- Show the aspects that are non-routine
- Be aware that work may come in bursts
- Allow for dreaming. Encourage imagination, and don't "burst their bubble"

THINKING TYPES

- Be brief and concise—don't ramble
- Emphasize logic
- List the pros and cons
- Be intellectually critical and objective
- Be calm and reasonable
- Don't assume feelings are unimportant; they are just valued differently
- Present emotions and feelings as facts to be weighed in the decision

FEELING TYPES

- Get to know the person before getting down to business
- Be personable and friendly
- Describe how the idea is valuable to people and how it will affect people
- Be aware that people with F preference have more difficulty being critical and giving negative feedback
- Pay attention to how you say things, being aware of body language and other non-verbal cues

JUDGING TYPES

- Present a timetable and stick with it
- No surprises; give warnings of coming changes
- Allow time to prepare
- Demonstrate that you also want to accomplish things and can be counted upon
- Show your achievements and past results
- Take a stand; don't be wishy-washy

PERCEIVING TYPES

- Allow for things to flow, not to follow your schedule
- Bring in new information and ideas
- Allow time for thorough discussion; complexity is okay
- Encourage autonomy
- Realize any change in direction is not necessarily impulsiveness

Adapted from "Talking in Type," Jean M. Kummerow, Ph.D., Center for Applications of Psychological Type

Personality type, character, and temperament

Learning about temperament and character   The work of David Keirsey and Marilyn Bates, authors of *Please Understand Me,* takes the concept of personality type one step further. One of their contributions is their identification of four basic types, which they call temperaments. Their research shows that temperaments can provide accurate predictions of behavior, such as how people teach, learn, lead others, entertain, manage money, and relate to other people. Since 450 BC, philosophers, psychologists, and others have identified four configurations of attitude and behavior. The concept of the four factor model includes the work of Edward Spranger, Eric Fromm, and can be traced back to the ideas of Plato, Aristotle, and Galen. Keirsey and Bates' application of it, combined with a more user-friendly system of labeling from *Nurture by Nature,* simplifies our discussion of type and temperament.

Now that you have taken the assessment, you should know the 4 letters, or dimensions, that describe you. Extensive research has shown that by focusing on two particular dimensions, we can identify significant characteristics that people share. **Look at your profile and if your second letter is S, match it up with the fourth letter. You will either be a SP or SJ. If your second letter is N, match it up with the third letter. You will either be a NF or NT.** Everyone should fit in to one of the following categories:

SP   SJ   NF   NT

This information, applied in the next several pages, will likely help to describe you and your family members and offers you a different point of view and a different language than you may have used before. Our hope is that it provides useful insight and understanding that will enable you to allow your children to become "actually what they are potentially" and that you'll give your children "ample room to grow into their true, mature character."[5]

E

There are two sides to personality—**temperament** and **character**. Temperament is a configuration of inclinations. Character is a configuration of habits. Character is disposition. Temperament is pre-disposition. Temperament is the inborn form of human nature; character, the emergent form which develops through the interaction of temperament and environment.

David Keirsey, Marilyn Bates, *Please Understand Me: Character and Temperament Types,* 20-26

Personality type, character, and temperament (cont.)

Parents often assume that their children are much like themselves, extensions of their personality, and they may expect that their child will experience the world as they do. This may, in fact, be far from the truth. Well meaning parents may miss cues from their children that provide information as to their natural needs and styles, yet parents who are tuned in usually figure out ways to communicate and care for their child effectively.

The study of temperament can help to bring to the surface the inborn preferences and traits, helping you the clarify and identify them so they become less of a mystery and more of a tool.

Before we get to the detailed description of the temperaments, let's review:

- There are 16 different personality types, based on the 4 dimensions we've been discussing.
- The temperaments are derived from 2 specific parts of your profile, as described on page 153, and there are a total of four temperaments.
- The labels of the temperaments may change depending on your source of information.

Use the instructions on page 153 to determine the temperament of each person who has taken the assessment. With that information in hand, read about the four temperaments on the next two pages, and apply to your family members.

If you say "Why can't you be more like your sister" one more time I think I'll explode. I can't be more like her simply because I'm ME, myself, and that's who I am always going to be. As your child, I would appreciate it if you accepted me.[6]

Nancy, 15

The Temperaments

NT "Conceptualizers"

NF "Idealists"

	NT "Conceptualizers"	NF "Idealists"
As Individuals	• Most analytical and independent of the four temperaments • Theorize and intellectualize everything • Problem solvers and original thinkers • Driven to achieve competence • Learn by challenging authority • Have their own standards against which they measure themselves and others • See the big picture as well as the underlying principles of internal logic • Speak and write clearly and precisely	• Most empathetic and philosophical of the four temperaments • Always searching for meaning in their lives • Experience life as a drama • Extremely sensitive to subtleties in behavior • Searching for authentic self-realization • Work toward a vision of perfection • Can be an "intellectual butterfly" • Believe the pen is mightier than the sword
As Parents	• Have high standards and sometimes their children can find them hard to live up to • Demand intellectual excellence from their children	• Provide unlimited warmth and affection • May provide a confusing role model to their children because of their on-going quest for self-identity • Defend their children always
As Children	• Thirst for knowledge; intellectual curiosity • Often precocious • Strong willed; independent • Set high standards for themselves • Intrigued by how things work • May act emotionally detached (but this does not mean there is a lack of caring)	• Usually loving and affectionate; can express rage and hold grudges • Highly sensitive and dramatic • Take things personally and are upset by rough or aggressive treatment • Boys can be seen as too emotional
As Students/ Learners	• Easily bored; need a steep learning curve to stay engaged • Tend to be independent learners; like to follow their own path • Change their interests or hobbies often once they've mastered them • Need help in establishing priorities • As original thinkers they can find themselves ahead of their parents, teachers, and others who are not NTs • May be loners in the classroom • Often do not have well developed social skills • May be an "intellectual snob"	• Like to please their teachers, but take criticism too personally • Naturally drawn to the arts • Need recognition and feedback • Frequently better at oral communication than written • Prefer people-focused subjects over abstract ones • Participate well in democratic process in classroom • Responsive to teachers who are nourishing, supportive, and who value being open with feelings • Have vivid imaginations • Thrive on personal attention, caring
As Spouses	• They intellectualize feelings and emotions; this can create misunderstanding as the feelings and emotions are really there	• They are "teddy bears" • Have a deep need to give and receive affection as well as to avoid conflict

The Temperaments (cont.)

	SJ *"Traditionalists"*	SP *"Experiencers"*
As Individuals	• Most responsible of the four temperaments • Stable, traditional, can take charge, respect authority • Conservative, practical, dependable • Organized, realistic • Comfortable with rules • May have difficulty with transitions	• Most adventurous and fun loving of the four temperaments • They look for action; live in the "here" and "now" • Look for careers with immediate tangible rewards, like EMT's, mechanics • Practical, resourceful • Adept at problem-solving skills, especially hands-on tasks
As Parents	• Provide structure and boundaries that many children need; can be overly rigid, however • Make expectations clear	• They meet child's immediate expectations well; may not plan for the future adequately
As Children	• Highly value membership in a group • Family oriented • Life is serious; work hard and play by the rules • May be distrustful of new experiences; not natural risk takers; approach life with caution • Toys and closets are usually in order • Adult feedback and approval must accompany tasks for them to be appealing • Thrive on stability	• Most adventurous and fun • Highly value freedom, exploration • May be in trouble a lot • Their belongings may be in disarray; messy rooms • Are often late and/or unprepared • Impulsive, spontaneous, cheerful, resist rules • Often they are risk takers • Usually good eaters
As Students/ Learners	• Respond well to teachers who are organized and meet their expectations • May not be as open to learning new things due to innate rigidity • Comfortable with traditional classroom structure and Socratic methods • Desire to please the teacher and "belong" to the group • Conscientious and responsible; prefer to be prepared • Prefer to study facts and procedures, not areas requiring improvisation or speculation • Learn best using step-by-step methods • Good team players in a group setting	• Not attracted to theory; look for practical applications • This group has the lowest correlation between academic ability and good grades • Most happy with activity and action, not passive learning or Socratic methodology • Can be behavior problem in school due to their need for activity, their impulsiveness, and low tolerance for waiting • Many drop out of school because the typical environment is opposite from the learning environment that suits their active nature • Do not like to plan or prepare • Prefer hands-on rather than passive learning • Excellent team players, love competition • Love involvement in dramatizations and performances
As Spouses	• Devoted to home life • Clearly defined roles • Value rituals and traditions *Note: When these children come into adolescence, parents may find their rebellious behavior particularly shocking because of the dramatic change from earlier behaviors.*	• Never a dull moment • Planning and structure are always low priorities

The Temperaments (cont.)

Who in your family is most like you in personality style? In temperament?

In what ways are you different from your teenager?

How does applying the information in this chapter enhance your understanding of your teenager?

What specific tactics can you use to improve communication between you?

How might you show a greater appreciation for the uniqueness of your child?

Brain development

The last decade has produced exciting new knowledge about teenagers and their developing brains. We now know that the human brain is not fully developed until between 21—25 years old! And what we know now can explain a lot of puzzling teenage behavior.

First, let's be reminded that the physical appearance of your teenager bears little resemblance to the maturity of the brain inside that head. Be careful not to believe that your six-foot high son can reliably think like an adult, because this is just not so. The wiring inside of the teen brain is flakey; one psychotherapist I know likes to reference a flakey light switch, because there is a lot of similarity. Sometimes the lights are on, and sometimes they are not, with seemingly random predictability. Parents of teens must learn to expect this; this is teens' "normal."

The brain grows in a two-step process; first is the adding of gray matter when the body intentionally over-produces synapses, or connections, a process which occurs just before puberty (age 11 in girls, 12 in boys). (The only other time the body does this is in the womb through the first 18 months of life.) The second step, occurring throughout the teen years, is the gradual "pruning" of connections, or remodeling of the brain tissue, as the brain begins to specialize in some areas, while not developing others. The activities in which the teenager engages determines what areas of the brain will be developed. Jay Giedd at the National Institute of Mental Health in Bethesda, Maryland is a leading researcher who calls this the "Use it or Lose It Principle." He has said: "If a teen is doing music or sports or academics, those are the cells and connections that will be hardwired. If they're lying on the couch or playing video games or watching MTV, those are the cells and connections that are going to survive."[7]

Current research indicates the area in the brain known as the "pre-frontal cortex" is still developing in teenagers. Sometimes referred to as the "executive," this area of the brain carries out executive-like functions such as planning in advance, exercising judgment, having insight, weighing information, and directing goal-oriented behavior. That it is still developing in teenagers is significant. It means that teens cannot be relied upon to always show good judgment or see consequences for their behavior in advance. Furthermore, because this pre-frontal cortex is not fully developed, teens evaluate situations and people from the *emotional* center of their brain. This can explain much of teenagers' highly emotional reasoning and behavior. And, it is reported that teens feel emotions more than twice as intensely as adults. Again, this is teenagers' "normal."

One study measured adolescents' responses when reading emotion on other people's faces. The results showed that teenagers use less of the prefrontal region when reading emotion, and that they were far less accurate in their assessment of facial expressions than were adults. While teens tend to respond from the "gut" section of the brain, the two regions interact with one another for a more accurate assessment in adult brains.

Brain development (cont.)

Think about how this applies—how many times has your teenager read you wrong? I've been accused of saying things I never said, and of thinking things I've never thought! And to think it's because she is "hard-wired" in a certain developmental stage gives me a far better understanding of where she's coming from!

Brain research confirms what you undoubtedly see: teens are more impulsive, more spontaneous, and more emotional. And you need to know that they are not developmentally ready to foresee the consequences of their actions. This comes with time.

These findings have implications for all of us in understanding communication with teenagers and in predicting their behavior. Think of it this way: they are different from adults in

- *what* is actually entering their brain (perceptions, visual cues)
- *how* the information is organized and processed (most processing going on without the benefit of the "executive")
- their ultimate *response* (or unedited "gut" reaction)

Now that explains a lot, doesn't it? And it highlights the importance of your role. Because teens have not developed the "executive" brain functions of planning in advance and exercising judgment, there are times we will need to help them with this. Some parents have trouble stepping in when their teenager is pushing back loudly, but you can see that if your child isn't mature enough to be making good decisions reliably you have a responsibility to get involved.

Yet taking over for him is not the answer, either. Children learn to make good judgment calls by practicing; these are like muscles that need to develop. Being aware that this brain functionality is still developing in your teenager should give you some much needed guidelines. Remember, he may *look like* an adult, but he is not.

Look inside yourselves. Try to remember what it was like to be a teenager, maybe even relive the past. I know it might not be easy, but it will help you to understand why I make mistakes and why we have so many arguments.[8]

Alba, 14

Brain development (cont.)

What types of positive activities is your teenager involved in that may be helping the development in his brain?

The "use it or lose it" principle supports the importance of enrichment activities for kids. How might this be balanced with concerns about our overscheduled children? Have you found the right balance for your family? What might need to change?

Think of an example of when you were "misread" by your teenager. Now that you know she is less capable than an adult at accurately reading facial expressions, will you be more careful and intentional about your communication?

Changing sleep patterns

Have your teenager's sleep patterns changed yet? Is she staying up later at night and sleeping in on weekends to make up for it? She really isn't necessarily being rebellious or lazy—it is common and normal for sleep patterns to change during adolescence.

Many factors play into the changes in sleep patterns that typically affect teenagers. Some of these factors are biological in nature, and some are more socially and environmentally based. Let's begin with the biological changes.

You may have heard references to our internal biological clock, which determines our sleep-wake cycle. With teenagers, the biological clock often seems to get out of rhythm with external clocks and schedules with which kids must comply. Researchers have shown that the biological clock of teens shifts forward, creating difficulty in sleeping at the time they previously went to bed. Their internal clocks prevent them from feeling sleepy until later in the night, and the internal systems that used to wake them up, refreshed and ready to go early, are also shifted to a later time. This is called a "sleep phase delay."[9]

Then there are the external factors that affect teens sleeping: school starts earlier, schoolwork or other commitments are likely to engage them later into the evening, and social interactions may also keep them up. The disparity between the school week sleep schedule and the weekend sleep schedule becomes more pronounced.

What is often unrecognized is that teens actually need at least as much sleep as they got as smaller children—nine and a quarter hours.[10] Teenagers frequently find themselves battling a sleep deficiency to their detriment.

Parents are probably well aware of the dangers of sleep deprivation, and driving a car presents an obvious danger. But sleep deprivation negatively affects all kinds of performance, including the ability to acquire information, retain it, and use it. School performance is directly affected by quality of sleep.

One additional challenge for teenagers in regards to sleep, is that they can get into a vicious cycle where emotions cause lack of sleep, and lack of sleep exacerbates emotional responses.

How can parents help? For one, understanding and supporting what is a new "normal" pattern for them will help. Encourage keeping a fairly regular schedule not just during the week, but without major aberrations over the weekend. Help your teens understand their performance is directly impacted by the quality and amount of sleep they get. Keep computers and cell phones out of their room; as parents you have that authority and right. As far as sleeping in an extra few hours on weekends, this helps, although it is less than ideal. Sleeping in late on Sunday morning makes getting to bed on time Sunday night even more difficult. But gaining an extra few hours helps more than not.

(Note that some teenagers do have sleep disorders and need to see their doctor for treatment.)

ISSUES TO EXAMINE AND DISCUSS

Refer to

1. Try and have a discussion about this chapter with your family members. Share with each other your personality types. Does this feel accurate? What insights have you gained about yourself?

    142-150

2. What did you learn about your similarities and differences with your various family members?

    146-152

3. Do any of you have male Fs or female Ts in your family? These people live in contrast to typical gender stereotypes. Do you see this? Discuss.

    150

4. How will you apply what you've learned about personality type and temperament to improve your relationships and communication in your family?

    –

5. What information stood out for you in the brain development discussion? What did you learn that's new? What insight does it provide? How will you apply it?

    155-157

6. Does the discussion on sleep give you a greater understanding of your child's needs? How might you support him better?

    161

TAKE-AWAYS

What are my "take-aways" from this chapter?

_____

_____

_____

_____

_____

_____

_____

_____

What specific things am I going to do differently as a result of what I've learned?

_____

_____

_____

_____

_____

_____

_____

_____

_____

ZITS

School, Parental Support, and Self-Esteem

A scenario

You have noticed your daughter's recent disinterest toward school. During a conversation with her 9th grade math teacher, you learn that her teacher is supportive but concerned; your daughter has not handed in a homework assignment all week, she is falling behind, and she has been late to class for several days. He tells you that he kept your daughter after class to express his concerns and to offer his help in getting her back on track. You agree to speak with your daughter and to encourage her to meet with her teacher for extra help and to make up missed assignments.

Your daughter comes home from school that same day furious with her math teacher. She angrily spits out that he kept her after class that day to speak with her about her "bad attitude" and "horrible homework." She feels angry and insists that you switch her out of her class because, she tells you, he doesn't like her.

How do you manage this conversation with your daughter?

Chapter Six: Overview and objectives

School is the center of the world for many teenagers; their social, academic, athletic and extra-curricular worlds revolve around school. And, to a large degree, parents gets shut out. It takes sensitivity, understanding, and the knowledge of how and when parents can appropriately participate in this important part of our child's world to have a positive influence on our kids' school experience.

In this chapter we will examine this important part of their world, what it's really like for them, and the important part that parents should play.

Objectives

You will:

- Tune in to the sources of stress in your child's life.

- Become aware of both your attitude and your teenager's attitude toward school, teachers, homework, and achieving academic success.

- Examine and identify how and how much you should involve yourself in his schooling. Identify strategies for involvement.

- Gain a better understanding of what school is really like for your teenager and begin to identify how you can best support him.

- Briefly examine learning styles and Gardner's theory of Multiple Intelligences.

- Understand the importance of self-esteem and the role it plays in your child's life.

> *"School is, after all, one of the few responsibilities we expect all youngsters to fulfill, regardless of their backgrounds or family origins. As a broad barometer, then, engagement in school is an indicator of children's commitment not only to education, but to the goals and values held by adult society."*
> Laurence Steinberg[1]

Chapter Six: Instructions

Reader Instructions

How to get the most out of this chapter:

- Read all of Chapter 6; you may want to highlight the areas that strike a chord with you.

- Don't be intimidated! Some very fine parents have told me that by the time they read this chapter they are feeling inadequate. Don't fall into this trap—nobody does everything right! You are living in a dynamic environment, and the very fact that you're reading this book says how much you value the relationship with your teenager. Just keep doing your best...and don't expect perfection.

- Prepare the exercises on pages 171, 173, 176, 178, 181, 183, 186, 189, and 194.

- Examine the issues and questions on page 196. Discuss the most relevant questions with a friend, spouse, or in your parenting discussion group, if you have one.

If you have a parenting discussion group:

Group Recommendations/ Reminders

- Begin by discussing how you were able to apply what you learned at the last meeting as you put your "take-aways" into action.

- Ask each group member to identify which of the issues on page 196 they wish to discuss.

- The facilitator for the meeting can guide the group discussion to ensure that the issues of greatest interest to group members are examined and explored, and that all group members participate.

- See page 11 for more recommendations for group leaders.

 Supporting parents as you help your teen in school is an area we consider very important. You'll find many helpful articles at www.PleaseStoptheRollercoaster.com. For those of you who are concerned with positive school-parent communication, you will also find helpful resources and information.

School and pressure

Parental involvement in a child's education can be one of the strongest predictors of a child's academic success.

Do you know what happens in your child's school life? For most parents, it's a mystery that gets deeper each year as your teen progresses further in school. And, to some degree, that's okay. Remember we're readying our teenagers for their next stage in life, and if we are overly involved in their schooling, we may be undermining their independence and the learning of important skills. On the other hand, there is much data that supports the fact that involved parents positively influence the success of their child in school. How do parents find that proper balance? How can we assist our teenager's growth and responsibility for learning, while at the same time have the right amount of involvement from which he will benefit? Parents are on tricky turf—again.

It helps to think about your experience in school. Yes, in some ways your teenagers' experience is quite different—there is an innocence lost and certain realities that are faced by this generation. Yet, at the same time, there is much that we share; the fundamental developmental stage that our teenagers are experiencing will, in many ways, be similar to what we experienced. It helps to tap into your experience; it will help you gain understanding and validate what your adolescent is going through.

School is important for many reasons, many of which are obvious, but not all. A teenager's engagement in school can actually be viewed as a barometer that offers some understanding about his emotional health and happiness. There has been proven to be a strong correlation between teens who are disengaged from school and their abuse of drugs and alcohol, experimentation with early sex, likelihood of suffering from depression, and committing acts of crime and delinquency[2].

Parental involvement in a child's schooling drops off dramatically in the teenage years—just at a time when students are making important decisions about their future.

And there is a strong correlation between student achievement and parental involvement. But, it gets tricky here for many parents. What kind of involvement is appropriate and effective? How do you manage it when your kid is pushing back and wants minimal involvement from you? There can be a dynamic tension between beneficial parental involvement on one hand, and the input we receive from our teenagers. Additionally, some parents feel intimidated in schools, unwelcome even. Whether this is the parent's issue or the school's, parents must not take the easy way out...too much is at stake.

Teenagers today feel a lot of stress and pressure around school. Pressures that show up at the top of their list are not those that show up in the

School and pressure (cont.)

School and academic expectations are a significant source of stress for teenagers.

headlines—drug and alcohol use, sex, gangs. Their concerns are with the social expectations of the adult world, which all have to do with *pressure:* the pressure to obey parents and teachers, to get good grades in school, to prepare for the future and to earn money[3]. Additionally, there are pressures to fit in, to attain membership in the crowd they admire, to succeed in sports or other extra-curricular activities of their choice…all while they are growing and changing dramatically.

Examining this academic pressure on a macro level requires us to look at an additional pressure source: government. Government is playing a larger role in our children's education by applying standards and requirements for graduation. Kids have to perform, because if they don't their school system will be penalized. Although the pressure put on kids is often from people who have their own best interests at heart, teens don't always make that distinction, they just feel the stress.

Most kids find themselves in an intensely competitive environment on many different levels.

Demographics play a part here, too. The pressures on many communities to build and expand schools to educate these youngsters generates demand for tax increases, sometimes pitting one generation against another in the fight for services. Our adolescents feel the population pressures in the intense competition for positions on sports teams, in plays, for admittance into limited enrollment programs and schools, and of course, in the college search. Pressure is on them from many directions,.

How can parents help? We'll discuss this in concrete terms, but remember this: balance is important—parents need to find the proper level of involvement without overdoing it. Knowing your child as you do will give you the knowledge for finding that balance. Just remember that a "keep out" sign on her door is not a valid excuse for you to be in the dark. And, in fact, it may be a sign that she needs you.

The school scene

What do teenagers think about school? Are they optimistic about their future? Richard W. Riley was a former Secretary of Education and he says they are! Excerpts from a speech that he gave while in office, although somewhat dated, provides an optimistic viewpoint about the adolescents' world and their view of school—a viewpoint that remains valid and yet different from much current rhetoric. This view fits with the perspective shared on page 115.

E

Over 20% of the students who were polled [in a national study] said flat out that they hated school or like it very little....They feel a great deal of pressure to get good grades (44%) and to get into college (32%), and those two pressures outweigh the pressure they feel to "fit in socially" (29%), use drugs (19%), or be sexually active (13%).

In my opinion, this is good news. America's teenagers are more worried about getting good grades than using drugs or being sexually active. Yet, the pressure to be sexually active is very strongly felt by 9th and 10th grade girls.

At the same time, America's teenagers in overwhelming numbers feel happy (90%), cared about (91%), confident (90%), motivated (86%) and fortunate (84%). Our children are optimistic, resilient, and three-fourths of them think the future looks very promising.

There is a wonderful hopefulness in our teenagers, which stands in sharp contract to a consistent negativity that all too often seems to define how we adults think about our young people.

Last year, for example, the Public Agenda released a study entitled "Kids These Days" which told us that a majority of adults in America viewed teenagers in the "negative" and saw them as "rude, irresponsible, and wild." This study went on to suggest that the majority of adults believed that our young people were "failing to learn such values as honesty, respect, and responsibility."

Yet our poll of American teenagers gives us a very different picture. They rank being honest, working hard, being a good student, and helping others as being far more important than all the things that make someone popular—like having lots of friends, being a great athlete, having a lot of money, or having a boyfriend or girlfriend.

Our young people seem to have their heads on their shoulders. They recognize that the stakes are high in this new time when learning how to learn and keep on learning is the key to future success.

Let's give our young people the vote of confidence they deserve. They may dress differently, look differently, and listen to music that is simply beyond us, but they are not a lost generation or a negative generation. They are quite the opposite of slackers. By and large, America's teenagers are thinking hard about their future. A large majority is planning to go on to college.

Eighty percent of our teenagers believe that "it's better to aim high and have big ambitions" rather than just play it safe or muddle through. These are encouraging findings. They suggest to me that we really do need to develop a new language and mindset that reflects the hope and aspirations our high school students have of the coming times.

Richard W. Riley; Former United States Secretary of Education

The school scene (cont.)

At what age and grade is your teenager? Think back to when you were that age. What was your life like? What happened at home before and after school? What were the sources of pressure? Compare and contrast this to the realities of your child's life today. How are they alike? How are they different?

I wish you'd trust me more than you do. I don't drink. I don't smoke or do drugs and I get decent grades in school. So I don't do the dishes perfectly? So what! I'm not saying I'm an angel, but you forget how good I am, and tend to overlook my accomplishments. There are a lot worse kids out there and I am tired of being treated like I'm a juvenile delinquent.[4]

Michael, 17

The school scene (cont.)

It really does begin at home   When the subjects of school or grades come up at the dinner table, does the mood quickly become less-than-desirable? Does it seem lately that "school" and "tension" are tied together inextricably? If school is becoming a hotbed for disagreement and frustration, your family is not alone. For many teenagers, middle and high school are difficult, confusing, and at some times overwhelming experiences. Although the ultimate responsibility for success in school belongs to your son or daughter, your attitude toward school and learning actually has a great impact on his or her ability to succeed. Examine your own attitudes; note the words you use and the feelings you share. Are they helping your child move toward success? Be honest, for it is true that "learning starts in the home," and your values toward education set the foundation for your child's future success, or failure, in school.

Whether it seems true or not, your teen is listening very carefully to everything you say. Are you generally supportive of your son or daughter's teachers and administrators? Or are you continually frustrated and vocal about your disapproval of teachers and school curriculum? Understanding that you do not need to agree with every teaching style or decision, do you rest the responsibility for academic success on your child, or on the school system? Are you setting a realistic, mature tone? Or do you tend to blame others for your child's academic disappointments?

Now that your teenager is in secondary school, your attitude matters more than ever. If you want to raise a child who can solve the problems she faces, who feels empowered and in control, you'll have to behave in ways that demonstrate this attitude. You will need to model this behavior and facilitate it in your teen as she develops the skills she'll need to be successful in school and beyond.

It would be unrealistic to expect that your child will love each and every one of her teachers and be wonderfully successful in every class without even a hint of conflict or challenge. If that is the case, you should feel extremely fortunate! Another perspective seems more realistic: your child will love a few of her teachers, despise a few, and the vast majority of her teachers will be nothing more than a neutral blur a few short years after high school. In life, your child needs to learn how to deal with all kinds of people. School is a great place to start learning this lesson.

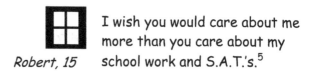

I wish you would care about me more than you care about my school work and S.A.T.'s.[5]

Robert, 15

The school scene (cont.)

Think about recent conversations you have had with your teenager about school. What words have you chosen to represent your feelings? What was the conversation like? Are you empowering your child when it comes to school or helping her find excuses?

What is really happening in those hallowed halls?   Chances are, you have not had the opportunity to follow your teenage son or daughter through an average school day. If you had, you might be amazed at the myriad decisions, pressures, and information overload that a typical teen experiences during a school day. School is a complex microcosm of the outside world. Peer interactions blend with classes, activities, sports practices, play rehearsals, and socializing. It is a dizzying world through which teenagers must navigate day after day.

Let's first focus on the academic aspects of school. In theory, academics are the reason your teenager boards the bus to school each day. On any given day, a student may attend somewhere between five and seven classes. With a minimal amount of time between classes, students must race through the halls to the next class, often without time to pick up forgotten books from lockers or even to go to the bathroom or get a drink of water. Arriving at the next class, the student must switch gears from French to math seamlessly. The student must adjust to that particular teacher's style and demands, recall material learned the day before, keep track of ongoing assignments, and absorb the current day's lesson before packing up frantically and racing to the next class. The added pressure of tests during the school day is exhausting to say the least. Lunch is often the only time students enjoy a sustained period of socialization and decompression during the day, but this period is sometimes as brief as twenty minutes, barely enough time to stand in line to buy food, sit down to eat, and get to the next class.

In addition to the academic pressures students face, their school world consists of social pressures, as well. Mixed in with classes may be arguments with friends, harassment from other students, confusion about identity, competition for sports teams or parts in a play, concerns about clothing and body image, sexual tension, invitations to parties (or exclusion from

The school scene (cont.)

them), and the overall pressure to "fit in" in some way or another. Teenage girls can be ruthlessly cruel in social circles; teenage boys are highly driven by their sexuality and can sometimes objectify the teenage girls around them. This mix makes for a highly charged array of stimuli which bombard teenagers on any given day in school, whether in middle school or high school.

Susan, a high school senior, describes the social scene in school in her own words. "It's not as if I don't like other kids who aren't my friends. It's just that girls can be so mean to each other. So cruel…if they aren't back-stabbing, then they are changing their 'best friends' as fast as they change their clothes. I don't trust many girls in my class."

Brian, a ninth grader, paints a picture of his experiences in the high school hallways: "I avoid this one certain hallway. I'm not afraid or anything, but the kids who hang out there…I guess they are some of the jocks, and some of the kids who party a lot… It's like I don't feel comfortable there. They're such a big group, and they're older. And so I just avoid it."

Not all of these pressures affect all teenagers. For some teens, middle and high school are happy, exciting times. For many others, the happy, exciting times are mixed with painful and awkward ones. It is a time of growth and discovery, extreme fun and extreme disappointment. And lots of experiences that fall somewhere in between.

For many students, much of what they study in school seems "unrelated" to the real world. They often wonder out loud to each other, "Why do I need to study chemistry? I'm never going to be a scientist," or "Why do we have to write so many papers about books we don't like and can't relate to?" Although this logic makes sense to them, students are not just in school to memorize dates and write papers. They are there to learn time management, to develop the ability to follow projects through to completion, and to understand that in school, as in life, they need to sometimes do the very things they do not want to do in order to be successful in the big picture.

Dad, you need to be more in tune to my life. I do huge projects and you don't even know they were assigned. Now you want input on where I should go to high school but how do you know what would be good for me in the next four years if you don't know what I'm doing now?[7]

Gina, 14

Motivation and influence

Unmotivated teens   Experts hear more complaints from parents about teenagers' lack of motivation in school than probably any other single complaint. While there are many factors that may contribute to an apparent lack of motivation, the trickiest thing for a parent is to try and discern whether this is a problem that will pass, or a more serious one requiring major intervention. Let's examine some of the possible causes for lack of motivation:

- Difficulty accepting authority: Teens who have difficulty with authority may resist it in school, even in some ways that are quite obviously self-defeating. A school setting requires adherence to rules and routine, which works against some kids' very temperaments.

- Learning disabilities, ADD and ADHD: It is not uncommon for learning disabilities and other issues to crop up in secondary school. As the curriculum becomes more challenging, teenagers who were previously able to cope in spite of unrecognized disabilities my find themselves much more challenged.

- Peer rejection: Teenagers who are different from the valued norm in school can be treated cruelly. Once labeled as a loser or outsider, teens may withdraw and choose not to engage or compete.

- Poor self-esteem: Teens who think negatively about themselves may choose not to compete. Whether to prove they are not capable, or because they fear that if they do try they will fail, poor self-esteem often presents as lack of motivation.

- Substance abuse: Teenagers who are involved with alcohol and drugs can see their motivation be sapped by the distractions and negative appeal of this lifestyle. It becomes a cycle that drags them downward as they spend time under the influence and with friends who share this value and priority.

- Negative influence from peers: As discussed in Chapter 4, teenagers are influenced by peers and tend to engage in similar activities as the peers with whom they hang out. It may not be easy to discern which comes first, the disillusionment with school or the friends who share this feeling, but these kids often do become reliant on one another for support as they check out of the system.

- Family stress: Family problems impact kids, no matter how hard adults may try to keep them separate. Issues of abuse, alcohol problems, marital or financial problems...they can't help but spill over, impacting kids of all ages.

- Lack of a positive vision for the future: Teenagers who do not have an optimistic vision for their future may not have enough of a reason to care about school. If they cannot see a connection between effort and results, if they don't understand what elements influence one's success, if they don't see value in education, they may have little reason to try hard.

- Average potential: not everyone is going to be an intellectual star. Very bright and successful parents can have children who are not at the top of their class.

Motivation and influence

What can parents do to address poor motivation? The first step needs to be an accurate diagnosis about what is behind this behavior and why. This can best be done in concert with the school, and most parents should begin with the school counselor. A school counselor will gather data from the various teachers and help you to piece together the various puzzle-parts. Together, and hopefully with your teenager's participation, you can decipher the sources of the problem and develop strategies to help him get back on track.

Keep in mind, that no child wants to fail. A teenager who is doing poorly in school can't be feeling good about himself. If the problems are getting so severe that you need to work with the school to address them, try and express an attitude that demonstrates to your teenager that you are one his side, not that you are the enemy. You don't want this dialogue to become a contest of wills.

Possible actions to take:

- Whenever possible, try and let your teenager take the initiative and be in charge. Obviously, for younger teens and those in serious trouble, parents may need to intervene more, but keep the ultimate goal of self-sufficiency in mind.

- Make sure that your home environment supports your teen's efforts in school. She needs a consistent and appropriate place to study. She may benefit from your help in establishing and keeping to a schedule. If she cannot manage this herself, support her efforts.

- When monitoring your teen's progress, communicate with the school. Parents should not be the primary overseer here, but rather, manage this in conjunction with teachers, counselors, or others from the school. Many find that weekly progress reports help facilitate communication and give the student an appropriate amount of supervision.

- Many schools offer peer support groups. Kids will often accept help from their peers, and well managed programs can be a "win" for all involved.

- Get a tutor. Another teaching method, another voice, more one-on-one instruction may do wonders for bringing a child along when she is facing difficulty.

- Hold your teen accountable. Let him know if he doesn't deliver on agreed-upon goals he'll be attending summer school to make it up.

- Some of the reasons behind poor motivation that we've pointed out on the previous page may be serious and will require professional assistance. If your child, or family for that matter, needs a therapist or special counselor, don't hesitate to find one. Again, the school can recommend appropriate resources, as can your health professionals.

Remember that doing well in school is not only important in its own right, it is an indication of your child's overall health and well-being.

Motivation and influence (cont.)

There is always hope   Although motivation levels may rise and fall, the worst thing to do is to lose hope. Some students who seem unreachable and uninterested can become inspired when least expected. A high school English teacher told me this story of one her students: David was a senior in a class of students who struggled with English all through high school. When she met him at the beginning of the year, he was awkward, immature, almost babyish in some of his mannerisms. He would scribble instead of listening to directions, rarely did homework, made inappropriate (often offensive and sexual) comments during class, and wrote papers on bizarre, unrelated topics. Even his appearance was awkward; he was gangly, too big for his own skin but too young to fill his 6-foot frame with confidence. David had no plans for college or work after high school. He earned an "F" for the first half of the year, and it seemed as if David would fail his entire year of English class and prevent himself from graduating. Then the class began to study *Hamlet*. Although exciting to teach, Shakespeare is often intimidating for students. As frequently happens, the class had a difficult time understanding the language and getting into the story. David, on the other hand, experienced an awakening through Shakespeare's language. It didn't take him long to realize that he was one of the only students in the class who could easily read and understand the play, both on its basic levels and in terms of its complex use of language. He began to realize that he was smart. *Very* smart. He began to contribute to class discussion and realized he could help other students to understand Shakespeare's word play. He gained confidence as he realized that he was capable of being an excellent student in English class. This was the beginning of a remarkable transformation. David went on to earn an "A" for the second semester, and was accepted to college. He made the Dean's list during his first two years, and transferred to a prestigious business school where he pursued his business degree in an honors program. He began to fill out his 6-foot frame with poise and confidence, a wonderful sense of humor, and a curiosity for learning.

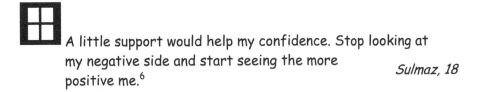

A little support would help my confidence. Stop looking at my negative side and start seeing the more positive me.[6]

Sulmaz, 18

Who owns the problem?   This is an important question when it comes to dealing with problems in school, and in many ways it is the crux of the matter. Aren't we trying to help our teenagers become self-sufficient? In my research I asked parents who have already raised their teens what they would do differently. Note these responses: "I would require more accountability on school grades." "I would make them responsible for their homework and not help them as much, as it impeded their development of responsibility." "I sat with my son as he did his homework in grade school, and as a result when he went to high school he found it difficult to work on his own."

Motivation and influence (cont.)

Mike Riera, author of *Uncommon Sense for Parents of Teenagers,* also believes in holding high school students accountable. While he gives some concrete advice about the way parents can influence and help, he is quite clear about who needs to claim responsibility.

E

Q: What can I do to help my teenager improve his poor grades?

In my mind, this is a case of natural consequences doing the work (anything else is probably at least inefficient and uncomfortable). Nagging your adolescent about homework is an unenviable task, and it usually doesn't work!...Essentially, school is your teenager's job, a job that has clear parameters and expectations. Have this conversation with your adolescent—usually sometime during freshmen or sophomore year. Include what is important to you, and ask what he thinks needs modification. Then ask him what role he wants you to play; expect a surprised look followed by, "Uh, what do you mean?" Then have a few options laid out to appeal to his creativity: "Well, we could agree to a specific homework time and we (Mom and Dad) could remind you of it when you forget and periodically checkup on you so you don't get distracted. Or we could go over each homework assignment with you to see how well you've done on each one. Or we could..." Eventually, you want him to assume honest responsibility for his homework and ask for your help periodically, though you might have regular, agreed-upon check-ins (once every week or two) to see how things are going. Build a means of support that allows you to feel active and that actually does support your adolescent. This is easier to say than do, but it can be done with some patience and persistence...

Michael Riera, *Uncommon Sense for Parents with Teenagers,* 110-112

Riera noted one couple's idea for encouraging communication with their teenage daughter. Instead of nagging her each night about her homework, the three chose a designated time each night (9:30 pm) to share ten minutes of tea and conversation—sometimes about homework, sometimes not. Flexibility in the plan allowed for the parents to become more involved if her grades began to drop. The family sincerely looked forward to their time together and the nagging was no longer necessary.

How might your strategy differ with junior high students vs. high school students?

Types of intelligence

Gardner's Theory of Multiple Intelligences   Using both biological and cultural research, Howard Gardner has created a new framework for viewing human intelligence. Gardner's research is useful to recognize the diverse abilities and talents students possess. It also gives insight into how students may struggle in one subject area while excelling in another. He points out that it helps to acknowledge that "while all students may not be verbally or mathematically gifted, children may have an expertise in other areas, such as music, spatial relations, or interpersonal knowledge." [8]

According to Gardner, both biology and culture play important roles in the development of intelligences. A culture may value different intelligences, or talents, to varying degrees, impacting the skills that are developed. Each of us has all eight intelligences, however, most people have one or two dominant intelligences or talents. It is possible to develop or increase an intelligence or talent area. Perhaps this information can be helpful in identifying your child's academic strengths and challenges.

Gardner defines the eight intelligences as follows:	Possible applications
Logical-Mathematical Intelligence: The ability to detect patterns, reason deductively and think logically.	Accounting, computer programming; often associated with scientific and mathematical applications
Linguistic Intelligence: Having mastery of language. Includes the ability to effectively manipulate language to express oneself rhetorically or poetically. Also allows one to use language as a means to remember information.	Journalists, lawyers, writers; any communications focused profession
Spatial Intelligence: The ability to manipulate and create mental images in order to solve problems. Not limited to visual domains, as spatial intelligence is also formed in blind children.	Artists, designers; ability to "visualize" can be applied to any field: sports, scientists, entrepreneurs
Musical Intelligence: The capability to recognize and compose musical pitches, tones, and rhythms.	Music related fields; can also be helpful in certain language learning
Bodily-Kinesthetic Intelligence: The ability to use one's mental abilities to coordinate one's bodily movements.	Mechanics, surgeons, craftsmen, athletes, dancers
Interpersonal Intelligence: The ability to understand and work effectively with others.	Social workers, teachers
Intrapersonal Intelligence: Concerned with self-understanding. Often linked with interpersonal intelligence.	Theologians, self-employed business people who can work alone.
Naturalist: Knowledge of the natural world.	Biology, ecology, forestry, etc.

Types of intelligence (cont.)

Sometimes very bright individuals find themselves marginalized by the institution of school. Jonathan Mooney and David Cole, two such men with learning disabilities, co-wrote a book entitled *Learning Outside the Lines* as a result of their meeting while students at Brown University. They assert that schools support and develop only a narrow range of intelligence, leaving large parts of our potential underdeveloped. They suggest the present educational focus today virtually ignores the creative, intuitive, emotional, and creative parts of ourselves.

Mooney and Cole also bring up the importance of recognizing the different learning styles people have. Educators have made progress in this regard; many teachers alter the way they deliver material to appeal to different learning styles. Do they do enough of this? Is it reflective of wide spread changes in the educational system? Do parents understand the implications of learning style differences? Many parents are not knowledgeable in this area and could benefit from gaining a better understanding of learning styles. Is it possible that your child's learning styles are not recognized and supported?

E

In addition to the concept of multiple intelligences is the separate concept of alternative learning styles, which challenges the common notion that all people learn the same way. Many educators believe that people process information and in turn learn in multifaceted and individual ways. Some alternative learning styles are tactile and kinesthetic, verbal, visual and spatial, and project based. Again, as a result of the structure of most schools and their underlying assumptions and values, our teachers teach to a universal learning process for all children: one teacher, one way of presenting the information, one way to learn.

Jonathan Mooney and David Cole, *Learning Outside the Lines*, 69

Emotional intelligence   Another form of intelligence, emotional intelligence (EQ), has received a lot of attention in the last few years. It is claimed that emotional intelligence is a better predictor than IQ for both personal and professional success. Studies have shown that IQ may only contribute, at best, about 20 percent to the factors that determine life success. Unlike IQ, EQ can be learned. Daniel Goleman, author of *Emotional Intelligence,* has identified these qualities in people high on emotional intelligence:[9]

- Self-awareness: they recognize feelings and pay attention to them.

- Self-regulation: they deal appropriately with emotions like anger, anxiety, frustration, etc.

- Motivation: they can marshal emotions and delay gratification to meet goals.

- Empathy: awareness of other's feelings, needs, and concerns.

- Social skills: they are adept at communication, influence, leadership, collaboration, etc.

Types of intelligence (cont.)

Emotional intelligence, also referred to as emotional literacy, has been associated with many positive outcomes for children and adolescents: improved academic scores and school performance, higher SAT scores, increased empathy, improved abilities to control impulses, manage anger, and find creative solutions to social predicaments.[10] In some schools emotional literacy courses are taught with measurable improvements in several areas. Some schools incorporate this instruction into other curricula while others debate its value in budget constrained times. As parents, what you need to know is to not diminish the importance of emotional literacy; it is one of the most important attributes your child can develop, and you can help her develop these skills. You may want to explore this topic more. (See Resources)

Can you identify your child's primary intelligences? Has your child struggled in school due to the emphasis on mathematical and linguistic intelligences in many schools? How can you encourage your child to both maximize her natural intelligences and develop other skills?

Does Gardner's theory seem useful to you? If so, in what way(s)? Is your child high in emotional intelligence?

Parental support

What matters most   Laurence Steinberg's *Beyond the Classroom* describes the results from the largest study done to date measuring the correlation between scholastic success and families. Specifically setting out to examine how events outside of the classroom impact students' engagement and performance in school, over 20,000 teenagers and their families in nine very different American communities were included in this study. Using surveys, interviews, and focus groups, the field research examined a diverse sample ethnically, economically, and in terms of intact or divorced households, and took three years to complete.

The facts from their study are these:[11]

- Nearly one in three parents is seriously disengaged from their adolescent's life—especially their schooling

- Only one in five parents consistently attend school programs

- Nearly one third of students say their parents have no idea how they are doing in school

- About one sixth of students report their parents don't care whether they earn good grades or not

- More than half of all students say they could bring home grades of C or worse without their parents getting upset.

- Parents' lack of interest is strongly associated with academic difficulties and low school achievement

What can parents do to turn around these dismal statistics? In what ways are parents of successful students involved in their schooling? Steinberg and his colleagues found that what matters the most is the *physical attendance* of parents to school events. This includes "back to school" nights, school programs, extracurricular activities—anything that brings a parent into the school.

Why is this so important? Because of the messages that it sends. The message that it sends to the teen is that school is important, valued, and that school and home are connected; it is a part of this family's life. Also of high importance is the message that it sends to the school: that school is valued by this family; that we are open to communication; in fact, we seek it out. They also "hear" that we encourage mutual accountability.

Parents of successful students do some things differently than parents of less successful students: they see their role as helping the school to better serve the child, rather than solving the problem themselves. Steinberg calls this "working the system," which means to mobilize the school on their kid's behalf. Engaged parents of less successful students will focus on "at home" solutions—like checking homework, monitoring homework time, etc. Steinberg's

Parental support (cont.)

research has shown this strategy to be less beneficial to the student than "working the system."
Steinberg gives three reasons why "working the system" is an effective solution:

- The school has the expertise and knowledge to diagnose a problem and implement a solution
- You are sending an important message to the school: that parents are involved and that they expect the school to serve the child and to solve the problem
- The parents support the school and trust and value their capabilities

This dovetails perfectly with the recommendations I received from a psychologist who specializes in working with adolescents. Dr. David Gleason[12] speaks passionately on the necessity of the adults in a child's life working together in a coordinated effort. When a kid is having trouble in school the *most effective* way to positively influence him is for the adults to meet (usually with the teen), to discuss the situation, and to agree on a coordinated plan. The adult group may be as small as the parents and one teacher, or the team may extend to school counselors, specialists from the school, outside therapists, or other specialists. The point is, the group provides a "safety net" through which the child is unlikely to fall. By involving all the appropriate adults in the process, and speaking together with one voice, all available resources are activated and coordinated.

Steinberg's study also examined other ways that parents have influence. Although this effect may be more indirect, parents can exert some control or influence over the friends the teen spends time with by selecting the environments in which the child spends his time—the neighborhood, the school, the weekend activities that consume her time. What should parents tune in to when selecting neighborhoods and schools? You should look for high levels of parental involvement in organized activities that serve the teenagers, as well as the degree of monitoring and supervision. These elements are visible to a large degree and should be an important criterion.

In what ways are you involved in your child's schooling? Are you giving the right messages to your child as to the importance of school? Specifically, what messages does he receive from you? What messages are you giving to the school? If you see room for improvement from your end, make a specific plan of action.

Parental support and middle school

For some parents their child's move to middle school or junior high can feel disconcerting. Parents tell one another in advance that "parents aren't involved as much" in junior high. This can be a challenging transition for parents, and many are confused as to how to approach it. Parents wonder:

- What is my role now that my child is in middle school?
- What level of involvement should I have with my child's homework?
- How much time should my child be spending on homework?
- What are the teacher's goals for my child?
- Will I only hear about problems? I'd like to hear about my child if she's doing well, too!
- How can I get involved? (without impacting my child who doesn't want me in his school!)

Parents may need to "feel their way" at the beginning, so expect an adjustment period. No matter what you hear though, don't be intimidated. There is a place for parents at the junior high level—in fact, they probably need you. Just be respectful. I've found the best way was to get involved on a committee, or to find a job that I could own. Just getting into the building on a regular basis took away much of the mystique and gave me an opportunity to build relationships. Parents who make assumptions that they are not wanted in the school are simply losing out, and depriving others in the process! Many committees and programs would love to have you. But things are done differently than in elementary school; listen and observe so you can fit in productively for everyone.

A teacher offers these wonderful suggestions to enhance your efforts to connect:

- *E-mail does wonders for teacher-parent communication.* Ask your child's teacher if s/he would be willing to give out an e-mail address where you can ask questions, request assignments, or proactively pass on information that might help the teacher better understand any home issues that might be preventing your child from completing work, etc. Often teachers prefer receiving e-mail instead of having to make phone calls. Ask the teacher how often s/he would like to receive contact from you. Try to respect those boundaries. Teachers are planning and grading in the evenings and on weekends; an occasional contact is wonderful. E-mailing every night and expecting detailed responses is not.

- *Teach your child how to use an assignment notebook.* Middle school is the time for kids to start learning organizational skills, as the amount of homework will increase. Ask to see it each night. To take the pressure off both you and your child, make a "date" to look at the assignment book at a designated time each night, after homework has been completed. This way, you will avoid nagging to get homework done and the check in can be a short, successful time. Use this opportunity to ask questions, your best way to support kids in school. How do you like the book you are reading? What is the paper topic about? What project are you doing in science class? Is this a fun way to learn math? Ask non-threatening, non-judgmental questions. Some teachers require parents to sign an assignment notebook each night, to ensure that homework is being done. Some teachers

Parental support and middle school (cont.)

also use it as a communication tool—they will write messages to you, and you can do the same.

- *Ask kids about what they are learning.* Make yourself available to help. Be sure that students have a quiet, well-lit place to study. Keep extra supplies on hand for projects. Asking questions about what they are learning is one of the best ways to let kids know that although you support them and want to be available if they need you, you also expect them to be held accountable for their own work.

- *Get involved in parent-teacher organizations.* Every school has one. They are the PTSO's, PTA's and Home/School Organizations at school. Although many are fund-raiser based, providing supplies and other much needed supports for teachers and students, parents can be creative about working together to problem-solve and increase communication. Host an evening for parents and a few teachers to discuss, in small groups, various difficult scenarios that may come up over the course of the middleschool years and possible solutions. Another event could bring a panel of teachers and administrators to discuss how to improve communication between the school and home. With a team of parents, offer to create a directory of parents, students, and teacher contact information. This type of information helps all stay in touch. Offer to help work on a newsletter and invite other parents to get involved.

- *Let your child's teacher know you are "up for hire."* You never know if your skills and experience could be of use to your child's teacher. Offer to come in and assist with research projects, speak on a particular topic, introduce students to your line of work or other skill/talent. One such parent has volunteered for five straight years to visit an English teacher's class and give an outstanding presentation about a controversial view of Shakespeare's works, information that adds wonderfully to the teacher's unit. Offer to write a class newsletter or team newsletter for your child's class. This can be a great way to celebrate successes and keep connected to the class community.

- *Attend all of the "givens" and as many "extras" as you can.* It goes without saying that parents of the majority of students who are successful in school attend Back to School nights and parent-teacher conferences regularly. Try to attend other events as well: plays, sports events, concerts, speakers, as many as your schedule allows without making you feel overloaded. Being present in the school building makes a difference. You'll get to know coaches, choir directors, other teachers, and other parents. You will feel more connected to the school community.

- *Propose a "Principal's Coffee" or other regular contact.* Parents often feel they'd like more time with the principal of their child's school. Many principals now offer "coffees" or other bi-weekly or monthly times when a group of parents can drop in to the office and, instead of talking about particular students, discuss larger issues regarding their child's school. The parent-teacher organizations can often help to pull this together.

Parental support and middle school (cont.)

- *School counselors hold the key to parental access to the school.* Get to know him or her. If you are feeling confused or unclear about anything, speak with the counselor, and express your concerns. The counselor will arrange for meetings with your child's entire team of teachers, if necessary. The counselor may have to carry a very large student load, so be respectful of this. Counselors are usually extremely helpful and sincere... and very busy. But, invariably, it benefits you and your child to become known by the counselor.

Starting a parenting group is a step toward feeling more connected, more empowered, and less alone in this process. Be persistent about staying involved in your child's education. Recognizing that teachers have limited resources and many students to support, take the initiative to ensure that you have open, successful communication. Seeing teachers as the other members on your "team," helping to support your child, makes this process go more smoothly.

Ultimately, parents need to take responsibility for figuring out the system. Each of you is likely to find a different way to participate in school activities that fits your schedule, and feels comfortable given your expertise. It's up to you to build relationships with the people who matter to you, so be proactive, and tune in thoughtfully. School will feel less intimidating and more understandable each time you interact there.

 "Parent involvement" is an important topic and one that is addressed both from a parent's and an educator's perspective at www.PleaseStoptheRollercoaster.com

Brainstorm additional ways in which you can find a comfortable level of involvement in your child's schooling.

Parental support and high school

A view from the school counselor's chair I have already mentioned the wonderful resource at our fingertips – the school counselors. Counselors are advocates for students, they are experts at dealing with adolescent issues, and adults who can relate to parents and their point of view. To not develop a relationship with your child's school counselor is to deny yourself a well placed resource who can support you and help you.

I asked a high school counselor to share his insight and observations. He was a counselor for over 25 years at both the junior high and high school levels. From his seat he saw all kinds of parent-student relationships, and he developed an interesting perspective about how parents can best support their kids in their school career.

Sue Blaney: As an experienced school counselor, and father of two grown boys, what comments would you share about the best ways parents can support their kids in school?

Counselor Andy Palmer: Parents need to find the right balance. Parents who know too little about their child's school life create problems. But some parents know too much, and that creates problems, too. At the elementary level, teachers and schools keep in close touch with parents. They include parents in most decisions, and are mindful about communicating with parents in many ways. At junior high, communication with parents remains an important part of the school's point of view, but parents are less involved. In high school, the school's major focus is on the students, and not on the parents. It is the school's job to prepare the students to be able to handle themselves after high school. Students must learn how to advocate for themselves, how to navigate through a variety of circumstances, and they need to be able to manage themselves without their parents' intervention. Students gain a voice, and it is important to allow them the opportunity to develop it. Parents who micromanage their kids' lives are doing them a disservice. As an example, when a student needs to get a form to me for one reason or another, I'm concerned when I see the parent dropping off the form. Parents are not teaching their kids responsibility if they take over their kids' jobs. And, when parents take over those responsibilities they are giving their child a message that their child is not competent— not a helpful message when you consider the overall objective.

Here's something that happened just recently: a student here was passed over for the National Honor Society, and she felt that she should have been recommended. We have a process in situations like this, and she had the opportunity to present her case to a review board of five staff members. The student and I discussed the situation at length, and I helped coach her as she prepared her presentation. She asked that I be present at the meeting, and she also asked if her mom could be present; both of us were there but neither of us said anything. This student did a great job. She presented her case clearly and thoughtfully. It was not an easy thing to do and I was very proud of her. In the end, however, she was still denied the Honor

Parental support and high school (cont.)

Society recommendation. The next day both of her parents were in my office. They wanted another shot at it, this time playing a larger role. They were upset that the father had not come to the meeting; they were upset that the mom had not spoken up. They felt that with their involvement they could change the outcome of the case. In reality, however, what they were doing was undermining their child. They were saying that the job she did wasn't good enough, that she needed them to be successful. It was not productive. Their child needed to deal with the disappointment—it won't be her first in life—without adding any feelings of incompetence. Can you see how their actions were hurting, not helping, their daughter?

SB: How much involvement is the right amount in our children's academic lives?

Counselor Andy Palmer: Again, there is a balance needed. It's great to meet the teachers at the fall open house. It's great to know the name of your child's English teacher, and there may be times when a conversation is appropriate. But parents who know their kid's schedule by heart are probably too close. Their involvement in their kids life may be diminishing the child, rather than allowing him the opportunity to be successful on his own.

SB: How about parents' involvement in their children's extracurricular lives? In sports, for instance, is it important to attend all the games?

Counselor Andy Palmer: It's great to go to your kids' games. That is important to many parents and their children. Again—the objective, however, is balance. Missing some games is perfectly fine. Never attending one isn't right.

SB: What problems do you see relative to the social life of students?

Counselor Andy Palmer: Problems arise when parents are on one extreme or the other; parents who don't know any of their kids' friends are living in the dark. That is not healthy. However, sometimes I see the other extreme. A mother whose daughter tells her everything may be behaving more like a girlfriend than a parent. It's very important to know the difference.

SB: Do you have any advice you'd give parents as to how they can better support their students?

Counselor Andy Palmer: Parents have selective memories, and that's a shame. They need to remember what their junior high and high school experiences were like and draw from those experiences. Yes, some things are different today, but much is the same. Parents can validate their kids' experiences by remembering their own, and this can help their children a lot.

(continued)

Parental support and high school (cont.)

Counselor Andy Palmer: One additional comment: I've noticed that some parents actually express a fear of teenagers. This can come across in subtle or overt ways, but it's not a healthy thing for kids. The kids tend to respond to that in one of two ways: either it empowers them, giving them a sense of power that can be dangerous, or it frightens the teenager. Neither one is healthy, and parents who realize they may be expressing this emotion need to recognize it, manage it, and deal with it because it's not helpful to anyone.

What is the name of your child's counselor? When was the last time you had a conversation with him or her? How might you enlist this resource to benefit you and your child? Brainstorm ways to be involved in your child's schooling at an appropriate level.

Fear of teenagers   Let's be honest about this: have you ever been afraid of a group of teens? This feels silly now, but I can remember actually feeling intimidated walking into my son's junior high school! Maybe it was because we were new in town; maybe it was because many of the kids were taller than me...but my feeling of discomfort was a very real thing. Once I identified it as *my* problem, I was able to get a handle on it and consciously work on gaining confidence.

What Mr. Palmer, the counselor in the interview you just read, says is very true: for kids to feel that adults are afraid of them gives them a dangerous message. And what they may need is your leadership, or friendship or mentorship...remember these youngsters may *look like* adults, but they are not.

I'll tell you what I did to solve this problem. I started out volunteering in the school by contributing to the newsletter that went home to parents. That way I got involved in a way that felt comfortable to me, on my terms. The result was I gradually grew more comfortable in the school environment and began to develop an appreciation for what was going on there. In time I volunteered to produce the school play, which gave me an opportunity to get to know many of the kids, which was wonderful. Once you get to know them as individuals you quickly understand they are kids—kids with enormous energy, excitement for life, and potential for great things. Getting to know them one by one was the best way to alleviate any fear or discomfort. Sometimes adults have to take a deep breath and remember we are adults, and we have to embrace that responsibly.

Self-esteem

Self-esteem is a personal evaluation of one's worth as a person. It measures how much you respect yourself:

- Physically...how happy you are with the way you look,
- Intellectually...how well you feel you can accomplish your goals,
- Emotionally...how much you feel loved,
- Morally...how you think of yourself as a good person.[13]

Self-esteem influences all of life's experiences; people who are high on self-esteem are more likely to be successful in endeavors of any kind. There is a direct correlation between high self-esteem and success, and in the teenage years it is one of the single most important attributes that can support a child's efforts. It merits discussion because parents need to be sensitized to how they can impact their child's self-esteem, and how it can be used as a positive tool.

One of the women in my group had a son who was in his freshman year of high school. He had been in a social slump, not uncommon for freshman boys, and she was worried about him. He never made telephone calls to friends, and few ever came in. His one close friend was clearly drifting away, and her son seemed to be unwilling to put himself out in any way. This lasted most of the fall and winter. In April, about a week before they were leaving for vacation on a cruise ship, she was surprised to hear him say "I guess I have to really get my self-esteem up for this trip." "What do you mean by that?" she asked. "Well, there will be teenagers on the ship, and I figure I had better get psyched up to meet them." That change of attitude intrigued her. She watched him when they arrived on ship, and the very first night all the teenagers had the opportunity to meet one another. Her son consciously took on the role of ringleader for this group of teenagers, pulling in all stragglers and encouraging the group to get together and have fun. He had deliberately and consciously corralled all the self-esteem and social confidence that he could muster, and was well rewarded for his efforts. This conscious effort on his part was, looking back on it, a turning point in his high school social life, and he taught himself the power of self-confidence. He went back to school after vacation with a new attitude, a new confidence, and was able to apply it in his social setting. It was all about his attitude; all about his self-confidence. And getting to "try it out" in neutral territory while away on vacation turned out to be an unexpected gift.

The National Association for Self-Esteem suggests that people with high self-esteem have some habits or outlooks in common:

- self-responsibility,
- mindful living,
- living purposefully,
- personal integrity,
- self-acceptance.

Self-esteem (cont.)

These are habits, skills and outlooks that take time to develop and we will spend our lifetime developing them. It helps to begin early.

The impact of self-esteem   People with high self-esteem are able to set personal boundaries, and not be exploited. They are able to speak up to get what they want. They are not reliant on approval from the outside, so they can develop their own identity. They are more able to accept their mistakes and failures, and are likely to be less critical of others. They can deal with rejection, and are willing to take risks to enhance learning and personal growth.

Nurturing individuality   Teenagers are more likely to develop a strong self-image in families where their individuality is encouraged. With guidance and support from their parents, teenagers can feel more confident about expressing themselves and being themselves. Conversely, adolescents who come from families that can't support their separate and unique individuality run the risk of developing a poor self-image. Parents who require their children to duplicate their own values and opinions, and become critical if their kids choose a different route, are doing a serious disservice to the development of their child's self-confidence.

Here are some pointers for nurturing your teenager's growth:[14]

*   Show her you love her; spend time with her doing things that please both of you, but don't *expect* her to share your interests.

*   The fear of making mistakes makes many teens timid. Encourage him, and help him to find opportunities where he can safely practice the skills he's developing.

*   Many parents inadvertently tend to curb their teens' drive for individuality. Show tolerance. Accept that she needs to explore and develop her own ways of thinking.

*   Even when you disagree with your teenager's views, show respect for them.

*   Clothes, hairstyles, and room décor are all natural expressions of her individuality. Don't let it become a battleground.

*   Encourage his involvement in an area in which he can feel competent, valued, and have membership in a group.

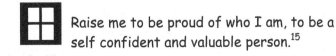 Raise me to be proud of who I am, to be a self confident and valuable person.[15]

Elizabeth, 13

Self-esteem (cont.)

How does one develop high self-esteem? Developing self-esteem is closely linked to developing confidence. How do kids develop confidence? Developing *competence* has a lot to do with it. Being good at something makes people feel confident. Competence comes from developing skills, knowledge, learning, and gaining experience. Within their world and the opportunities that are available to them, there are many ways that teenagers can gain skills, competence, and confidence.

Let's talk about some examples.

Athletics Not all kids are great athletes. Those who are have felt the pleasure of success, and have basked in the glory athletics can provide. And those children who are not the stars but simply members of the team, gain tremendous value from the participation. Let's examine what kids gain from team sports beyond the obvious skill development and fitness benefits:

- a sense of camaraderie and team spirit ,
- a sense of identity and belonging ,
- going after a goal and seeing their hard work pay off,
- participating in sports provides "markers" they can see and feel as they gain skill over time,
- a team commitment and serious discipline—sometimes more so than the kids get in their academic experiences. (One junior high student was quoted to have said they have more discipline on the football field than in the classrooms. Think about that—he may be right!)

Participating in a team, whether the child is an athlete or the equipment manager, can be one of the biggest esteem boosters available during these developmental years.

The arts Participating in band, chorus, or other similar endeavors can provide the same benefits of team membership, a sense of accomplishment, and skill development, which translates into important boosters of self-confidence. Even if your child is a pretty poor clarinet player, if he wants to be in the band, think long and hard before you discourage it. There is little downside to such activities, and what he gains may have little to do with the clarinet, and much to do with the development of confidence and team camaraderie.

I'm fortunate enough to live in a town that highly values and supports the arts. We have a gifted community member who believes that no child who desires to be in the annual junior high musical should be cut. And, with a cast numbering about 120 each year, she manages to direct a musical spectacular that *changes kids lives*. That is not overstating it; I've seen what it does to kids. A few years ago I offered to produce the annual junior high musical—a new experience for me. Watching the auditions, seeing these kids up close as they, shaking from head to foot, tried to sing and act to the best of their ability, was an experience I'll never

Self-esteem (cont.)

forget. It took enormous courage for the shy, quiet, unconfident children to get up on the stage and give it all they had for their audition; I came away from that experience with respect for each and every one of them. The naturally talented actors, singers, and dancers were assigned most of the leads; those kids who didn't manage to leave a big impression were cast in the chorus positions they didn't really want, but realistically earned. But the transformation that was most fascinating was with the kids in the chorus. The youngsters that had the least poise, the least natural ability in this area—they were transformed.

This director believes that if a child can walk she can dance. If a child can speak, she can sing. Believing they can do it is the single most important element that creates the success of these shows. And they *can* do it! Year after year she is able to demonstrate that her philosophy is correct. The productions are wonderful by anyone's standards—but the best part is the experience the kids all share. After our last performance, one of the "chorus" girls was hanging in the wings, and she signaled for the director to come over so she could speak with her. The child was crying, and the director was afraid something was terribly wrong. As the young girl tried to speak through her tears, it soon became evident that these were tears of joy, and high emotion. "Thank you," she said. "This was the best experience of my entire life. I have never had the opportunity to be on a stage before; nobody ever believed I could do it. Thank you for giving me this chance." This child may not grow up to be a singer or actor, but she knows she can perform. She has felt the power and thrill of being on stage and "wowing" an audience. She knows she can be an effective member of a group who can create something wonderful. She will never forget it.

Community and spiritual connections   Although athletics and the arts are valued ways for teenagers to participate in their schools, they are by no means the only types of activities that can positively influence self-esteem. What opportunities are there for community service? What types of faith-based programs are available to your kids? They can tutor, join clubs, help out at a retirement home, wash dishes at community supper. There really is no limit to the ways in which they can get involved. And that is the key to self-esteem: *involvement*. Involvement in anything that is productive adds to their confidence and competence. Go out of your way to encourage it.

Rebecca, 13

I wish you guys would take my music more seriously, because I like to sing and play the guitar and you don't seem like you really care. I mean, you listen to me, but you don't actually hear what my words mean when I say them. It's like when I'm talking. You look at me, but you don't really pay attention. [16]

Self-esteem (cont.)

A mistake parents can easily make   A high school counselor has told me how common it is for parents to prevent a student from participating in extra curricular activities if the student is not performing well academically. This is understandable; parents will frequently believe the poor academic performance is a result of lack of effort, and it may well be. But there is another element that should be taken into consideration, and it is to evaluate what the extra curricular activity provides for the child. The counselor, referring to athletes, said "Many of my students do better in season than out of season." I can understand how this can happen; structure and discipline is a part of most athletic teams, and this can carry over into other areas. Laurence Steinberg's research has demonstrated that as long as the time commitment doesn't exceed 20 hours per week, there are important benefits to extra-curricular activities.[17] It is important to become aware of the ways in which your child's activities help him to feel competent, even if they are activities that you may not value. Everybody has to find a place in their life where they feel competent and receive positive feedback, and it is especially important when they're dealing with performance challenges in a key area in their life. If "success" isn't happening in school for your child, be careful about denying him access to an activity from which he gains an important sense of accomplishment.

What self-esteem boosters play a part in your teenager's life? How do you build him up and add to his self-confidence?

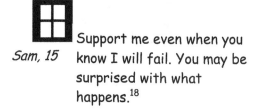

Sam, 15   Support me even when you know I will fail. You may be surprised with what happens.[18]

Self-esteem (cont.)   From Harriet, age 14

Running Cross-Country

This year, I started to run cross-country. All my brothers have run cross-country: it is a family tradition. Ever since my brother Andy started running, I have thought about running myself. When I was little, I wanted to run, because my brothers did. But as I got older, I was not so enthusiastic. When I got to be about in third grade, I realized that I was not an athlete. Even when we were that young, we were pretty much divided up into cool people and non-cool people. The cool people were always the athletes, and ever since third grade, I have felt inferior to them. The cool boys always walked with a swagger, their body language saying that they were the best, and that nobody could dethrone them. The cool girls were also athletes, but they did not swagger. Even in third grade, they would have the best clothes. All the cool girls had identical outfits from identical stores. I never got out of my geeky third grade persona, really. I will never be an athlete in the way that the cool kids are.

I did not want to do cross-country because I was afraid of what people would think. They would think it pathetic that a person like me, a social outcast who has never done sports, who is most definitely not an athlete, to do a sport. Of course, a lot of people consider cross-country to not be a sport, but even so, it is physical work. I was afraid because of all the older people on the team, who were real athletes, and me, who at best did not come in last in running in gym class.

One day, my mother somehow convinced me to try cross-country, saying that she thought that I would be good at it and gain a lot from it. I was still undecided, but I did try to start running over the summer, to get into reasonable shape. I kept on running, and I think I did improve. Some days, it was agony, and some days I just quit running, I couldn't do it; but I did finally complete the training schedule, and it did work. I am now an official member of the cross-country team, with my name in the town newspaper. I am probably the slowest or second slowest person on the team, and I came in last in my first real meet, but I do not feel too bad about it. I have gained several things from cross-country. I am more physically fit, and I can now run longer distances. I think I have become mentally tougher, because in order to keep running, I have to deal with the fact that I am not a good runner, and I have to keep on running, even though I get very tired. In life, it is important that one does not become a perfectionist. Cross-country helps me with that, because I really am a bad runner, and I think that being able to accept that can make me a better person. Without cross-country, I might become obsessed with grades and scores, and not think of the greater issues in life. Perhaps what I like most about cross-country is that I have been able to make many friendly acquaintances who might turn into friends. I don't talk much and feel very out of place in social situations, so I feel great that a lot of upperclassmen say "hi" to me when I pass them in the halls.

It is odd, because when I look back to who I was at the end of 8th grade, I seem to be very different. I am still me, but I don't think I could imagine then how well things would work out. Of course, there is still time for me to hate high school and cross-country, but I think that I am a lot happier than I expected myself to be. On the team, every person is interesting and friendly. I feel glad that I have started cross-country.

ISSUES TO EXAMINE AND DISCUSS

Refer to

1. How does your child describe his school, teachers, and school work? How do you respond when conversations about school, teachers, and grades come up? — 172

2. Do you think the figures Richard Riley shared in his speech on page 170 are overly optimistic? Have you run into people who have negative opinions about this generation of young people? How do you feel about that? — 170

3. Look again at the exercise you did on page 171. Discuss with a peer, or your group if you have one, and identify the traits that were common to your generation growing up. Contrast this to the experiences and traits of today's teenagers. — 171

4. Is your child overwhelmed with school pressures? Discuss with a friend or peer strategies that parents can use to support a teenager in this situation, doing additional research if possible. What resources are available in your school and community? — 173-178

5. What do you think of the "evening tea" described on page 178? What other ideas do you have for ways to open discussion and provide support in a non-threatening way? — 178

6. Have you noticed your teenager hanging out with a homogenous group of kids? Or do you notice that she has a diverse group of friends? How would your teen describe the social landscape at school? Is she comfortable within that landscape?

7. How can you use the information regarding types of intelligence and learning styles to better understand and support your child's learning experience? — 179-181

8. In what ways do you get involved in school? What do you get out of it? What does your child get out of it? Share your observations from the brainstorming exercise on page 186. — 182-189

9. Do you feel your child's self-esteem is pretty well intact? What activities and experiences build it up? What diminishes her self-esteem? How might you provide guidance in the right direction? — 190-195

 Be sure to access supplementary and current information on this topic at www.PleaseStoptheRollercoaster.com.

TAKE-AWAYS

What are my "take-aways" from this chapter?

_____

_____

_____

_____

_____

_____

_____

_____

_____

What specific things am I going to do differently as a result of what I've learned?

_____

_____

_____

_____

_____

_____

_____

_____

_____

ZITS

7

A scenario

As you open your e-mail you're delighted to see a note from an old friend who moved to another part of the country. Her life is so exciting— a new home, a special trip to Paris; she sounds great. And she boasts that her 7th grader was voted "Student of the Year." Your friend points out that not only does this award stand for her daughter's outstanding academic performance, but it reflects on citizenship, leadership, and community service. You actually feel a stab in your belly. "Why isn't my child able to compete in such ways?" you ask yourself. She's bright enough, but she's never been a candidate for any award at all! Nor does that seem likely to change. She's a follower, and you're hard pressed to identify any way in which she stands out in her peer group. It's not what you imagined for her, or for you. Is that feeling in your belly actually *jealousy?*

Are you disappointed in her, or are you disappointed with yourself and the feelings of jealousy and inadequacy this correspondence generated?

Chapter Seven: Overview and objectives

Imagine yourself sitting in a living room, looking through a lovely bay window. Your teenager is outside doing what he loves to do—whether that's reading, talking with friends, playing football—whatever. But the window through which you are looking at him is not clear; the glass is tinted blue. Your child's face has a tint of blue. You know he's not really blue, so you hardly even notice that the glass is colored.

We're going to take a good close look at this window—at the colored glass. Because this represents our "lens," or our perspective, as parent. We never look at our child through clear glass; we cannot separate ourselves from this role of parent. We're going to examine that perspective, and how it colors our adolescents.

Then we're going to turn the focus onto ourselves. How are we doing in *our* journey? Are we headed in the direction we want to go? There's lots of food for thought in this chapter.

Objectives

In this chapter you will:

- Examine and challenge your expectations of your teenager and look at your motives.

- Uncover some of the baggage and unresolved issues that you bring to this role, and examine how these issues impact your adolescent.

- Identify areas where you would like to grow as an individual, and begin to make plans to make it happen.

- Examine failure and why it's not a bad thing for your kids to experience.

> *"We may not sacrifice our children to our unfulfilled dreams."*
>
> Wolf[1]

Chapter Seven: Instructions

*Reader
Instructions*

How to get the most out of this chapter:

- Read the entire seventh chapter; you may want to highlight the areas that strike a chord with you.

- The exercises are particularly important in this chapter and require some serious self-contemplation. Complete the exercises on pages 204, 206, 210, 211. Spend some extra time with the exercise on page 215 as your honest answers may yield important insight. Finish with the exercises on pages 216, 218, 219, 220, and 221.

- Examine the issues and questions on page 222. Discuss the most relevant questions with a friend, spouse, or in your parenting discussion group, if you have one.

- Be sure to write down your "take-aways." These insights will help you translate your intentions into actions.

If you have a parenting discussion group:

*Group
Recommendations/
Reminders*

- Begin by discussing how you were able to apply what you learned at the last meeting as you put your "take-aways" into action.

- Ask each group member to identify which of the issues on page 222 they wish to discuss.

- The facilitator for the meeting can guide the group discussion to ensure that the issues of greatest interest to group members are examined and explored, and that all group members participate.

- Take a quick look at the parenting plan (pages 242-245) that you'll each create in Chapter 8. Decide as a group if you want to do this on your own as homework, or if you want to create your plans together at the next group meeting.

- See page 11 for more recommendations for group leaders.

  Be sure to access supplementary and current information on this topic at www.PleaseStoptheRollercoaster.com.

Examining your motives

Perfection. Of course we don't expect our children to be perfect. "How absurd," you say. But, look closely at the expectations you have, and listen to the messages you give your children. Under closer scrutiny you may see that your standards and expectations are really very high.

What does it mean to have a "perfect child?" Why do we dress them "just so" for special holidays? Why are we ashamed if she brings home a D? Why does it bother us if he wears sneakers when dress shoes are more appropriate? One reason may be that *what our children do reflects on us.* If we have a "perfect child" then we must be a "perfect parent," right?

If a child is "perfect" does that mean that the parents are perfect?

- Your child brings home a report card with 3 A's, 1 B, and 1 C. What is your first comment? Is it about the A's, or about the C?

- Your child has been told that he cannot go out until his room is cleaned up. He spends 2 hours cleaning; you hear the vacuum cleaner going, you see him drag two bags of trash down to the barrels in the garage, and finally he announces he is ready to leave. You go in his room for the big inspection and what do you say? Do you congratulate him on what he accomplished, or on the guilty looking pile that remains in the corner?

- You overhear one of your friends complaining about her daughter being lazy and unfocused about her school work. She is in 3 honors courses and is bringing home B's—her mother is not pleased. You think "This mom needs to have her head examined–she has no idea how good she has it. My kid is struggling with B's and C's in college prep classes."

What if your child is less than perfect? What does that say about you?

- You received a call from the local police Saturday night that your son was at a party where there was alcohol. As you accompany him to court on Monday morning you wonder if your hurt and humiliation are in proportion to the crime. Why do you feel ashamed to show your face in the community? Why does it matter so much?

Are our kids being supported and built up by our responses to them? Or are they feeling inadequate and undermined? What's the right balance? What is the difference between a proper amount of *push* from us, and an improper amount? How do we know when to congratulate on a job well done, and when to admonish for not living up to their potential?

Examining your motives (cont.)

These are not easy questions to answer. And as we begin to examine these questions we come face to face with our motivations. Why do we push our kids? What do we expect from them? We need to look at our expectations and where they come from.

Do we have a right to expect certain things from our children? When do our hopes and dreams for people we love turn into the very tethers that tie their hands?

Many parents who have weathered their child's adolescence call it a humbling experience. High hopes for "doing it differently" are often exchanged for hope of just getting through it. "I'll never let her…" gets replaced with "I never thought I'd be allowing this." Experiencing the reality of parenting teenagers is an equalizing experience. There's not much room for moralizing to others.

 *Josh, 16*

If you don't expect perfection all the time, you won't be disappointed all the time.[2]

Alex, 16

Don't pressure me so much on the future while I'm still trying to figure out the present.[3]

E

Often our children do not live up to our hopes for them. They rarely can, and often we are disappointed. This too is normal and not bad. But sometimes we take our disappointment out on our children. This may be normal but it is *not* okay. It's not fair to our children to get angry at them because they have not become what we had wanted. That's our problem, not theirs.

Anthony Wolf,
*Get Out of My Life,
but First Could You Drive Me
and Cheryl to the Mall?*, 57

Examining your motives (cont.)

Do your children reflect on you? In what way? How do their accomplishments reflect on you? What about their failures?

Think for a moment about what your kids would need to do or be for you to be considered a "perfect parent." What attributes would they have? What accomplishments would they achieve?

This is important to think about because it is unlikely that your child has achieved this level of perfection in your eyes. Try and identify the difference between your ideal and her actuality. Do you want to diminish her because she doesn't live up to your ideal? Or would you rather intentionally celebrate her strengths and help her live into *her* potential?

Jenny, 13

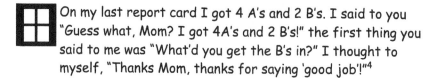

On my last report card I got 4 A's and 2 B's. I said to you "Guess what, Mom? I got 4A's and 2 B's!" the first thing you said to me was "What'd you get the B's in?" I thought to myself, "Thanks Mom, thanks for saying 'good job'!"[4]

Examining your motives (cont.)

I have struggled to examine these questions and issues myself. The essence of our challenge is to connect our role and growth as a *parent* to our growth as an *individual*. In the vast stores of current literature exploring parenting and adolescence, there is not a lot of discussion to help us explore this essential territory. But I was happy to find a few resources that are helpful in this quest.

Girl in the Mirror, by Snyderman and Streep, has a wonderful chapter entitled "Reflections" that examines the very issues we are addressing together here; I encourage you to read it. Although they focus their book on the mother–daughter relationship, much can be applied to fathers and sons, and all parent-teen relationships. Encouraging the type of self-reflection we are embracing in this chapter, they write: "The introspection that is a hallmark of authoritative parenting at its best may feel foreign to us or make us uncomfortable. We may feel caught in turmoil as our relationships and our own definitions of success and self-worth suddenly seem to be built on shifting sands."[5] Indeed, our teens are experiencing major developmental shifts during adolescence, at a time that often coincides with significant mid-life changes for parents. So the questions we are exploring on behalf of our teenagers are important for us to ponder in the context of our own lives. Snyderman and Streep say, "As the closest thing to a mirror our daughters have, we each have to look within and discover what we think is of value in our own lives…"[6] The very questions we ponder in the next few pages are of key importance to us and to our families as well.

Begin to think about:

- the definition of success

- effort vs. achievement

- the significance of failure

- success vs. fulfillment

- the lessons you've learned

- the values you cherish

- your response to your child's individuality

- how to nurture your spirituality

- continuing your intellectual growth

...and how all of this is shared with your children.

Examining your motives (cont.)

I've noticed in many situations that it is much easier for us to be objective about other peoples' children than about our own. When we step back from the intense personal involvement that is inherent in our parent-child relationship we can see things differently, and many times we give the others outside of the family more slack and understanding. See if you can apply this objectivity to your child for a moment, isolating and eliminating for the moment that parenting "lens" that colors his world.

Think of a situation your child has recently faced in which he let you down or failed in some way. Give advice to him as though you are a family friend, not his parent. Begin the conversation with giving him positive feedback before you give him advice.

Did you feel that you handled this imaginary conversation differently in your role as family friend vs. the way you handled it as parent? How was it different for you? How do you think your child would respond to this new version of the conversation?

What motivates you as parent to handle your child as you do? How are the motivations different when you are in the role of family friend?

The Very Energy of the Universe

Your children are not mere lumps of clay
waiting for your expert hands.
They are the very energy of the universe
and will become what they will become.
They are sacred beings.
If you tamper with them
you will make everyone miserable.

They will find success,
and failure.
They will be happy,
and sad.
They will delight you,
and disappoint you.
They will be safe,
and at great risk.
They will live,
and they will die.

Stay at the center of your own soul.
There is nothing else you can do.

My son almost lost his life as a teenager.
There was nothing I could do.
I remember accepting that he might die.
I cried for hours.
I got up and returned to my life and to my loves.
Years later, he is a happy, strong, wonderful young
man–
all because of his choices,
not mine.

From The Parent's Tao Te Ching, a New Interpretation
by William Martin

What others have learned

Ask yourself "What do I bring to my role as parent?"   Lorraine has three kids, all teenagers. Her one daughter is "just like me, only better." Her oldest son is like her husband, physically and emotionally–it's uncanny at times. Her youngest son is very different. "I feel as though someone left a bird from a different family in our nest," she says. His rejection of their values has been deliberate, and has caused them pain. "It's hard not to take it personally," she says. "He's ours, and we love him very much, but he is so different from us, it's hard."

These are rather strict, thoughtful parents who are intentional about what they do. What does she bring to parenting? "Real baggage" about the value of possessions. Lorraine is one of eight kids, and her father left when she was fourteen. She had to work to buy her own clothes, and to put herself through college. "It's a hindrance coming from a different economic background than the one in which you are raising your children," she says. On the one hand, she believes in *not* spoiling children; on the other hand, it's difficult not to when one has the means. She's tried it both ways, and interestingly enough, the children who received less materially seem to appreciate it more than the one who was spoiled.

In preparation for the college selection process for her daughter, Lorraine set out on a mission to *not* get sucked in to the competitive nature of this endeavor. In her town, the atmosphere for high school seniors looking for college acceptances is very intense and very competitive. Not buying into that scene, she thought, would be something she could manage.

But it didn't work out that way. She did play a role in the college search: "I think our kids need us to push them. I think that failure is proof of a truly noble effort. In a funny way, failure is a form of success. It can speak to character. So I don't really regret pushing my daughter toward 'reach' schools. What causes me shame is the comparative/competitive element that I found myself participating in, if only privately. The name of the college became a very high priority. It's a consideration, sure, but there are about a dozen other considerations that should have preceded it. And I wanted to be able to say 'my daughter will be attending BC' both because I want her to be able to declare that as a success and because I liked the way to sounded to ME."

Examining her motives and paying attention to the big picture helps Lorraine to stay her course, as parent of three teenagers. Her youngest son has "found a way to be oppositional and generate discord in his family just about every day of his life." This "different bird" has taught his parents many lessons, including appropriate detachment from both his misdeeds and accomplishments. In learning that she does not need to accept responsibility for his mistakes, she has also learned that she cannot accept responsibility for her children's successes. "I can't have it both ways," she says.

Her best advice to other parents is to "pull up and gain perspective. They will get through this stage—these kids will not always been teenagers. Parents need to learn to not hyper-focus on today's crisis. Things will change. We need to learn to trust our instincts."

What others have learned (cont.)

Is love enough?   Carolyn, 45, was saying goodbye to her dying mother. As they were quietly conversing, Carolyn was compelled to apologize to her mom for the trials and trouble she had brought to her family during her rebellious adolescence. "What trouble?" her mother asked. "You were perfect."

Pondering that made Carolyn realize that to her mother, she probably was perfect. And it was because her mother had had no expectations of her. They shared their love unconditionally.

Her mother was not an empowered person. She didn't make much money, she had low self-esteem and low power in the household compared to her husband, Carolyn's father. But she was able to offer her daughter all that she had to give—her complete love. And in the absence of high expectations, Carolyn couldn't fail. All her life she has felt the support of the unconditional love of her mother.

Is love enough?

Big opportunities and high expectations   Dan is a high school history teacher looking to move back to his home state. In interviewing in one school system he is struck by the level of intensity articulated by the principal. "We intend to deliver the finest education available today. We set our sights high and we prepare our young people to excel. There is no room for mediocrity here in any way. We have dedicated, creative, motivated teachers and staff who deliver, and we prepare our students to be accepted into the finest colleges and universities in the country. This is what is expected by our citizens and parents. We are producing leaders."

When does a focus on excellence and opportunity turn into too much pressure? Do big opportunities and a value for excellence bring expectations that are so high they work against our ability to love our children unconditionally?

Perfection is an illusion   Amy says that her first two children looked "perfect" from the outside in. But she knows better, now.

Katie was self-motivated and excelled in her honors courses in high school. A lovely dancer, she was busy, successful, and focused. She identified the college of her choice early on and was accepted early decision. She worked hard, played by the rules, and was rewarded.

Younger brother, Jeff, was a model citizen. Successful in school, sports, a leader with his peers, respected by adults and teachers…his acceptance at Yale was no surprise.

It took a while, but reality came crashing down, as it tends to do. Katie fell in love while in college and married young. The day after the wedding she found herself living in a physically abusive relationship. It took Katie six months to tell her mother of the abuse; the challenge and pain of extricating herself from the relationship took even longer. Amy says when the image shattered, "it shattered like glass exploding on the floor."

Examining your motives (cont.)

Jeff was at ground zero September 11, 2001. He survived by running to safety and hiding along the beachfront until rescued by a boat. His survival is a miracle.

Amy's third child, Jennifer, was different from the moment she was born. She came into life a fighter, and hasn't stopped yet. Another bright, talented, beautiful child, Jennifer wanted to challenge the system, her parents, and all authority. And most of all, she didn't want to be like, or be compared to, her older sister.

What was it that made Jennifer different? Temperament? Different life experiences? Challenges in the family dynamics? Changes in family finances? Sure, all of the above contributed. And who knows what it is that makes one child respond one way, and another child respond differently.

It was challenging for Amy and her husband to manage Jennifer, and to manage themselves as their attempts to parent her were thwarted continually. This child's dress, her manner, her friends, her behavior at home and at school—all were rebellious in nature. This child was dearly loved, as were they all…but these parents were tested time and time again. Amy felt the pain and despair of a mother whose children are not a always a source of pride, but are sometimes a source of embarrassment. As she struggled with her older daughter's painful marriage and her younger daughter's rebellious adolescence, she came to terms with the realities of parenthood. "We do the best we can, and then we let go." Having put much of her rebelliousness behind her, Jennifer, today, is happy with herself and with her family.

Amy's comments for parents: "Empower children with the knowledge that life isn't easy; life is not perfect, and we're not going to get everything we want. But families are strong, and together big problems can be faced and managed. I have learned over and over that we are stronger than we realize. And most importantly, good comes from bad. I've seen it happen over and over again."

What do you bring to parenting...what hang ups, what baggage, what unresolved issues?

What can you learn?

Our strengths and weaknesses   What do I bring to parenting? I bring the same hang ups, issues, strengths, and weaknesses that I struggle with as a human being. I need to be careful not to project these issues onto my children and color their world.

My memories of my junior high and high school experiences are more filled with pain than with pleasure—at least socially. Never quite confident enough or comfortable enough to negotiate the social scene smoothly, my memories are of awkwardness and lack of confidence. It probably did not show on the outside. I'm reporting the truth of my inner experience.

Today, sharing my children's experiences as they navigate the social minefield of junior high and high school is dangerous business for me. As I've felt their pain, I've had to remind myself that I'm not the person who is in junior high—I've already lived that and I don't need to do it again. This is my son's own experience, and that of my daughter. I must be very careful not to project my issues, fears, and pain on them. They are very different people. They don't need my limitations.

> What are the things you'd most like to change about yourself? How do these traits affect your parenting style?

As we raise these intimate questions and mull them over, we are again reminded how delicate the balance is, the balance between the appropriate level of parental involvement versus giving our kids their freedom. A friend of mine has told me her story, and I share it here with you. It holds our concerns about finding the right balance between intervention, and not. Parents don't always get the balance right; perhaps you can learn from her lessons.

What can you learn? (cont.)

E

Jeffrey always had better things to do than read. Although he kept his grades up, his mom, Brenda, never felt that his reading skills were what they should have been. Teacher after teacher reassured her, but as Jeff entered 7th grade, his testing showed him to be reading at a 4th grade level. Brenda felt no satisfaction in being right.

Middle school was a struggle on all fronts. Jeffrey wanted little to do with his parents, and any discussions about schoolwork felt like the start of a war. Brenda and her husband Bob disagreed about the best approach to take. Bob wanted to run things with a heavy hand, Brenda was more concerned about Jeffrey's feelings. So many dinner conversations ended in indigestion and arguments that finally Bob gave up and handed over the problem to Brenda. She wasn't sure she wanted to own it.

Although Jeff's grades were unspectacular, he was a good kid who rarely got into trouble. He didn't spend much time studying, but his teachers indicated they didn't see any real problems.

High school brought on some major changes, including a precipitous drop in grades. Jeff's once active social life also took a dive once his junior high friends were disbursed into the larger social scene. In December, it became very to clear to Brenda that Jeff was in trouble, academically and socially. She immediately went into action.

She had the school test Jeff and, along with results indicating that Jeff was highly intelligent, the school psychologist identified some issues with his learning style. But she was quick to add that Jeff was "not disabled in any way and was not eligible for services." It was recommended that Jeff acquire strategies to accommodate for his imbalanced style of learning.

Brenda was relieved and delighted! Now Jeff did not have to feel that he was stupid, he had confirmation that he was very bright indeed. He just needed to work a little harder in some specific areas, and things would work out. They hired a tutor and waited hopefully.

Thank heavens Jeff was an accomplished musician; this was the one bright spot in his life. Brenda grew to appreciate what a lifeline it was. Tutors and all, sophomore year brought continued disappointing academic results. Family dynamics were tense; Bob had completely withdrawn from the problem, and to some extent from Jeff. Brenda had many sleepless nights worrying.

Then Jeff got in trouble with the police. His involvement in a senseless act of vandalism was entirely out of character. Brenda was devastated. "Is he trying to say something?" she wondered. "Is this a red flag?"

Brenda felt she had some leverage and could demand that Jeff see a psychologist, an offer he had previously refused. She brought it up to Bob. "Over my dead body!" he said. "That's not going to do any good! What Jeff needs to do is buckle down, work hard, and stay straight!"

Brenda stewed for another day or two, and approached Bob again. "You don't have to agree, you don't have to participate, but I don't want to do this behind your back. Jeff needs to see a psychologist, and I need to make that happen." This time Bob agreed.

Brenda met with the psychologist on the first day of school of Jeff's junior year. She went alone for the first meeting, armed with the school evaluations. Five minutes into the conversation the psychologist said "This boy has a learning disability. What's the matter with them?" Brenda started to cry. To think that Jeff was now a junior in high school, and they were just now getting the real story.

The experts went into high gear; Jeff was diagnosed depressed, and with an attention deficit. He went on Ritalin and found he could focus much better; the positive results he saw made the depression disappear quickly. By the time the second term was finished he was on the honor roll and he finished his junior year with mostly A's and B's. His confidence grew visibly every week. While he was undeniably getting taller, it was the way he projected himself that made his growth appear even more dramatic.

LESSON #1: NEVER BELIEVE THE TEST RESULTS FROM ONE WHO HAS A VESTED INTEREST IN A PARTICULAR OUTCOME.
LESSON #2: RED FLAGS AREN'T ALWAYS RED.
LESSON #3: PARENTS WON'T ALWAYS GET IT RIGHT, BUT GO WITH YOUR GUT, AND NEVER GIVE UP.

What can you learn? (cont.)

Raising children is an opportunity for tremendous growth. We learn to view the world in a new way. We learn that we are not the center of the universe. We learn acceptance, generosity, and the meaning of unconditional love. And that is just the beginning of what we learn in our course of life through parenting.

There is an interaction between the developmental changes parents experience and those of their adolescent children. As A. Rae Simpson reports in her *Raising Teens* report, "some scholars…observe that parents interpret their teenager's behavior, decide on courses of action, and communicate with their teen differently, depending on their own level of development." She points out that "raising teens can be a stimulus for further development in adults, as well as vice versa."[7]

Reviewing again Carolyn Moore Newberger's "Level Four" parenting from Session 2, it's significant to note the reciprocity inherent in the parent-teen relationship, and that both individuals are experiencing developmental shifts.

Newberger raises an important question for parents: Are you growing? How? What are you doing to enhance your personal growth? Are you enhancing your life spiritually? Emotionally? Intellectually? These questions merit honest examination.

Laurence Steinberg's *Crossing Paths: How Your Child's Adolescence Triggers Your Own Crisis* offers insight into the dynamic of this relationship, too. His point of view is particularly interesting because he notes that most of the psychological literature available about families focuses on "the impact parents have on their children, not the other way around." This book examines the reverse: the impact teenage children have on their parents. He says: "The child's entry into adolescence is a crucial time for mothers and fathers, for it is a period in which a critical developmental transition in the child's life, puberty, coincides with a critical developmental transition in the adult's life, midlife."[8] The opportunities for growth in this period for parents is tremendous, and exciting. However, so dramatic are the adolescent and midlife transitions, that the opportunity for "psychological turmoil" exists as well.

Parent-teenager interactions—What do they mean? The way in which a parent responds to her child's adolescent development and journey is reflective of her mental health and happiness, as well as a product of it. Steinberg's book is based on extensive field research, and in interviewing several hundred families with teenagers, he identified five most frequent types of responses from parents.

- *Jealousy versus joy*: Most parents respond with joy to their child's development and achievements. Parents' joy may be derived from seeing their child's accomplishments and the pleasure it brought to him, or because they see their child's achievements as a positive

What can you learn? (cont.)

reflection on their parenting. Some parents appreciate the beauty of the child's development in its own right. Although a minority, the parents who feel jealousy feel it strongly. Jealousy can come from parental reactions to their sacrifices (often to what they perceive as unappreciative children), envy for the teenager's exciting and romantic sexual adventures, or achievements the child may accomplish that the parents wish they themselves had achieved.[9]

- *Abandonment versus rejuvenation*: Parents who suffer from an unfulfilling emotional life may tend to over-rely on their relationship with their teenager as a means to fill their gap. Those who compensate in this way are more likely to feel a sense of abandonment as their adolescent begins to focus on her life outside of home. A parent who enjoys an emotionally satisfying relationship with a spouse or friends is more able to remain close to her child while allowing her to grow apart. These parents are more apt to find a sense of rejuvenation in their child's development.[10]

- *Loss versus freedom*: Some parents who feel an intense sense of loss as their child enters adolescence find themselves dealing with depression. This is not surprising as psychologists note that most instances of depression are linked to some sort of loss. The bigger challenge in this situation, however, is that exactly what one is "losing" is not clear. Many parents have a difficult time identifying exactly what is going on inside of them. The sense of loss may be difficult to name, examine, and address. There are those parents who, on the other side of the spectrum, see their child's adolescence as a time and opportunity for their own freedom and rebirth. These individuals are more likely to fare well through this stage in their families' life.[11]

- *Powerlessness versus assurance*: Steinberg identified three dimensions of parenting—guidance, affection, and authority. Parents agree that children need all three, but parents will differ in their emphasis in these three areas. Interestingly, parents who focus most heavily on their role as authority figures are most likely to feel a sense of powerlessness with their teenagers. Conversely, parents who emphasize their roles as providers of guidance or affection are less likely to feel this sense of powerlessness.[12]

- *Regret*: Living through a child's adolescence, for some parents, brings them face to face with their own adolescence which can surface strong feelings of regret about their life and choices.[13]

Examine the common parental responses discussed in Steinberg's work. What kinds of feelings do you have regarding your child's passage into and through adolescence? (This is intensely personal work: be as honest with yourself as you can. You need not share this with anyone unless you choose to.)

How do you respond to each of the areas he identified:

Jealousy versus joy

Abandonment versus rejuvenation

Loss versus freedom

Powerlessness versus assurance

Regret

What can you learn? (cont.)

Additionally, Steinberg's study identified four risk factors that increase the likelihood that parents will have a rocky road through their child's teenage years. If you meet any of these criteria it does not mean that you'll necessarily have trouble, just that the chances are increased and go up for each additional risk factor that applies to you. They are:

- being the same sex as the child making the transition;

- being divorced or remarried, especially for women;

- having few sources of satisfaction outside the parental role;

- having a negative "cognitive set" about adolescence.

This last risk factor is simply the famous old concept of the self-fulfilling prophecy. Steinberg's research determined that the mind set—positive or negative—with which a parent approached adolescence "became psychological filters through which the adolescent's behavior was interpreted and explained. What began as an emotional reaction to the onset of adolescence became an interpretive framework for subsequent events."[14]

What does your "parenting lens" look like? What color is it? When does it change color? Our "parenting lens" provides a framework for how we interpret our parent-child relationship, and for the way we respond to our child and our life's events. Let's make sure we're enhancing this journey, not undermining it.

 There are many articles that explore various aspects of the parenting journey at www.PleaseStoptheRollercoaster.com

Which of the above four risk factors apply to you? How might you ensure that these factors don't undermine your ability to enjoy, flourish, and grow during your child's teenage years?

What can you learn? (cont.)

What do you want?   It's essential to keep ourselves on a path of personal growth. Sometimes, in the busyness of life, we get off track. Raising our families puts some parents in the position of putting themselves at the bottom of their list as they make their kids the priority. It is dangerous to prioritize anyone over oneself...even our children.

Cheryl Richardson, the well known personal coach, calls what we need to exercise "extreme self care."[15] Few parents exercise the self care they deserve, and it may require a concerted effort on your part to make this change. It will have many benefits, however, and one is actually a benefit to your children as they witness a healthy example of how one should take care of oneself. We need to consciously examine how we approach our life, our priorities, and our goals as we begin to exercise this level of self care.

Parents who become overly invested in their identification with their children run the risk of losing their own identity. It is not healthy to live life vicariously. I fully expect to suffer and miss them when my kids leave and go off to college—and yet I've been raising them to launch them, that is the job as I accepted it. So how do I prepare myself for this change? I must tap into my resources, and my desire to explore new horizons and new opportunities for growth. And so must you. No matter where your kids are in their adolescent journey, this is a good time to focus on you and what you hope to achieve in your future.

Applying the lessons   So what can we learn from Steinberg's research? We learn that the parents who manage well through their child's teenage years have an optimistic attitude along with a full life. Specifically Steinberg shares these "lessons for living:"[16]

- *Make sure you have genuine and satisfying interests outside of being a parent.*

- *Don't disengage from your child emotionally.*

- *Try to adopt a positive outlook about what adolescence is and how your child is changing.*

- *Don't be afraid to discuss what you are feeling with your mate, your friends, or, if need be, with a professional counselor.*

Let go of your watch and your cellular phone and LIVE![17]

Bryan, 15

Do more things for yourself. Go out once in a while. Start dating again.[18]

Josh, 15

What can you learn? (cont.)

What are you doing to grow intellectually? How are you sustaining this? In what ways are you challenging yourself? Is this an area that needs improvement? How might you increase your intellectual growth?

What are you doing to grow spiritually? To what new ways of thinking or being are you exposing yourself? Is this an area that needs improvement? What actions might you take to increase your spiritual development?

What are you doing to grow emotionally? How might you get support from others in this part of your journey?

Create your future

How do you define "success"? What does success look like to you? What would be embodied in your life if you met your definition of success? What would you have to achieve, or acquire, or do? Usually we think of success in concrete terms—and it usually can be measured by external measures. For example, attaining a certain level of income, a certain type of home, or the perfect job. Maybe it's writing a book, or mastering a musical instrument to a certain level of accomplishment. Take a moment to think about what success looks like to you.

Now think about fulfillment. This is a different dimension than success. Fulfillment comes from the drive to answer questions like "Who am I?" and "What do I want?" Fulfillment is usually measured by internal measures, not external ones. You cannot find fulfillment by chasing success. Fulfillment is likely to come from creativity and meaningful work; from relationships and love; from our ability to change our attitudes and manage ourselves positively as we move through the various stages in our lives. What will make you feel fulfilled? What does fulfillment look like?

These are important questions to ask as your role in parenting is changing and as your children prepare to launch into their new lives. But it's just a beginning...

What does "success" look like to you? What will you need to achieve to be successful in your own eyes?

What does "fulfillment" look like to you? What will you need to achieve to be fulfilled in your own eyes?

Failure is an option

We've talked a little about success. Now let's examine failure. That's a loaded word, and a loaded concept. While we're usually taught to focus on success most people recognize that failure is something that may happen along the way. We don't make *every* team, and we don't win *every* game; it's important for kids to know that risking failure is the only way to success.

As our children get ready to leave home, the possibility of failure—and the fear of it, can become overwhelming to them. The high suicide rate of college freshmen is an alarming way of highlighting this fact. Some teenagers make mistakes when they leave home, and of course while they still live with us, too. Mistakes can run the gamut from trouble with police for under age drinking, flunking out of college, getting into trouble financially...the list is endless. These problems are likely to feel like disasters to them. And, indeed, they may be very serious problems. But, as parents, we must recognize the importance of helping our kids develop coping skills that will facilitate their ability to get through the tough times and not make them feel there is no way out. They must know that they will survive failure. And they must know that, while they have to take the consequences of their actions, they have our unconditional love. Taking a good close look at failure, and your relationship with it, can help you come to terms with this concept.

Do you give your child enough freedom to fail? When was the last time she failed in an attempt to succeed at something? What was your response? When was the last time you failed in an effort to achieve something? How did you respond? What did you learn?

Failure is an option (cont.)

Examples of failure surround us. It is our attitude that colors our relationship with it. Do we want to see the glass as half empty or half full? Do we appreciate that for Thomas Edison to achieve his end results he first had to fail over and over again? As parents this can be challenging territory. But do we want our children to be afraid to attempt new things?

E

...Failure builds character, helps you hone your skills, tests your determination, fortifies you with eight essential vitamins, and gives you the inner strength and courage to go back out there and fall flat on your face all over again.

...Just remember, everyone falls down. You're not a failure until you don't get back up.

Joey Green, *The Road to Success is Paved with Failure, 7*

The Power of Failure[19]

- Charles Conrad, the third astronaut to walk on the moon, flunked out of Haverford, a prestigious private boys school in Pennsylvania, where he was known as a prankster.

- Steven Spielberg's mediocre grades prevented him from getting into UCLA film school.

- Katie Couric was banned from reading news reports on the air by the president of CNN because he felt she had a high pitched, squeaky voice.

- Ronald Reagan lost the 1968 Republican nomination for president to Richard Nixon. He lost the 1976 Republican nomination for president to Gerald Ford.

Ask yourself this question: Are you helping your teenager develop the resiliency to manage, survive, and learn from failure?

ISSUES TO EXAMINE AND DISCUSS

Refer to

1. Did your parents have expectations of you? How did you respond to that? — -

2. Do you have a right to certain expectations of your children? — 202-203

3. In what ways do your children reflect on you? What happens when their goals and desires conflict with the goals and desires you have for them? — -

4. Are you more understanding and do you give more leeway to other people's children than your own? Is this right or fair? — -

5. Can unconditional love and an emphasis on excellence co-exist in a parent-child relationship? How does one affect the other? — -

6. Raising children has undoubtedly taught you things about yourself. What have you learned? Refer to the list of issues on page 205. — 205

7. Think about what you bring to parenting: what kind of baggage, history, expectations? What impact does this have on your parenting style and relationships? — 208-211

8. Review Steinberg's parental responses on pages 213 and 214. Do you recognize yourself having any of these responses? Think back to your parents' responses to your adolescence. Do you see their responses reflected here? What can you learn from this? — 213-214

9. How many of Steinberg's risk factors apply to you? How might you ensure that they don't undermine your growth? — 216

10. Brainstorm with a friend or as a group, if you have one, ideas for ways in which you might enhance your spiritual, emotional, and intellectual growth. — 218

11. Think about your experience with failure and what you learned from it. What messages about failure do you give your kids? Do your actions correspond with your words? — 222-223

➡ *TAKE-AWAYS*

What are my "take-aways" from this chapter?

_____

_____

_____

_____

_____

_____

_____

_____

What specific things am I going to do differently as a result of what I've learned?

_____

_____

_____

_____

_____

_____

_____

_____

ZITS

Reflections

A scenario

You just received a telephone call from your son's history teacher. She has informed you that there is a cheating ring taking place in her classes, and she suspects, but does not know for sure, that your son is involved. Although you are upset, you don't let your emotions and fears take over. You try and apply some of the points you've taken away from your parenting discussion group and this book. One of your tendencies is to react first and ask questions later. But this time, you tell yourself you're going to calmly ask your son to share with you what is giving his teacher this impression. You take a deep breath and say a little prayer.

Later that evening, after you and your son have had a calm discussion about this incident, he says to you, "You know, Mom, you handled this really differently. Normally you would have gone off the deep end, and I'd be found guilty before the trial even started. I like you better this way!"

Will you respond to the crises of life differently now?

Chapter Eight: Overview and objectives

In this chapter you'll summarize what you've learned so far in this program, and you will make plans to continue to apply it. By identifying the key take-aways and the most relevant points that apply to you in your relationship with your teen, you will write advice to yourself and set some goals for applying your learning.

Objectives

In this chapter you will:

- Review what you've learned and gained as a result of completing the chapter, the exercises and the reading.

- Examine the "Five Basics" of Parenting Adolescents.

- Examine some true life stories that illustrate the challenging situations you may have to face and think about what you would do.

- Put together advice and a plan to remind yourself of points you want to remember and actions you plan to take.

> *If I could*
> *I would teach you all the things I've never learned*
> *And I'd help you cross the bridges that I've burned*
> *Yes, I would*
>
> *If I could*
> *I would try to shield your innocence from time*
> *But the part of life I gave you isn't mine*
> *I've watched you grow*
> *So I could let you go...*
> *Miller, Hirsch, Sharron[1]*

Chapter Eight: Instructions

***Reader
Instructions***

How to get the most out of this chapter:

- Read through Chapter 8. As you read the "What would you do" section, you'll undoubtedly want to discuss this with others. It's great for generating thought provoking conversation.

- Read through the previous sections of this book, paying particular attention to your "take-aways" in each chapter, as well as the reflections and exercises. Remind yourself as to the most important points and strategies that you feel are pertinent to your family.

- Complete the Parenting Plan on pages 242-245.

If you have a parenting discussion group:

***Group
Recommendations/
Reminders***

- Begin by discussing how you were able to apply what you learned at the last meeting as you put your "take-aways" into action.

- If the Parenting Plan was completed as homework, ask each member to share his/her plan. If they haven't been completed yet, take the necessary time for each participant to create her plan at the meeting, and then share it.

- After everyone has shared their Parenting Plans, discuss the scenarios in the "What would you do?" section. Devise strategies, discuss alternative responses, identify the first steps parents might take in each situation to keep calm and to ensure an appropriate response.

- Discuss ways the group can continue to stay in touch and support one another in the future. Consider planning a celebration for your accomplishment.

 **Be sure to access the "Tools for Groups" area on our website
www.PleaseStoptheRollercoaster.com.**

Putting it all together

Parents need to know how essential their involvement is. Our teens are unlikely to tell us that directly, but we must believe we truly are the right person for this job and we must not allow them to push us away.

T he overriding message that comes through loud and clear from all the authors we've resourced and quoted is basically the same: *Parents must stay actively involved with our teenagers. This is not the time to pull back from the relationship.*

And yet, each day as I interact with my two teenagers I frequently feel their discomfort with my presence. Often they don't want to be with me. The "allergy" to parents that Anthony Wolf talks about is, at times, alive and well in my house. And other times they actually sit happily and hang out with me. The patience and understanding it takes to parent through this stage is overwhelming at times. I must constantly remind myself not to take their rejection personally. I speak to other parents whose children are now in their twenties; they all say the kids "come back," that families become close again. I look forward to that.

I remember how close we were before the teenage years came upon us. One precious tradition was every Friday night we'd rent a movie and we'd all lie together— cuddling up while we enjoyed our evening reconnecting after a busy week. When our puppy joined the family, we moved our pile of bodies to the floor so we could include her. The weekend trips to the amusement park, or the country fair are precious memories of time shared. Now I have to be very creative to find events that we might share together. Perhaps I should look for "moments," not events. We do have special moments of connection, of shared laughter. Should I be satisfied with these? I yearn for more.

Each family has its own unique dynamic, and each parent-teen relationship is a unique and special thing.

Not all teenagers are like mine. I observe other families that have different dynamics. One friend of mine in particular comes to mind. Always smiling, she has a sense of herself, a confidence, really, that enables her to project a practical, realistic attitude. She seems comfortable with her kids pulling away and doesn't seem to get hurt in the process. That is who she is, though; she is practical and realistic in all her affairs and relationships, rarely succumbing to second thoughts or wavering confidence. Another friend is always lighthearted and fun to be around. Kids love her jokes and teasing. I wish I could be more like her. I notice however, her child rejects her just as mine rejects me.

We all bring to this role of parent who we are. We bring our best, and we bring our worst. Our good traits and our bad traits will show up; we can count on that. And the areas in which we aren't sure or lack

Putting it all together (cont.)

confidence—these show through in our parenting, too. If you always think you are right and have trouble seeing other people's point of view, then you are probably going to be somewhat inflexible with your children. If you suffer from a lack of confidence you may find it difficult to put your foot down and keep it there against the push back from your teenager. If you are hungry for attention you may be so "soft" with your kids that they run all over you.

You are who you are. You bring many wonderful qualities to this relationship, too. And nobody loves your children as deeply as you do.

I know I can't waver too far off base as a parent if I remain in touch with two things:

- how I want to improve myself and grow
- what kind of parent I want to be

The very traits that are our strengths become our weaknesses when they are expressed in the extreme.

We need to be intentional and thoughtful in our parenting. We need to be realistic about our strengths, motivations, shortcomings, hang ups, skills, and weaknesses so that we can make adjustments for these as we parent. And we must consciously expose ourselves to opportunities to learn and better ourselves. That may be all we can do. We won't be perfect. I won't be like my friend who doesn't stew over a nasty interchange. I am extremely sensitive, probably overly so, and while this is at times a shortcoming, it is also one of my biggest strengths. For all of us, our strengths can become our weaknesses when present in the extreme.

What have you gained from this program? Have you clarified your beliefs and can you defend your stand when your teenager challenges it? What have you learned about adolescent development that has helped you better understand your child? Can you get into her shoes now, and understand her responses? Do you feel more empowered and comfortable with your changing role?

Be reassured that much of what you are experiencing is similar to what happens in other homes.

One of the best results from participating in this program, whether you were in a discussion group or not, is the experience that you're not alone. Most parents of teenagers are going through something similar to what you are. We all benefit from one another by sharing our experiences and feelings, and learning from each other. The knowledge that you gain is what helps you smooth out your ride on this rollercoaster we call adolescence.

Putting it all together (cont.)

It is so easy for parents to feel isolated. Without the benefit of honest conversation with your peers, you may feel the issues that your family faces are unique to you. As you now know, that is probably not the case. All the experts encourage parents to talk to one another. And, it's important to be honest and to talk about both the good and the bad. Michael Riera says, "If you just focus on the good (and keep the negative silently to yourself) you'll walk away worse than ever, convinced that you really are an atrocious parent. If you only talk about the bad, you'll walk away depressed and hopeless, which isn't much better."[2] Hopefully the discussions you've had with others have provided you with a perspective on what is typical in other homes with teenagers, and have likely provided you with a better perspective on your situation.

What have you learned from this program? How has your relationship with your teenager improved? Let's review a few things so that we may see how far we've come.

Laurence Steinberg's 2004 book titled *The 10 Basic Principles of Good Parenting* offers a principle-based examination of what parents should do as we raise our children. His 10 basic principles are[3]:

1. What You Do Matters

2. You Cannot Be Too Loving

3. Be Involved in your Child's Life

4. Adapt your Parenting to Fit Your Child

5. Establish Rules and Set Limits

6. Help Foster Your Child's Independence

7. Be Consistent

8. Avoid Harsh Discipline

9. Explain Your Rules and Decisions

10. Treat your Child with Respect

Over the course of this program you have addressed all of these areas, sometimes *several* ways and in different chapters. I hope you are finding many varied ways to apply your discussions and learnings; whether you are tuning in to the importance of your child's self-esteem, finding a more appropriate level of support in his schooling, learning more about her temperament, or simply listening more without interrupting, you've undoubtedly been changed through this process. Keep it up. It's rewarding work.

Putting it all together (cont.)

The North Star helps us create a metaphor that's effective in it's message for teenagers as well as for parents. All our lives we'll need to be diligent to stay our own course, and not allow ourselves to be blown off course by outside influences. Our teens must learn to tune into their essential self, and to develop the confidence to seek their North Star.

As parents we can get off course. We will find ourselves criticized—by our kids, our relatives, our peers, the schools, the media; criticism is in no short supply. We, like our children, can get buffeted by the storm. But by staying true to your values, beliefs, and objectives you will be a great parent, and you'll do a great job. Stay tuned in. Stay engaged. Take what you've learned from this program to stay on your course as you've defined it.

And we must help our teens develop their own sense of self, their own sense of "true north." In a way, that is the developmental task of the adolescent. Our role in that couldn't be more important.

To quote Mary Pipher, "True freedom has more to do with following the North Star than with going whichever way the wind blows. Sometimes it seems like freedom is blowing with the winds of the day, but that kind of freedom is really an illusion. It turns your boat in circles. Freedom is sailing toward your dreams."[5]

I think of our kids as sailing yachts, with keels heavy and deep. They may get blown off course, and they may stray far, but they will weather the storms, no matter how severe, and always right themselves because of this deep stabilizing force. We've already helped to build those keels, and they were created by our love. Soon, we'll see our teenagers set sail.

E Young adults in their early twenties provide the following advice for parents of teenagers:
- "Do not spoil them [teens]; you're not doing them any favors."
- "Be strict with boundaries but rich in love."
- "Know what they are doing and who they are hanging out with."
- "Be consistent! Follow through on rewards and consequences."
- Don't be their friend; it's not your job."
- "Listen to them. Make them feel comfortable talking to you."

Excerpted from *Parenting Teenagers: The Agony and The Ecstasy* by Sue Blaney
Downloadable from www.PleaseStoptheRollercoaster.com

I'm glad you always let me know you love me no matter what. Don't ever change that.[6]

Doug, 16

Putting it all together (cont.)

What's the bottom line? According to *Raising Teens:A Synthesis of Research and a Foundation for Action,*[7] published by Harvard's School of Public Health, there are five areas in which parents of adolescents must focus.

E

The Five Basics of Parenting Adolescents

I. Love and Connect
Most things about their world are changing. Don't let your love be one of them.

Strategies for Parents:
- Watch for moments when you can express affection, respect, and appreciation
- Acknowledge the good times
- Expect increased criticism
- Spend time just listening
- Treat each teen as a unique individual
- Appreciate and acknowledge new areas of interest, skills, and strengths
- Spend time together

II. Monitor and Observe
Monitor your teen's activities. You still can, and it still counts.

Strategies for Parents:
- Keep track of your teen's whereabouts
- Keep in touch with other adults
- Involve yourself in school events
- Stay informed about your teen's progress
- Learn and watch for warning signs
- Seek guidance if you have concerns
- Monitor your teen's experiences
- Evaluate the level of challenge

III. Guide and Limit
Loosen up, but don't let go.

Strategies for Parents:
- Maintain family rules [with] non-negotiable rules around...safety
- Communicate expectations
- Choose battles [that are important]
- Use discipline as a tool for teaching, not for venting or taking revenge
- Restrict punishment to forms that don't cause emotional or physical injury
- Renegotiate responsibilities and privileges

(continued)

Putting it all together (cont.)

The Five Basics of Parenting Adolescents (cont.)

IV. Model and Consult
The teen years: parents still matter; teens still care.

Strategies for Parents:
- Set a good example around risk taking, health habits and emotional control
- Express personal positions about social, political, moral and spiritual issues
- Model the kind of adult relationships that you would like your teen to have
- Answer teens' questions
- Maintain or establish traditions
- Support teens' education
- Help teens get information
- Give teens opportunities

V. Provide and Advocate
You can't control their world, but you can add to and subtract from it.

Strategies for Parents:
- Network within the community
- Make informed decisions
- Arrange or advocate for preventive health care
- Identify people and programs to support and inform you

A. Rae Simpson, Ph.D., *Raising Teens: A Synthesis of Research and a Foundation for Action*, 7-11

Sarah, 16

I am not that embarrassed by you and I don't want to change you. What's kind of scary is that I will probably be the same kind of parent to my kids as you are to me.[8]

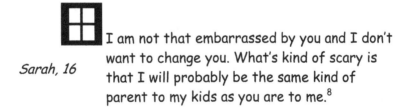

Young adults' comments are particularly helpful as they were very recently teenagers, and have clear memories. Hear what advice they have for parents by downloading our research-based report *Parenting Teenagers: The Agony and The Ecstasy* at www.PleaseStoptheRollercoaster.com

Putting it all together (cont.)

Remember a special, favorite memory from your teenage years that includes one of your parents.

Step 1: Write down how you were feeling at the time.

Step 2: Write down what you were doing.

Step 3: Write down what your parent was doing with you.

Step 4: This exercise usually highlights how simple activities facilitate connections that are meaningful. How might you create or find some opportunities with your child that can generate similar special feelings?

What would you do?

What would you do?   Truth is stranger than fiction, and here are some true stories that may curl your hair. You will probably be faced with problems and situations that will test you beyond your comfort zone. In an effort to prepare, you need to think about these, and other, real stories. Ask yourself how you would respond. Discuss it with your group members. Identify the core issues at hand, and various options for appropriate responses. There isn't just one "best" response.

E-mail Intercept
The phone rings, and you see on your caller-ID that it is a familiar name from your church. "Hello?" you say, picking up the phone. "Hello, Nora. This is Sandy Brown. This is a difficult call for me to make." Your heart sinks. You know this is not a good way for a telephone call to begin.

"I don't know your son well, and I don't believe our boys hang out together at all." (They don't, as far as you know.) Sandy goes on to tell you that she occasionally monitors her seventh grade son's e-mail account without him knowing. She and her husband have been shocked to see some nasty and filthy messages going around among many kids in the class. Most of the kids were using code names so they were not able to discern who was involved. But they were getting increasingly concerned as the messages became more and more graphic and violent with some frightening remarks about "hitting on" a particular boy after school this Friday. Finally some real names came out in the communication. It seems one of the boys involved in the plans is your son!

What would you do?

The Pool Party
It's a lovely summer evening and Sharon's son, Jason, had a group of friends over for a cookout and pool party. This group of friends spends a lot of time at Jason's home, which is just as Sharon likes it. When they installed the pool, part of their intent was so that their children, and the children's friends, would want to spend time at their home. She keeps better tabs on things that way.

This particular evening Sharon's husband was not at home, so she had manned the grill, cooking hamburgers and hot dogs for this group of twelve soon-to-be high school sophomores, kids she considered friends of hers, as well as friends of her son. After she had cleaned up the kitchen and the kids were out swimming in the pool, she headed up to her bedroom to change her clothes. It was beginning to get dark, and something made her look out the window toward the pool. What she saw shocked her. Two girls were standing on the end of the diving board minus their bathing suit tops. And two boys were standing at the opposite end of the pool with nothing on at all!

What would you do?

What would you do? (cont.)

Bagged by the Pipe

Danielle, a high school sophomore, was settling in to a good year. She had her academics in good shape, she could be counted upon to make the honor roll, and her Math teacher had called to say that she had received the highest grade in the class on a major exam. Her friends were lively, athletic, and studious. Her parents thought all was going well.

One of her friends, Lauren, had just moved to town at the beginning of this year. Danielle's mom, Nancy, who took pride in reading people intuitively, instinctively liked Lauren. When Lauren's mom asked if Lauren might spend 5 days with them so she could join her husband on a business trip to San Francisco, there was no hesitation. "Of course!" Nancy said. "I'm so glad you asked us! This will be fun!" So it was arranged.

School and soccer practice kept the girls busy the first couple of days. The weekend was full of events with a scrimmage on Saturday morning, shopping in the afternoon, and a party at a friend's home Saturday night. Nancy and her husband had hesitated to make plans for themselves, thinking they needed to provide dinner for the girls, but they found out that the girls planned on eating at a friend's home anyway, so once the girls were gone the adults settled in to watch a movie. The girls had an eleven o'clock curfew, and it had been arranged that another friend's dad would drop off both Danielle and Lauren. At 11:00 Nancy was in bed already, struggling to stay awake; her husband was gently snoring. Once the girls came and checked in with her she immediately fell asleep.

An early riser, Nancy was the first person downstairs in the morning. She sat to read the paper with her cup of coffee and noticed a chair in the family room oddly out of position. Walking over to straighten it, she noticed an ashtray on the table. She hadn't had an ashtray in her home in years! Upon closer inspection she got a feeling in her stomach that something was very wrong. The ashes looked odd, and they smelled particularly strong. Then she noticed a small glass pipe that was sticking out from under the chair. It was marijuana! Someone had been smoking drugs here in her home! She was dumbstruck!

She waited until the girls got up. As she came down the stairs, Danielle found herself faced with a big frown on her Mom's face. "Do you recognize this?" she was asked as her mom held up the glass pipe. "How did Mom find that?" she asked herself. "Oh, man," she thought, "I'm bagged."

"Yes, Mom. We used it last night when we got home."

What would you do?

What would you do? (cont.)

Rumors and Sex

Mary's eighth-grade daughter was starting to enjoy an active social life--group trips to the movies, pool parties, sleepovers, and an occasional party on a weekend night. She was happy that her daughter seemed well-adjusted and had many friends. The outings usually included boys and girls, and the kids seem to get along well mixing together in one large group.

At a school meeting one evening with other parents, Mary heard a group of them saying that some kids in this grade were engaging in oral sex at parties. She was shocked! It was incomprehensible to her that her daughter might be exposed to, or engaging in, such behavior. But, to make matters worse, she learned that many of the parties she had been told were supervised were actually un-chaperoned.

Although she thought she trusted her daughter and thought they had relatively open communication, the sudden realization that her daughter had lied on several occasions about the unsupervised parties put everything into a new perspective.

What would you do?

Making the Grade

Tom's grades came in for the third term of his freshman year. His parents were shocked to see that the grades had dropped significantly in all of his classes. They confronted him, and his hostility made conversation impossible.

Not knowing what to do, they made contact with his counselor at school. The counselor checked in with all of Tom's teachers and the word they got back was not good. Tom had stopped turning in homework regularly and was occasionally cutting classes. His mom began thinking back and realized that Tom had been spending an inordinate amount of time in his room and in front of the tube. He hadn't been out with friends in over a month, and the telephone rarely rang. Wishing she had tuned in to this earlier, she wondered with panic in her belly, "Is this what depression looks like?"

Her response to Tom changed from anger and blame to one of concern about what was going on. But that didn't change his demeanor toward her. He was withdrawn, sullen, and would not share what was going on inside of him.

What would you do?

What would you do? (cont.)

Copy Cat

Sally's son James was in his junior year and seemed to be enjoying his classes and doing well. He made good grades and still made time for several after school activities including working on the yearbook, and playing on the basketball and baseball teams. He seemed happy and well-adjusted with his friends and teachers.

In the spring of James' junior year, Sally received a call from his English teacher. He told her that James had plagiarized a paper he had handed in earlier in the week by researching on the Internet and copying more than half of his paper from the Internet source. He told Sally that as a result of this plagiarism, James will have a permanent note in his academic record and an "F" for the term in English class. Sally was furious when she hung up the phone.

What would you do?

Overdue

Pat was enjoying her mid-afternoon cup of tea as she was catching up on reading one of her magazines. Her daughter Julie, a sophomore, was upstairs getting changed and visiting with her best friend Stephanie, who had come home from school with her. Pat looked up as the girls came into the kitchen, happy to have them around. But they looked serious, and her sixth sense was awakened.

The girls sat down with her and Julie asked if they could talk. She said that Stephanie needed someone to talk to. Pat looked at her face closely and realized that Stephanie was just barely containing tears. Stephanie was terrified. She told Pat that her boyfriend had been pressuring her to have sex with him for about three months, and that she had finally given in. She didn't really like it, and she didn't feel good about doing it, but he seemed pleased with her and that meant something to her. Now, however, in addition to her feelings of confusion about this new activity, her period was one week overdue. She wanted Pat to help her figure out what to do.

What would you do?

What would you do? (cont.)

A Midnight Rendezvous

Mike's mother, Lorraine, had made it a point to get to know as many of her son's friends as possible. It wasn't easy, as he did not invite them over often. But when the opportunity would arise she tried to get to know them without making herself overbearing, or making Mike uncomfortable. Some kids were more responsive to her than others. She particularly enjoyed one girl, Kristin, who was warm, friendly, and always willing to spend a little extra time in the kitchen talking with her. Mike's girlfriend, Laura, was elusive and difficult to reach.

Lorraine learned from comments from Mike and others that Kristin's parents were particularly restrictive. Lorraine had met Kristin's dad at her door when she had been dropped off, but she had never met Kristin's mom.

Lorraine was rather pleased with Mike's choice of friends. They appeared to be a lively group of good students, and kids with good values. They were late in their freshman year when the following incident took place.

Mike had asked on Monday after school if Jake, one of the boys in the group, could sleep over on Friday evening. Lorraine said, "Sure." She did note that it was the first time Mike had had a sleepover all year, and she also noted that of all the boys in the group, Jake had struck her as the one least like Mike. But she didn't think about it any further than that. She was glad that he wanted to have a friend over, and her philosophy was "the more close friends for her son the better."

Friday evening came and the boys had a pleasant dinner with Lorraine and her husband. After dinner they all went out for ice cream. The boys seemed content to hang out, and they had rented a couple of movies for later in the evening. About 10:30 Lorraine said goodnight, and shortly thereafter Mike's dad retired as well. The boys were planning to "camp out" in the playroom, which was the preferred mode for entertaining friends.

About 12:30 am the phone rang. "This is Officer Campbell at the Police Station. We have your son Mike here with us. He has been arrested for transportation of a controlled substance."

In shock, Lorraine and her husband went to the police station to find Mike and Jake trembling. The story was hard for them to believe. Obviously this had been planned for the whole week. Jake works at a convenience store that sells beer and wine. He had stolen several six packs of beer and brought them with him to Mike's home. After midnight the boys had left Mike's home to cross town on foot to meet with Mike's girlfriend, Laura, and Kristin. The girls had prearranged to spend the night at Laura's house, and were planning to sneak out to meet the boys at 1:00 am. The boys never made it to the meeting place; a policeman stopped them

What would you do? (cont.)

early in their trip. The boys, who had consumed no alcohol yet, were arrested and were to appear in front of a judge on Monday morning.

The next morning Lorraine and her husband discussed the appropriate punishment for Mike.

What would you do?

Another problem for Lorraine was how, and if, she should address the girls involved. Should she call them? Should she call their parents? Should they be dragged into this mess? Knowing that Kristin's parents were reputed to be harsh and punitive made this issue particularly challenging for Lorraine.

What would you do?

Rescue

Your high school sophomore, Sara, is at a party with her friends. This time you did not call the parents to confirm their presence—you took your daughter's word for it. You know the kids she is going to the party with, and you had met the family where the party is taking place; they seemed nice.

Curfew is at midnight; you stay up watching TV, to wait until she gets home.

The phone startles you at 11:50. Answering it, you hear Sara's anxious, breathless voice at the end of the line. "Mom," she whispers into the phone. "Please come get me. I'm at the Store 24. I'll be waiting outside." Panicked, you say, "Are you all right? Are you hurt? " "No, Mom. I'm OK. But remember when you told me you'd come and get me anytime, no questions asked? Well, this is that time."

When you get there she is standing in the shadows across from the store. You watch her as she limps to your car. Her jeans are ripped, she is wearing only one shoe, her hair is in her face, and you see a little dried blood on her cheek next to a sizable scratch.

You don't know if you can contain yourself, but she's right. You promised "no questions" if she ever needed rescuing.

What would you do?

Putting it all together (cont.)

My grandmother lived to be 100 years old. When I think of what her life was like it gives me a very different sense of time. She was born years before electricity would come to her central Maine home, and before cars existed. She raised a child struck with polio in his adolescence, lost her husband to a brain tumor when barely fifty, with a young child still to raise. If I have hardships, they look like nothing compared to hers.

The years when we are living with adolescents are relatively short. We'll be through this phase, and on to another one before we know it. Soon enough, our days of child-rearing will be behind us entirely, and we'll move into another new and exciting stage. Perhaps our careers will still be growing, and changing. We have many new skills to learn yet in front of us, many new experiences to enjoy. Maybe we'll even have the chance to be involved in raising another generation of children, this time from the perspective of a grandparent.

The opportunity we've taken in this process to examine, to discuss, to dissect even, our relationship with our teenager and our role as parent, has caused us to learn a lot more about adolescents, and about who we are and who we want to be. Reading the words of the many experts in this field gives us a tremendous amount of knowledge and perspective, and you will want to read many of the books in their entirety.

But reading alone isn't enough. In fact, reading alone doesn't give you a very high rate of retention—only about 10% of the material you've read is likely to be retained after 30 days.[9] If you discuss the material, the rate of retention increases to 50%. That's quite a difference. But it's when you put what you learn into action that you not only retain what you've learned (to a level of 75%), but more importantly, *you can see the changes you want to see.* You are the one who must act; as much as you may like to make your teenager act in a certain way you have little control over that. You do have 100% control over the actions you take, however. And through your actions you affect everyone around you.

In the next few pages you are going to put a plan together that will help you put into action what you've learned in this program*. You will give yourself advice, you will remind yourself of things that are important and relevant, and you will set some goals. I suggest you page through your entire book in preparation. Review the exercises that you've written. Pay particular attention to your "take-aways" at the end of each chapter. Give yourself some good reflective time to prepare this plan, and you will have a tool from which you can create the changes you wish to see.

*Some people like to share their plans with their family. As a result of parent requests, we've created an abbreviated one-page format for your Parenting Plan that you can post on your refrigerator, if you desire. It is downloadable from the *Tools for Groups* section of our Web site at www.PleaseStopTheRollercoaster.com.

My Parenting Plan

Adolescent Development (Chapter 1)

You've identified that some specific behaviors your child exhibits are a result of his/her developmental stage.

> ***Write advice to yourself on what you need to remember about this stage and how you want to support your teenager.***

Example: I must remember that her behavior doesn't always show how she is truly feeling, and it may be a mask. I also must be more understanding of her "black and white" view of the world.

Your Role as Parent (Chapter 2)

In Session 2 we examined 3 models for parenting:

- Mentorship
- Parenting levels
- The Authoritative Parenting model

> ***Write yourself two points to remember.***

Examples: 1) As a mentor, I must remember to let my child take ultimate responsibility for her outcomes. 2) In Level 4 parenting we are both growing. I must be aware that our relationship is evolving and I must learn to express my needs in this relationship. 3) Being strict is a positive, not a negative thing, as long as I continue to express my love.

My Teenager's Social Life (Chapter 4)

What can you do to become more tuned in to your teenager's friends and social life?

> ***Set two goals for yourself. Be specific.***

Examples:

Goal #1—I will encourage Jack to have his friends over to our home once a month.

Goal #2—I will meet Carolyn's mom for lunch next week to get to know her.

My Parenting Plan

Adolescent Development: *advice to myself*

_____

_____

_____

_____

Your Role as Parent: *two points to remember*

1) _____

_____

2) _____

_____

My Teenager's Social Life: *two goals*

1) _____

_____

2) _____

_____

My Parenting Plan

Communication (Chapters 3 and 5)

This important topic was covered in several chapters. Reexamine the guidelines you wrote for yourself on page 75. Now that you've practiced Active Listening and other strategies, let's reconsider them.

> ### *Update your guidelines and write them as advice to yourself.*

Example: Remember to listen first and get the whole story BEFORE I react.

Revisit the recommendations on communicating to the various personality types on page 152.

> ### *Based on your teenager's profile, write notes to improve your communication by choosing one point from each section.*

Example: If your child's profile is INTJ, pick one point from each section on page 152.

Risk Behavior (Chapter 4)

What is your stand on teenage alcohol consumption and drug use?

> ### *Articulate it here.*

Example: When my child graduates from high school I will consider offering beer and wine to him for consumption here at home.

School (Chapter 6)

Are you involved? If not, what are you going to do to increase or decrease your involvement so it fits the balance you desire?

> ### *What is the name of your child's counselor at school? Set a goal for yourself to find an appropriate level of involvement in your child's school and schoolwork.*

My Parenting Plan

Communication:

Updated guidelines:

1) _____

_____

2) _____

_____

My teenager's Personality Type Profile: _____ _____ _____ _____

When communicating with him/her, I will do the following: (from 152)

1)

2)

3)

4)

Risk Behavior:

_____

_____

_____

School:

Counselor's name: _____

My goal for involvement: _____

_____

_____

Reflections

We have talked a lot about parenting in this program. For me, being a parent is the most cherished and valued role in my life. It's more than a role for me, actually; it is part of my identity. It has changed me in ways I never could have foreseen. And I'm sure it has made me a better person. The story that follows profoundly captures the essence of motherhood, and I imagine fathers will share many of these same feelings. My thanks to its author, Dale Hanson Bourke for sharing this very special story.

E Time is running out for my friend. We are sitting at lunch when she casually mentions that she and her husband are thinking of "starting a family." What that means is that her biological clock has begun its countdown and she is forced to consider the prospect of motherhood.

"We're taking a survey," she says, half-joking. "Do you think I should have a baby?"

"It will change your life," I say carefully, keeping my tone neutral.

"I know," she says, "no more sleeping on weekends, no more spontaneous vacations..."

But that is not what I meant at all. I look at my friend, trying to decide what to tell her.

I want her to know what she will never learn in childbirth classes. I want to tell her that the physical wounds of child bearing will heal, but that becoming a mother will leave her with an emotional wound so raw that she will forever be vulnerable.

I consider warning her that she will never again read a newspaper without asking "What if that had been my child?" That every plane crash, every fire will haunt her. That when she sees pictures of starving children, she will wonder if anything could be worse than watching your child die.

I look at her carefully manicured nails and stylish suit and think that no matter how sophisticated she is, becoming a mother will reduce her to the primitive level of a she-bear protecting her cub. That an urgent call of "Mom!" will cause her to drop a soufflé or her best crystal without a moment's hesitation...

I feel I should warn her that no matter how many years she has invested in her career, she will be professionally derailed by motherhood. She might successfully arrange for childcare, but one day she will be waiting to go into an important business meeting and she will think about her baby's sweet smell. She will have to use every ounce of discipline to keep from running home, just to make sure he is all right.

I want my friend to know that routine decisions will no longer be routine. That a visit to McDonald's and a five-year-old boy's understandable desire to go to the men's room rather than the women's will become a major dilemma. That right there, in the midst of clattering trays and screaming children, issues of independence and gender identity will be weighed against the prospect that a child molester may be lurking in the restroom. I want her to know that however decisive she may be at the office, she will second guess herself constantly as a mother.

Looking at my attractive friend, I want to assure her that eventually she will shed the pounds of

Reflections (cont.)

E pregnancy, but she will never feel the same about herself. That her life, now so important, will be of less value to her once she has a child. That she would give it up in a moment to save her offspring, but will also begin to hope for more years—not to accomplish her own dreams, but to watch her child accomplish his. I want her to know that a cesarean scar or shiny stretch marks will become badges of honor.

My friend's relationship with her husband will change, I know; but not in the way she thinks. I wish she could understand how much more you can love a man who is careful to always powder the baby or who never hesitates to play "bad guys" with his son. I think she should know that she will fall in love with her husband again for reasons she would now find very unromantic.

I wish my modern friend could sense the bond she will feel with women throughout history who have tried desperately to stop war and prejudice and drunk driving. I hope she will understand why I can think rationally about most issues, but become temporarily insane when I discuss the threat of nuclear war to my children's future.

I want to describe to my friend the exhilaration of seeing your son learn to hit a baseball. I want to capture for her the belly laugh of a baby who is touching the soft fur of a dog for the first time. I want her to taste the joy that is so real that it hurts.

My friend's quizzical look makes me realize that tears have formed in my eyes. "You'll never regret it," I say finally. Then I reach across the table, and squeezing my friend's hand, I offer a prayer for her and me and all of the mere mortal women who stumble their way into this holiest of callings.

Dale Hanson Bourke, *Everyday Miracles; Holy Moments in a Mother's Day*, 1

Congratulations! You've come to the end of a program that hopefully has helped you smooth out your ride as your teenager maneuvers through adolescence. Appreciate the effort you've taken to complete the reading and the exercises in this book. Your efforts will pay dividends in the most rewarding area of your life.

How are you different now than when you began? Have the dynamics in your household changed? Have you developed any new friends? What have you learned? What stands out for you as highlights from this program and experience? Whether you've elected to join a parenting discussion group or to participate in discussions in a less formal way, I hope that you have gained and learned from the input from others.

You may find that issues that were addressed through this program merit addressing again in a year or so, when your teenager is in a different place developmentally. I've been amazed at how much information I forget over time, and how points that don't seem important one day are incredibly relevant at another time. You'll enjoy reading through your notes and reflective exercises in a few months, and I encourage you to visit these pages often.

Now—Celebrate! You've done a great thing.

ISSUES TO EXAMINE AND DISCUSS

Refer to

1.   Find someone and discuss the scenarios in the "What would you do?" section. Create possible responses for each story and discuss the benefits and drawback of each one.

235-240

2.   Once you've made your *Parenting Plan* share it with a friend, spouse, someone in your group if you have one...or with your teenager. Make a commitment to keep to your goals, recommendations, and advice.

242-245

3.   If you have been in a group, discuss how you might want to continue to provide support to one another. Here are some suggestions: You could agree to arrange a meeting in a couple months, at the beginning of the next school year, or you could meet socially for a cup of coffee or a glass of wine. Perhaps you'll want to share e-mail addresses and keep in touch that way.

-

When you meet in the future you can revisit this book, review some of the most significant points, and touch base on your results with your Parenting Plan.

In the meantime, help each other be aware of local lectures and books that you would recommend.

How else might you support one another?   Discuss and agree on next steps.

4.   Visit our Web site for updates, information, and to receive our e-mail newsletter. Also, please let me hear about your results, thoughts, and comments about this program. Contact me at www.PleaseStoptheRollercoaster.com.

ChangeWorks Publishing & Consulting
P.O. Box 3085
Acton, MA 01720-7085

www.PleaseStopTheRollercoaster.com

ZITS

Appendix

Personal Style Inventory (for use in Chapter 5)

Instructions

The following items are arranged in pairs (a and b), and each member of the pair represents a preference you may or may not hold. Rate your preference for each item by giving it a score of 0 to 5. 0 means you strongly dislike the choice; 5 means you strongly prefer the choice. The scores for a + b MUST ADD UP TO 5. Use 4 and 1 or 3 and 2 if you feel less strongly, *do not use fractions such as 2 1/2.*

Generally,

1a. _____ I make decisions after finding out what others think.

1b. _____ I make decisions without consulting others.

2a. _____ I prefer being called imaginative or intuitive.

2b. _____ I prefer being called factual and accurate.

3a. _____ I make decisions about people based on available data and systematic analysis of situations.

3b. _____ I make decisions about people based on empathy, feelings, and understanding of their needs and values.

4a. _____ I allow commitments to occur if others want to make them.

4b. _____ I push for definite commitments to ensure they are made.

5a. _____ I am quiet, thoughtful, and like time alone.

5b. _____ I am active, energetic, and like other people around me.

6a. _____ I prefer using methods I know will get the job done.

6b. _____ I prefer to think of new methods to do tasks.

7a. _____ I draw conclusions based on unemotional and careful step-by-step analysis.

7b. _____ I draw conclusions based on what I feel and believe based on past experience.

8a. _____ I avoid making deadlines.

8b. _____ I set a schedule and stick to it.

9a. _____ I have inner thoughts and feelings that others don't see.

9b. _____ I prefer activities that involve others along with me.

10a. _____ I prefer the abstract or theoretical.

10b. _____ I prefer the concrete or real.

Personal Style Inventory (cont.)

Generally,

11a. _____ I like to help others explore their feelings.

11b. _____ I like to help others make logical decisions.

12a. _____ I communicate little about my inner feelings and thinking.

12b. _____ I communicate my inner thoughts and feelings freely.

13a. _____ I plan ahead.

13b. _____ I prefer to "wing it" at the last minute.

14a. _____ I like to meet new people.

14b. _____ I like to be alone or with one person.

15a. _____ I like ideas.

15b. _____ I like facts.

16a. _____ I prefer convictions based on personal thoughts.

16b. _____ I prefer verifiable conclusions based on facts.

17a. _____ I use appointment books and notes to myself as much as necessary.

17b. _____ I do not use appointment books or notes except when I must.

18a. _____ I am precise and lay out a detailed plan of action.

18b. _____ I like to design plans but do not feel I have to carry them out.

19a. _____ I prefer to do things on the spur of the moment.

19b. _____ I like to know in advance what I am expected to do.

20a. _____ I prefer emotional situations, discussion, and movies.

20b. _____ I prefer analytical situations where I can use my ability.

Source: "Personal Style Inventory," Jewler and Gardner, 1993, p. 51-56. Available online: <http://mets.maine.edu/life/personindic02.html>

Personal Style Inventory (cont.)

Scoring instructions

Transfer your scores for each item of each pair to the appropriate blanks. **Check the a and b letters to be sure you are recording scores in the right blank spaces**. Add up each column. The total of each *pair* of columns must equal 25.

E	I
1a.	1b.
5b.	5a.
9b.	9a.
12b.	12a.
14a.	14b.
E Total:	I Total:

S	N
2b.	2a.
6a.	6b.
10b.	10a.
15b.	15a.
18a.	18b.
S Total:	N Total:

T	F
3a.	3b.
7a.	7b.
11b.	11a.
16b.	16a.
20b.	20a.
T Total:	F Total:

J	P
4b.	4a.
8b.	8a.
13a.	13b.
17a.	17b.
19b.	19a.
J Total:	P Total:

Source: Muskingum College: http://muskingum.edu/~cal/database/PSIscore.html. Available online: <http://mets.maine.edu/life/personindic02.html>

Personal Style Inventory (for use in Chapter 5)

(This second copy is provided for your convenience. Use with scoring sheet on page 259.)

Instructions
The following items are arranged in pairs (a and b), and each member of the pair represents a preference you may or may not hold. Rate your preference for each item by giving it a score of 0 to 5. 0 means you strongly dislike the choice; 5 means you strongly prefer the choice. The scores for a + b MUST ADD UP TO 5. Use 4 and 1 or 3 and 2 if you feel less strongly, *do not use fractions such as 2 1/2.*

Generally,

1a. _____ I make decisions after finding out what others think.

1b. _____ I make decisions without consulting others.

2a. _____ I prefer being called imaginative or intuitive.

2b. _____ I prefer being called factual and accurate.

3a. _____ I make decisions about people based on available data and systematic analysis of situations.

3b. _____ I make decisions about people based on empathy, feelings, and understanding of their needs and values.

4a. _____ I allow commitments to occur if others want to make them.

4b. _____ I push for definite commitments to ensure they are made.

5a. _____ I am quiet, thoughtful, and like time alone.

5b. _____ I am active, energetic, and like other people around me.

6a. _____ I prefer using methods I know will get the job done.

6b. _____ I prefer to think of new methods to do tasks.

7a. _____ I draw conclusions based on unemotional and careful step-by-step analysis.

7b. _____ I draw conclusions based on what I feel and believe based on past experience.

8a. _____ I avoid making deadlines.

8b. _____ I set a schedule and stick to it.

9a. _____ I have inner thoughts and feelings that others don't see.

9b. _____ I prefer activities that involve others along with me.

10a. _____ I prefer the abstract or theoretical.

10b. _____ I prefer the concrete or real.

Personal Style Inventory (cont.)

Generally,

11a. _____ I like to help others explore their feelings.

11b. _____ I like to help others make logical decisions.

12a. _____ I communicate little about my inner feelings and thinking.

12b. _____ I communicate my inner thoughts and feelings freely.

13a. _____ I plan ahead.

13b. _____ I prefer to "wing it" at the last minute.

14a. _____ I like to meet new people.

14b. _____ I like to be alone or with one person.

15a. _____ I like ideas.

15b. _____ I like facts.

16a. _____ I prefer convictions based on personal thoughts.

16b. _____ I prefer verifiable conclusions based on facts.

17a. _____ I use appointment books and notes to myself as much as necessary.

17b. _____ I do not use appointment books or notes except when I must.

18a. _____ I am precise and lay out a detailed plan of action.

18b. _____ I like to design plans but do not feel I have to carry them out.

19a. _____ I prefer to do things on the spur of the moment.

19b. _____ I like to know in advance what I am expected to do.

20a. _____ I prefer emotional situations, discussion, and movies.

20b. _____ I prefer analytical situations where I can use my ability.

Source: "Personal Style Inventory," Jewler and Gardner, 1993, p. 51-56. Available online: <http://mets.maine.edu/life/personindic02.html>

Personal Style Inventory (cont.)

Scoring instructions

Transfer your scores for each item of each pair to the appropriate blanks. **Check the a and b letters to be sure you are recording scores in the right blank spaces**. Add up each column. The total of each *pair* of columns must equal 25.

E	I
1a.	1b.
5b.	5a.
9b.	9a.
12b.	12a.
14a.	14b.
E Total:	I Total:

S	N
2b.	2a.
6a.	6b.
10b.	10a.
15b.	15a.
18a.	18b.
S Total:	N Total:

T	F
3a.	3b.
7a.	7b.
11b.	11a.
16b.	16a.
20b.	20a.
T Total:	F Total:

J	P
4b.	4a.
8b.	8a.
13a.	13b.
17a.	17b.
19b.	19a.
J Total:	P Total:

Source: Muskingum College: http://muskingum.edu/~cal/database/PSIscore.html. Available online: <http://mets.maine.edu/life/personindic02.html>

Endnotes
Chapter One: Adolescent Development

[1]Robert Brooks, Ph.D. and Sam Goldstein, Ph.D., *Raising Resilient Children* (Chicago: Contemporary Books, 2001), 1.

[2] Brooks, and Goldstein, 7.

[3]Michael Riera, *Uncommon Sense for Parents with Teenagers* (Berkeley: Celestial Arts, 1995), 35.

[4]Ava Siegler, Ph.D., *The Essential Guide to the New Adolescence: How to Raise an Emotionally Healthy Teenager* (New York: Penguin Group, 1997), 16, 18.

[5]Siegler, 16, 19-20.

[6]Siegler, 16, 28.

[7]Siegler, 16, 28.

[8]Siegler, 16, 17.

[9]Riera, 11.

[10]Anne Moir and David Jessel, *Brain Sex...the Real Difference Between Men and Women* (New York: Dell Publishing, 1992), 36.

[11]Mary Pipher, Ph.D., *Reviving Ophelia: Saving the Selves of Adolescent Girls* (New York: Ballantine Books, 1994), 59.

[12]Pipher, 60.

[13]Pipher, 60.

[14]Riera, 14.

[15]J. S. Salt, *Always Accept Me for Who I Am: Instructions from Teenagers on Raising the Perfect Parent, by 147 Teens Who Know* (New York: Three Rivers Press, 1999), 117.

[16]Riera, 60.

[17]Riera, 60.

[18]Riera, 60.

[19]Riera, 60.

[20]Anthony Wolf, *Get Out of My Life but First Could You Drive Me and Cheryl to the Mall?* (New York: Farrar Straus and Giroux, 1991), 16.

[21]Salt, 61.

[22] "Reflection," Music by Matthew Wilder, Lyrics by David Zippel, Walt Disney Music Company, 1998.

[23] John Mayer, "83," from *Room for Squares,* Sony Music Entertainment Inc., 2001.

[24] The Dave Matthews Band, "Dancing Nancies," from *Under the Table and Dreaming,* December 2001, http://www.lyrics.com.

[25] Asher, *"Choices,"* from *Neptune's Satori,* 2006, http://www.asherssatori.com

[26] Pipher, 38.

[27] Pipher, 37.

[28] Pipher, 61.

[29] Pipher, 54.

[30] Kalergis, Mary Motley, *Seen and Heard: Teenagers Talk About Their Lives,* (New York: Stewart, Tabori & Chang, 1998), 61.

[31] Salt, 17.

[32] Wolf, 82.

[33] Wolf, 80.

[34] Siegler, 21.

[35] Riera, 2.

Chapter Two: Parenting: Our Changing Roles and Relationships

[1] Wolf, *Get Out of My Life but First Could You Drive Me and Cheryl to the Mall? ,* 60.

[2] Wolf, 4-6.

[3] Patricia Hersch, *A Tribe Apart: A Journey into the Heart of American Adolescence* (New York: Ballantine Books, 1998), 19, 23.

[4] J. S. Salt, *Always Accept Me for Who I Am: Instructions from Teenagers on Raising the Perfect Parent, by 147 Teens Who Know* (New York: Three Rivers Press, 1999), 127.

[5] William Bridges and Associates, "Leading Organizational Transition," *Facilitators Guide,* 1999.

[6] Salt, 21.

[7] Families First Former Executive Director Linda Braun. Families First is a non–profit organization located in Cambridge, MA.

[8]Carolyn Moore Newberger, "The Cognitive Structure of Parenthood: Designing a Descriptive Measure," *New Direction for Child Development, 7,* 1980.

[9]Laurence Steinberg, *Crossing Paths: How Your Child's Adolescence Triggers Your Own Crisis* (New York: Simon & Schuster, 1994), 19.

[10]Laurence Steinberg, *Beyond the Classroom: Why School Reform Has Failed and What Parents Need to Do* (New York: Simon and Schuster, 1996), 108.

[11]A. Rae Simpson, Ph.D., *Raising Teens: A Synthesis of Research and a Foundation for Action* (Boston: Center for Health Communication, Harvard School of Public Health, 2001), 42.

[12]Steinberg, *Beyond the Classroom,* 111-114.

[13] Steinberg, *Beyond the Classroom,* 187.

[13]Steinberg, *Beyond the Classroom,* 187.

[14]Steinberg, *Beyond the Classroom,* 130.

[15]William Pollack, *Real Boys* (New York: Henry Holt and Company, 1998), 102.

[16]Eli Newberger, MD. *The Men They Will Become* (Reading, MA: Perseus Books, 1999), 31.

[17]Pollack, 119-121.

[18]Pollack, 119-121.

[19]Roni Cohen-Sandler and Michelle Silver, *"I'm not mad, I just hate you!"* (New York: Penguin Books, 1999), 13-14.

[20]Cohen-Sandler and Silver, 16.

[21]Cohen-Sandler and Silver, 17.

[22]Nancy Snyderman and Peg Streep, *Girl in the Mirror: Mothers and Daughters in the Years of Adolescence* (New York: Hyperion, 2002), 31,34.

[23]Terri Apter, *Altered Loves* (New York: St. Martin's Press), 16.

[24]Joe Kelly, *Dads and Daughters* (New York: Broadway Books, 2002), 9.

[25]Kelly, 29.

[26]Wolf, 34.

Chapter Three: Improving Communication

[1]Simpson, *Raising Teens: A Synthesis of Research and a Foundation for Action,* 41.

[2]Salt, *Always Accept Me for Who I Am: Instructions from Teenagers on Raising the Perfect Parent, by 147 Teens Who Know,* 48.

[3]Robert K. Cooper, *The Other 90%: How to Unlock Your Vast Untapped Potential for Leadership and Life* (New York: Crown Business, 2001), 49.

[4]Dr. Thomas Gordon, *P.E.T. Parent Effectiveness Training: The Tested New Way to Raise Responsible Children* (New York: Plume, Penguin Books, 1970), 41-44.

[5]Brooks and Goldstein, *Raising Resilient Children,* 41-46.

[6]Jan Lewis, "Learn to Listen," www.ifas.ufl.edu, June 1997.

[7]Madelyn Burley-Allen, *Listening: The Forgotten Skill* (New York: John Wiley & Sons, 1995), 14.

[8]Stephen Covey, *The 7 Habits of Highly Effective Families* (New York: Golden Books, 1997), 201-243.

[9]Covey, 45-61.

[10]Salt, 58.

[11]Waybridge Associates, Nashua N.H.

[12]Mira Kirshenbaum and Charles Foster, *Parent/Teen Breakthrough: The Relationship Approach* (New York: Penguin Books, 1991), 37.

[13]Kirshenbaum and Foster, 8.

[14]Thomas Mattera, Highland Consulting, Sudbury, MA.

[15]Cooper, 23.

[16]Salt, 51.

[17]Wolf, *Get Out of My Life but First Could You Drive Me and Cheryl to the Mall? ,* 96.

[18]Riera, *Uncommon Sense for Parents with Teenagers,* 78.

[19]Riera, 82.

[20]Siegler,*The Essential Guide to the New Adolescence: How to Raise an Emotionally Healthy Teenager,* 93.

[21]Wolf, 62.

Chapter 4: Friends, Culture, and Risk Behavior

[1]Riera, *Uncommon Sense for Parents with Teenagers*, 21.

[2]Salt, *Always Accept Me for Who I Am: Instructions from Teenagers on Raising the Perfect Parent, by 147 Teens Who Know*, 84.

[3]Newberger, *The Men They Will Become*, 62.

[4]Steinberg, *Beyond the Classroom: Why School Reform has Failed and What Parents Need to Do*, 41.

[5]Riera, 22.

[6]Steinberg, *Beyond the Classroom*, 138-141.

[7]Steinberg, *Beyond the Classroom*, 41.

[8]The National Center on Addiction and Substance Abuse at Columbia University, *National Survey of American Attitudes on Substance Abuse XII: Teens and Parents*, August 2007, http://www.Casacolumbia.org.

[9]Steinberg, *Beyond the Classroom*, 148.

[10]Steinberg, *Beyond the Classroom*, 148.

[11]Hersch, 212.

[12]Pipher, *Reviving Ophelia: Saving the Selves of Adolescent Girls*, 44.

[13]Simmons, Rachel, *Odd Girl Out*, (New York: Harcourt, Inc.), 3.

[14]Simmons, *Odd Girl Out*, 3.

[15]Kelly, Joe, *Dads and Daughters* (New York: Broadway Books, 2001), 83.

[16]Pollack, *Real Boys*, xxii.

[17]"The Boys Are All Right," *TIME*, 6 August, 2007, 44.

[18]"The Boys Are All Right," *TIME*, 6 August, 2007, 47.

[19]Howe, Neil and Strauss, William, *Millennials Rising: the Next Great Generation*, (New York: Vintage Books), 8,9.

[20]Ralph J. DiClemente; Gina M. Wingood; Richard Crosby; Catlainn Sionean; Brenda K. Cobb; Kathy Harrington; Susan Davies; Edward W. Hook; M. Kim Oh; "Parental Monitoring: Association With Adolescents' Risk Behaviors," *Pediatrics*, June 2001: 1363.

[21]The National Center on Addiction and Substance Abuse at Columbia University, *National Survey of American Attitudes on Substance Abuse XII: Teens and Parents*, August 2007, http://www.Casacolumbia.org.

[22]The National Center on Addiction and Substance Abuse at Columbia University, *National Survey of American Attitudes on Substance Abuse XII: Teens and Parents,* August 2007, http://www.Casacolumbia.org.

[23]The National Center on Addiction and Substance Abuse at Columbia University, *National Survey of American Attitudes on Substance Abuse XII: Teens and Parents,* August 2007, http://www.Casacolumbia.org.

[24]The National Center on Addiction and Substance Abuse at Columbia University, *National Survey of American Attitudes on Substance Abuse XII: Teens and Parents,* August 2007, http://www.Casacolumbia.org.

[25]Salt, 81.

[26]Salt, 73.

[27]Salt, 96.

[28]The National Center on Addiction and Substance Abuse at Columbia University, *National Survey of American Attitudes on Substance Abuse XII: Teens and Parents,* August 2007, http://www.Casacolumbia.org.

[29]The National Center on Addiction and Substance Abuse at Columbia University, *National Survey of American Attitudes on Substance Abuse XII: Teens and Parents,* August 2007, http://www.Casacolumbia.org.

[30]The National Center on Addiction and Substance Abuse at Columbia University, *National Survey of American Attitudes on Substance Abuse XII: Teens and Parents,* August 2007, http://www.Casacolumbia.org.

[31]The National Center on Addiction and Substance Abuse at Columbia University, *National Survey of American Attitudes on Substance Abuse XII: Teens and Parents,* August 2007, http://www.Casacolumbia.org.

[32]The National Center on Addiction and Substance Abuse at Columbia University, *National Survey of American Attitudes on Substance Abuse XII: Teens and Parents,* August 2007, http://www.Casacolumbia.org.

[33]"Alcohol Use and Abuse: A Special Health Report from Harvard Medical School," Harvard Health Publications, Boston, 2001, 22.

[34]"How to manage Teen Drinking (The Smart Way): Colleges are reducing abuse by telling kids their peers are not as reckless as they think," *TIME,* 18 June 2001: 42.

[35]The National Center on Addiction and Substance Abuse at Columbia University, *National Survey of American Attitudes on Substance Abuse XII: Teens and Parents,* August 2007, http://www.Casacolumbia.org.

[36]Kate Kelly, *The Complete Idiot's Guide to Parenting a Teenager* (New York: Alpha Books, 1996), 212-213.

[37]Siobhan Gorman, "Why They Don't Just Say No," *National Journal,* 18 Aug. 2001: 2600.

[38]Kate Kelly, *The Complete Idiot's Guide to Parenting a Teenager* (New York: Alpha Books, 1996), 212-213.

[39]Substance Abuse and Mental Health Services Administration, *"2006 National Survey on Drug Use and Health: National Results",* http://oas.samhsa.gov/nsduh/2k6nsduh/2k6Results.cfm#1.1.

[40]Substance Abuse and Mental Health Services Administration, *"2006 National Survey on Drug Use and Health: National Results",* http://oas.samhsa.gov/nsduh/2k6nsduh/2k6Results.cfm#1.1.

[41]National Institute on Drug Abuse, *"Info Facts: Monitoring the Future Study: Trends in Prevalence of Various Drugs for 8th-grade, 10th-grade, and High School Seniors,"* 2006, www.drugabuse.gov/InfoFax/HSYouthtrends.html.

[42] Kaiser Family Foundation, *U.S. Teen Sexual Activity,* January 2005, http://www.kff.org.

[43]Kaiser Family Foundation, *U.S. Teen Sexual Activity,* January 2005, http://www.kff.org.

[44]Kaiser Family Foundation, *U.S. Teen Sexual Activity,* January 2005, http://www.kff.org.

[45]Roffman, Deborah, *Sex and Sensibilities: The Thinking Parent's Guide to Talking Sense About Sex,* (Cambridge:Da Capo Books, 2001), 176—178.

[46]The Henry J. Kaiser Family Foundation, *Survey Snapshot: Teens, Sex and TV,* May 2002.

[47]Kaiser Family Foundation and seventeen magazine, "Birth Control and Protection", July 2004.

Chapter 5: Personality Type and Brain Development

[1]David Keirsey, http://www.Kiersey.com/parent/html; excerpted from *Please Understand Me II.*

[2]Otto Kroeger and Janet Thuesen,*Type Talk* (New York: Dell Publishing, 1998) 8-10.

[3]Salt, 71.

[4]Paul D. Tieger and Barbara Barron-Tieger, *Nurture by Nature: Understand your Child's Personality Type-and Become a Better Parent* (Boston: Little, Brown and Co., 1997), 15-34.

[5]Keirsey, excerpted from *Please Understand Me II.*

[6]Salt, 91.

67Jay Giedd, National Institute of Mental Health, "Interview: Jay Giedd," www.pbs.org/wgbh/pages/frontline/shows/teenbrain/interviews/giedd.html.

[8]Salt, 85.

[9]Sleep Needs, Patterns and Difficulties of Adolescents: Summary of a Workshop," National Academics Press, http://www.books.nap.edu/books/030907071771.

[10]Sarah Spinks, *"Adolescents and Sleep,"* http://www.pbs.org/wgbh/pages/frontline/shows/teenbrain/from/sleep.html.

Chapter 6: School, Parental Support, and Self-Esteem

[1]Steinberg, *Beyond the Classroom: Why School Reform Has Failed and What Parents Need to Do,* 16.

[2]Steinberg, *Beyond the Classroom,* 17.

[3]Hersch, *A Tribe Apart: A Journey into the Heart of American Adolescence,* 101.

[4]Salt, *Always Accept Me for Who I Am: Instructions from Teenagers on Raising the Perfect Parent, by 147 Teens Who Know*, 95.

[5]Salt, 30.

[6]Salt, 22.

[7]Salt, 13.

[8]Amy Brualdi, "Multiple Intelligences: Gardner's Theory,"*Practical Assessment, Research & Evaluation*, 5(10).

[9]Daniel Goleman, *Emotional Intelligence* (New York: Bantam Publishing, 1995), 34.

[10]Goleman, 102.

[11]Steinberg, *Beyond the Classroom*, 19,187.

[12] David Gleason, Psy.D., Personal interview, July 24, 2002.

[13]Sandra Arbetter, "Taking a Look at Self-Esteem," *Current Health 2*, 2 Apr. 1996: 6,7.

[14]Michael Ryval, "Nurturing Individuality: It Can Boost Your Teen's Self-esteem," *Chatelaine*, June, 1993: 22.

[15]Salt, 19.

[16]Salt, 86.

[17]Steinberg, *Beyond the Classroom*, 176.

[18]Salt, 18.

Chapter 7: The Myth of Perfection

[1]Wolf, *Get out of My life but First Could You Drive Me and Cheryl to the Mall?*, 66.

[2]Salt, *Always Accept Me for Who I Am: Instructions from Teenagers on Raising the Perfect Parent, by 147 Teens Who Know*, 99.

[3]Salt, 31.

[4]Salt, 98.

[5]Snyderman and Streep, *Girl in the Mirror: Mothers and Daughters in the Years of Adolescence*, 292.

[6]Snyderman and Streep, 292.

[7]Simpson, *Raising Teens: A Synthesis of Research and a Foundation for Action*, 37.

[8]Steinberg, *Crossing Paths: How Your Child's Adolescence Triggers Your Own Crisis*, 261.

[9]Steinberg, *Crossing Paths*, 87-97.

[10]Steinberg, *Crossing Paths*, 111-112.

[11]Steinberg, *Crossing Paths* , 118-120.

[12]Steinberg, *Crossing Paths*, 144-145.

[13]Steinberg, *Crossing Paths*, 152.

[14]Steinberg, *Crossing Paths*, 231.

[15]Cheryl Richardson, *Take Time for Your Life* (New York: Bantam Doubleday Dell Publishing Group, 1998), 24.

[16]Steinberg, *Crossing Paths*, 259-260.

[17]Salt, 106.

[18]Salt, 139.

[19]Joey Green, *The Road to Success is Paved with Failure* (Boston: Little, Brown and Company, 2001), 42, 145, 177, 212.

Chapter 8: Reflections

[1]Ronald L. Miller, Kenny Hirsch, Martha V. Sharron, "If I Could," sung by Barbra Streisand on her album *Higher Ground*. 1997.

[2]Riera, *Uncommon Sense for Parents with Teenagers*, 205.

[3]Steinberg, Laurence, *The 10 Basic Principles of Good Parenting,* (New York: Simon & Schuster,2004), xi.

[4]Pipher, *Reviving Ophelia: Saving the Selves of Adolescent Girls,* 254.

[5]Pipher, 254-255.

[6]Salt, *Always Accept Me for Who I Am: Instructions from Teenagers on Raising the Perfect Parent, by 147 Teens Who Know*, 143.

[7]Simpson, *Raising Teens: A Synthesis of Research and a Foundation for Action*, 7-11.

[8]Salt, 101.

[9] National Training Laboratories, Bethel, Maine, http://www.eleaston.com/pyramid.html.

Selected Bibliography

Alcoholism and Drug Abuse Weekly. "Survey Links Hands-off Parenting, Teen Drug Use." 26 Feb. 2001: 6.

"Alcohol Use and Abuse." Harvard Medical School, Boston, MA: Harvard Health Publications, 2001.

Apter, Terri. *Altered Loves.* New York: St. Martin's Press, 1990.

Arbetter, Sandra. "Taking a Look at Self-Esteem." *Current Health 2,* April 1996, 6(7).

Bassoff, Evelyn. *Cherishing Our Daughters.* New York: Penguin Group, 1999.

Bernstein, Neil I. *How to Keep Your Teenager Out of Trouble, and What to Do If You Can't.* New York: Workman Publishing: 2001.

"Birth Control and Protection," *Kaiser Family Foundation and seventeen magazine.* Kaiser Family Foundation, November 2000.

Blake, Susan M., Linda Simkin, Rebecca Ledsky, et al. "Effects of Parent-Child Communications Intervention on young Adolescents' Risk for Early Onset Sexual Intercourse. *Family Planning Perspectives.* March 2001: 52.

Bourke, Dale Hanson. *Everyday Miracles; Holy Moments in a Mother's Day.* Dallas: Word Publishing, 1989.

Branden, Nathaniel. *The Power of Self-Esteem.* Deerfield Beach, FL: Health Communications, Inc., 1992.

Brualdi, Amy. "Multiple Intelligences: Gardner's Theory." *Practical Assessment, Research & Evaluation,* 5(10).

Burley-Allen, Madelyn. *Listening: The Forgotten Skill.* New York: John Wiley & Sons, 1995.

Cohen-Sandler, Roni and Michelle Silver. *"I'm not mad, I just hate you!".* New York: Penguin Books, 1999.

Cool, Lisa Collier. "The Secret Six Lives of Kids." *Ladies Home Journal.* March, 2001: 157-159.

Covey, Stephen. *The 7 Habits of Highly Effective Families.* New York: Golden Books, 1997.

DiClemente, Ralph J., Gina M. Wingood, Richard Crosby, et al. "Parental Monitoring: Associate with Adolescents' Risk Behaviors." American Academy of Pediatrics; *Pediatrics.* June, 2001: 1363.

Ellickson, Phyllis L., Joan S. Tucker, David J.Klein, et al. "Prospective Risk Factors for Alcohol Misuse in Late Adolescence." *Journal of Studies on Alcohol,* November 2001: 773.

Family Education .com "Let's Talk About Sex." http://www.familyeducation.com/article 9/11/00.

Gallagher, Richard. "Teenagers in Trouble," *Frontline, The Lost Children of Rockdale County,* http://www.pbs.org/wgbh/pages/frontline/shows/georgia/isolated/gallagher.html, 16 Feb. 2002.

Goleman, Daniel. *Emotional Intelligence.* New York: Bantam Publishing, 1995.

Gorman, Siobhan. "Why They Don't Just Say No." *National Journal,* 18 Aug. 2001: 2598-2601.

Selected Bibliography (cont.)

Green, Joey. *The Road to Success is Paved with Failure*. Boston: Little, Brown and Company, 2001.

Gurian, Michael. *The Good Son: Shaping the Moral Development of our Boys and Young Men*. New York: Jeremy P. Tarcher/Putnam, 1999.

Gurian, Michael. *The Wonder of Girls: Understanding the Hidden Nature of Our Daughters*. New York: Pocket Books, 2002.

Henkart, Andrea and Journey Henkart. *Cool Communication*. New York: Berkley Publishing, 1998.

Hersch, Patricia. *A Tribe Apart*. New York: Ballantine Books, 1998.

Howe, Neil and Strauss, William. *Millennials Rising*. New York: Vintage Books, 2000.

"How to Manage Teen Drinking (the Smart Way): Colleges are reducing abuse by telling kids their peers are not as reckless as they think." *Time*. 18 June 2001: 42.

"Info Facts: Monitoring the Future Study: Trends in Prevalence of Various Drugs for 8th-grade, 10th-grade, and High School Seniors." *National Institute on Drug Abuse. 2004,* www.drugabuse.gov/Info/Fax/ HSYouthtrends.html.

Kalergis, Mary Motley, *Seen and Heard*. New York: Stewart, Tabori and Chang, 1998.

Keirsey, David and Marilyn Bates. *Please Understand Me: Character & Temperament Types*. Del Mar, CA: Prometheus Nemesis Book Company, 1978.

Kelly, Joe. *Dads & Daughters*. New York: Broadway Books, 2002.

Kelly, Kate. *The Complete Idiot's Guide to Parenting a Teenager*. New York: Alpha Books, 1996.

Kindlon, Dan and Thompson, Michael. *Raising Cain, Protecting the Emotional Life of Boys*. New York: Ballantine Publishing Group, 1999.

Kroeger, Otto and Janet Thuesen. *Type Talk*. New York: Dell Publishing, 1998.

Kindlon, Dan. *Too Much of a Good Thing, Raising Children of Character in an Indulgent Age*. New York, Hyperion. 2001

Kirshenbaum, Mira and Charles Foster. *Parent/Teen Breakthrough: The Relationship Approach*. New York: Penguin Books, 1991.

Martin, William. *The Parent's Tao Te Ching, A New Interpretation*. New York: Marlowe & Company, 1999.

Moir, Anne, and David Jessel. *Brain Sex...the Real Difference Between Men and Women*. New York: Dell Publishing, 1992.

Mooney, Jonathan and David Cole. *Learning Outside the Lines*. New York: Simon and Schuster, Inc., 2000.

Selected Bibliography (cont.)

Murphy, Elizabeth. *The Developing Child: Using Jungian Type to Understand Children.* Palo Alto, CA: Davies-Black Publishing, 1992.

National Council on Alcoholism and Drug Dependence Brochure. New York: NCADD, 1996.

"National Survey of Teens: Teens Talk about Dating, Intimacy, and Their Sexual Experiences," *Kaiser Family Foundation and YM Magazine.* Kaiser Family Foundation, Spring 1998.

Newberger MD., Eli. *The Men They Will Become.* Reading, MA: Perseus Books, 1999.

Nichols, Hans S. "Getting Drunk on Rebellion (under-aged drinking)." *Insight on the News,* 16 July 2001: 18.

Painter, Kim. "The Sexual Revolution hits Junior High. The kids are doing more than baring bellies: They're shocking adults with their anything-goes behavior." *USA Today Online.* http://www.usatoday.com/usatonline/20020315/3944779s.htm.

Pipher, Mary. *Reviving Ophelia, Saving the Selves of Adolescent Girls.* New York: Ballantine Books, 1994.

Pollack, William. *Real Boys.* New York: Henry Holt and Company, 1998.

Richardson, Cheryl. *Take Time for Your Life.* New York: Bantam Doubleday Dell Publishing Group, 1998.

Riera, Michael. *Uncommon Sense for Parents with Teenagers.* Berkeley CA: Celestial Arts, 1995.

Roffman, Deborah. *Sex and Sensibility: The Thinking Parent's Guide to Talking Sense About Sex.* Cambridge: Da Capo Press, 2001.

Rodriguez, Cindy. "Deep Pockets are In." *The Boston Globe,* 18 Feb, 2002: B6.

Ryval, Michael. "Nurturing individuality: it can boost your teen's self-esteem." *Chatelaine,* June 1993: 22(1).

"Safer Sex, Condoms and 'the Pill,'" *Kaiser Family Foundation and seventeen magazine.* Kaiser Family Foundation, *November 2000.*

Salt, J.S. *Always Accept Me for Who I Am, Instructions from Teenagers on Raising the Perfect Parent, by 147 Teens Who Know.* New York: Three Rivers Press, 1999.

Saltmarsh, N.R. "Adolescent Risk Taking Tied to Perceived Parental Monitoring." *Women's Health Weekly,* 28 June 2001: 18.

Santor, Darcy A., Deanna Messervey, Vivek Kusumakar. "Measuring Peer Pressure, Popularity, and Conformity in Adolescent Boys and Girls: Predicting School Performance, Sexual Attitudes, and Substance Abuse." *Journal of Youth and Adolescence.* April 2000: 163.

Scott, Jerry and Jim Borgman. *Don't Roll Your Eyes at ME, Young Man!.* Kansas City: Andrews McMeel Publishing, 2000.

Selected Bibliography (cont.)

Scott, Jerry and Jim Borgman. *Humongous ZITS*. Kansas City: Andrews McMeel Publishing, 2000.

Siegler, Ph.D. Ava. *The Essential Guide to the New Adolescence: How to Raise an Emotionally Healthy Teenager*. New York: Penguin Group, 1997.

Simpson Ph.D., A. Rae. *Raising Teens: A Synthesis of Research and a Foundation for Action*. Boston: Center for Health Communication, Harvard School of Public Health. 2001.

Snyderman, Nancy and Peg Streep. *Girl in the Mirror: Mothers and Daughters in the Years of Adolescence*. New York: Hyperion, 2002.

Simmons, Rachel, *Odd Girl Out, the Hidden Culture of Aggression in Girls,* New York: Harcourt, 2002.

Stepp, Laura Sessions. *Our Last Best Shot*. New York: Riverhead Books, 2000.

Steinberg, Laurence. *Beyond the Classroom: Why School Reform Has Failed and What Parents Need to Do*. New York: Simon and Schuster, 1996.

Steinberg, Laurence. *Crossing Paths: How Your Child's Adolescence Triggers Your Own Crisis*. New York: Simon & Schuster, 1994.

Steinberg, Laurence. *The 10 Basic Principles of Good Parenting*. New York: Simon & Schuster, 2004.

Stoop, Dr. David. *Understanding Your Child's Personality*. Wheaton, IL: Tyndale House Publishers, Inc.,1998.

"2003 National Survey on Drug use and Health: Results," *Substance Abuse and Mental Health Services Administration*. http://oas.samhsa.gov/NHSDA/2k3results.htm#ch2.

Tieger, Paul D. and Barbara Barron-Tieger. *Nurture by Nature: Understand your Child's Personality Type – and Become a Better Parent*. Boston: Little, Brown and Co., 1997.

Tolman, Deborah L. "Asking Some Unasked Questions." *Frontline, The Lost Children of Rockdale County*. http://www.pbs.org/wgbh/pages/frontline/shows/georgia/isolated/tolman.html, 16 Feb. 2002.

"Virginity and The First Time," *Kaiser Family Foundation and seventeen magazine*. Kaiser Family Foundation, October 2003.

About the Author

Sue Blaney is a communications expert and has spent 25 years in training and development, marketing and sales. She is a Certified Professional Behavior Analyst and a graduate of Northwestern University with a degree in communications. Prior to her present work with parents of teenagers and educators, she worked with businesses, ranging from Fortune 500 businesses to small start-ups.

As the parent of two, the challenges of raising teenagers hit her hard when her eldest entered adolescence. To deal with the new stresses of raising a teen, Sue created a parenting discussion group with her peers in Acton, Massachusetts, who met regularly while their teens were in junior high and high school. What they experienced in their group dramatically impacted their experiences in parenting teenagers. This inspired Sue to apply her communications and training background to develop a discussion group program for other parents. After extensive research, she published *Please Stop the Rollercoaster! How Parents of Teenagers Can Smooth Out the Ride* in 2003. Since then, the value of this program with its peer-to-peer approach, has been demonstrated across the country as an effective way for parents to learn together, improve relationships with their teenagers and build strength in their communities.

Sue observes that many parents of teenagers are bombarded with conflicting messages and feel unsure about their changing role. She provides tools that empower and connect parents of teens while helping them explore the range of issues they are likely to face. She is in demand, speaking regularly to parent groups in live workshops as well as through tele-seminars and podcasts. Additionally, she provides workshops for educators and other professionals who work with parents of teenagers to improve communication strategies and understanding. Sue has been interviewed in national media in print, radio and on television.

Sue has founded ChangeWorks Publishing Company to educate, empower and connect parents of teenagers through print and audio products and programs.

Also available from ChangeWorks Publishing :

Leader's Guide and Program Manual
Our Leader's Guide provides the materials for a facilitator-led parenting discussion group program using the *Please Stop the Rollercoaster!* curriculum. It contains clearly written, step-by-step instructions so that almost anyone can lead a group, and it is flexible so a leader can customize the program further to meet a group's specific needs. Materials and instructions are provided for organizing and promoting the groups, and can be useful for all delivery models. On-site facilitator training is available, as well as training by tele-class, for those desiring it.

Christian and Jewish Leader's Guides
These two Leader's Guides have been customized for Christian and Jewish faith communities in partnership with experts in these areas. Faith communities are a natural place for parents to gather and discuss their parenting journey. The Leader's Guides will allow Christian and Jewish educators and lay leaders to run this program easily as they are guided step-by-step through planning and running each meeting. (Free excerpts are available from our website for your review.)

Note: The text used by group participants, *Please Stop the Rollercoaster! How Parents of Teenagers Can Smooth Out the Ride* is secular in its approach, while the program is customized for faith-based communities through the Leader's

Practical Tips for Parents of Young Teens; What You Can Do to Enhance Your Child's Middle School Years
This is a hands-on, quick-to-read 28 page booklet that answers the cries of parents who say *"Just tell me what to DO!"* Specifically written for parents of middle schools students, this is a booklet parents refer to over and over again. Many middle schools purchase these in bulk quantities for the parents of their students; consider passing this tool along to your child's principal, guidance counselor and PTO.

Tele-Seminars, Podcasts and Workshops
Sue Blaney, author of *Please Stop the Rollercoaster!* is an experienced speaker and workshop leader, offering various single-session and multi-session tele-seminar programs and workshops. Using her acclaimed curriculum and communications expertise she delivers reassurance to parents of teens, while providing essential information enhancing skills and understanding.

In addition to her ongoing tele-class programs, she is available for **on-site training sessions**, **lectures** and **keynote programs**.

Visit www.PleaseStoptheRollercoaster.com
for more information

NOTES